Extend Microsoft Access Applications to the Cloud

Andrew Couch

PUBLISHED BY
Microsoft Press
A division of Microsoft Corporation
One Microsoft Way
Redmond, Washington 98052-6399

Library of Congress Control Number: 2014946864
ISBN: 978-0-7356-6768-6

Printed and bound in the United States of America.

First Printing

Microsoft Press books are available through booksellers and distributors worldwide. If you need support related to this book, email Microsoft Press Book Support at mspinput@microsoft.com. Please tell us what you think of this book at http://aka.ms/tellpress.

Acquisitions and Developmental Editor: Devon Musgrave
Project Editor: Rosemary Caperton
Editorial Production: Waypoint Press (www.waypointpress.com)
Technical Reviewer: Jeff Conrad
Copyeditor: Roger LeBlanc
Indexer: Christina Yeager
Cover: Twist Creative • Seattle and Joel Panchot

For Charlotte and Michael. Thanks for all the fun and the way you have enriched our lives.

—ANDREW COUCH

Contents at a glance

Contents

What do you think of this book? We want to hear from you!

Microsoft is interested in hearing your feedback so we can continually improve our
books and learning resources for you. To participate in a brief online survey, please visit:

microsoft.com/learning/booksurvey

What do you think of this book? We want to hear from you!

Microsoft is interested in hearing your feedback so we can continually improve our books and learning resources for you. To participate in a brief online survey, please visit:

microsoft.com/learning/booksurvey

Introduction

If you are already experienced in working with Microsoft Access desktop databases, now is the time to suspend all your existing knowledge and prepare for something completely new. Even though you will find a familiar development interface, it looks a bit different. And even though the user interface is similar to past versions of Access, you will need to become familiar with a lot of new concepts.

If you have never used Access, you should realize that the product can be used to construct both desktop database solutions (which is not covered in this book) and the new web app database solutions. You can use these new web app solutions to quickly and productively deliver solutions in a browser window.

The new Access web apps fit into a strategic initiative to move the world of Microsoft Office into the cloud. Although each Office product offers its own isolated web experience, they all seem to be moving in a similar direction, and they have been consolidated onto the single common platform, Microsoft Office 365. You also can host these technologies with your own on-premise Microsoft SharePoint 2013 Server with Access Services—in which case, you should read the references to Office 365 within this book as meaning "your own SharePoint 2013 Server instance." This book is written from the perspective of Office 365, so you might find that some of the terminology varies from what you see when using your own on-premise solution.

Historically, there was a time when communicating between Access, Excel, and Word on the desktop was quite difficult. Then, in Office 95 and later when a number of issues were resolved in Office 97, we had seamless integration between the Office products. The process of integration required the adoption of a common programming language called Visual Basic for Applications (VBA). In the new web browser–based interface, VBA is not supported. We hope that Microsoft will improve integration though web services or other technologies, and the addition of new "Apps for Office" features is a step toward offering better integration between the Office products and other technologies.

Microsoft has tried twice in the past to leverage Access into a web browser; both times the technologies did not have great longevity. The first attempt, called *Data Access Pages*, delivered individual web pages and never got a great deal of support from the Access community. The second attempt, called *Access 2010 Web Databases*, took the cloud ideas further and had a lot of great features, but it suffered from too much reliance on storing data within SharePoint's internal structures and a publication model that was lengthy and prone to problems; both these issues have been addressed in the new web app technology.

Access 2013 demonstrates how the Access product is being transformed to deliver exceptional productivity in creating a web browser–based experience.

Product updates and Office 365

Office 365 gives Microsoft a platform on which to offer a more frequent mechanism for delivering updates and enhancements to the Office products. These updates, which are scheduled on a monthly basis, are automatically applied. In general, updates to the desktop products will continue to be available on a basis similar to the existing service packs.

However, because Access web apps have such tight integration with the cloud, the Access development team can deploy more significant updates on a shorter, more regular basis as service updates. Some of these updates are visible through the desktop experience of designing a web app.

As an example of the benefits of this approach, in July 2013 new updates were made to Access Services within Office 365 that provide a great new synchronization feature between combo box controls and include more diligent checking for inconsistent objects when creating packages.

In the first quarter of 2014, Microsoft released the first service pack for Office 2013 on Office 365. This service pack includes three significant enhancements to web-app development. This book reflects these changes:

- The first change was to provide a mechanism for developers to deploy changes to web apps without needing to apply those changes directly into the live system. Changes now can be made in a test environment and then subsequently deployed to a production environment.

- The second change is also related to deploying changes—it introduces the idea of locking an application to protect a developer's intellectual property rights and limit permission to modify the web app. This feature is aimed at software houses that plan to make applications available in the Office Store and need to provide an upgrade path while locking down the source code for the application.

- The third change is of great significance. For some time, Office products such as Excel have benefited from the ability to augment an application with an App for Office—for example, enabling map data to be seamlessly displayed in a spreadsheet. This feature now has been extended to support Access. This opens up opportunities to download a component from the Office Store, as well as to create your own components that, for example, can read and write data through to external company data sources. A long time ago, Access developers benefited from the introduction of OLE Automation, which allowed for interoperability between the Office products. You can view this new integration feature as offering a similar capability in the new development environment.

If you have an on-premise SharePoint 2013 environment, you might find that some newer features are available only at the point of applying service packs. The main use of service packs is to remedy problems, not to provide additional features. Major releases of the product for the desktop environment are still planned to take place. When you consider these updates together with the service update schedule, it is evident that Microsoft intends to compress the overall release cycle.

Because Office 365 can be updated on a regular basis, some of the screen shots might not match what you see on your screen as you follow along with the examples in this book. I also made the decision to focus on Small Business Premium and Enterprise subscriptions; for other subscriptions, you might also see differences in the screen shots, although the basic techniques and concepts will be similar to those I describe.

Choosing Access to develop in the cloud

In Visual Studio a number of years ago, Microsoft created the Entity Data Model as a scaffolding process where, after defining data structures, the tool then created web-browser forms to navigate between related information areas. This approach can be seen as a precursor to some ideas in Access 2013 web apps. Access 2013 uses the relationships in the same way Visual Studio did to create a scaffolding interface where most of the layout work is automatically constructed. This enhances productivity for you as the app developer.

If you are looking for .NET programming–style features, you will find this supported only when developing with the Apps for Office features, because the approach taken when developing with Access will not give you that "dig down deep" opportunity to endlessly extend your own code and functionality. The product is just not designed with that mindset. Currently, most new features in Access are aimed at the power user, with an emphasis on simplicity of use.

If you build sophisticated Access desktop applications and products and regard yourself as a serious Access developer, this book was written for you. But you need to bear in mind that the technology is still evolving, and the chances of reconstructing all your existing Access desktop applications into browser-based apps are slim. However, you will enjoy both the exposition of how to embrace the new technology and starting to see how you can use this technology on new projects and to extend existing projects. I also strive to demonstrate in the book how you can go beyond the built-in features and extend your web app.

If you have a new project where you or a potential client of yours might have increased geographical reach, and you want to save money by not funding infrastructure and get ahead of the competition, this technology offers a uniquely productive experience.

Before you decide to use Access, you need to consider the alternatives. Because you picked up this book, I assume you want a solution in the cloud. So, what are the alternative technologies that can deliver a pure browser-based experience?

The most obvious choice within the Microsoft product portfolio is Visual Studio. The advantage of using Visual Studio is it can give you everything you could ever want on the web. The disadvantage is that you will need to make a serious commitment to understanding how to write complex code. In our experience, people who develop Access applications can find this challenge to be a bit too difficult a step to take, and this is where the new web app technology will help you to take a big leap forward in the browser.

Here are some key benefits to consider in choosing Access 2013 web apps with Office 365:

- Your data is held in Azure SQL, so you have a scalable and efficient platform in which to store your data.

- Unlike many of the competing tools, you have a true graphical, easy-to-use GUI for positioning controls in the browser window, writing program code, and customizing the user experience.

- Although you cannot indirectly (using a tool like SQL Server Management Studio) change the database design in Azure SQL, you can dig down deep into the design to ensure that processing is performed correctly. You also can use the standard Microsoft SQL Server Management Studio (SSMS) to bulk modify data and investigate the database structure.

- You can link existing desktop Access database applications and other Office applications, such as Excel spreadsheets, to the data sets held in Azure SQL.

- You can use PowerPivot to display drill-down charts and summaries of your data in a browser interface.

- SQL Server Reporting Services (SSRS) can be used to supplement a web app delivering up reports in a browser.

- The automatic creation of views and drill-down capabilities will create a rich interface for slicing and dicing views of your data.

- When you change the design of tables, the views (unless customized) are automatically updated to reflect the design changes made in the dependent tables.

- The web app shares and builds on other technologies, such as SharePoint and Azure SQL.

- It offers a low-cost model for creating a functionally rich web experience for your users and provides an easy and intuitive path to get started.

- You can use Visual Studio 2013 to create completely standalone, browser-based Web Form applications linked to your Access data held in the Azure SQL Database.

- You can use Apps for Office targeted for Access to add new features to a web app you developed yourself or to one you obtained from the Office Store.

The preceding list contains just some of the great benefits of choosing Access 2013 to deploy a solution in a browser window. Here are the restrictions:

- The Azure SQL Database does not provide any permission on the master database. This means that other products such as Visio and older versions of Visual Studio will not work with the Azure SQL Database. Some useful standard features in SSMS are not supported, such as setting identity insert on tables (which would enable repeated, indirect uploading of data, replacing primary key values in the data). Another unsupported feature is scripting out the database design (although I have a workaround for this in Chapter 9, "Looking under the hood at Microsoft Azure SQL Database," in the section "Extracting information on relationships").

- Although reporting can be achieved in a browser using SSRS or PowerPivot, there is no native reporting features in a web app. This also means there is no ability to acceptably print out a screen of data. (I demonstrate a workaround you can use for small layouts in Chapter 7, "Programming a web app by using macros," in the section "Presenting a view for printing.")

Web app software life cycle

You'll find it worthwhile to consider how you will make changes to your application after the application is in use. An Access web app consists of both data and data-related design objects (such as queries and data macros) that are held in an Azure SQL Database as objects and execute in Azure SQL. The user interface design objects (such as UI macros and web app views) are also held in Azure SQL in system tables, but they execute in the browser interface.

Prior to service pack 1, there was no feature allowing you to upload a new set of user interface components without also replacing the Azure SQL Database data, but now there are new features enabling developers to evolve and test changes to a design deploying updates to the application without replacing live data.

In Chapter 1, "Finding your way around Office 365," I describe a simple approach to downloading your design and creating a backup using a package suitable for use either when you start developing an application or when you are the only user of the application. Following this, in Chapter 2, "Finding your way around Access 2013," I provide a more detailed description of the deployment techniques required when maintaining an application for which software updates are required. There is a further related topic, called the *On Deploy Macro*, which is discussed in Chapter 7.

Access 2013 web apps present a unique opportunity to deploy an extremely productive user experience. The scaffolding functionality is fantastic, and the integration into an Azure SQL back end provides a solid scalable platform.

A critique of the initial release of Access 2013 would point toward a lack of support for both upgrading and extending web apps and integrating with external data. Both these issues were addressed in the first service pack, and the remedies for them point toward Access continuing to be an exciting and rich development tool.

Reference material

If you find that you would like to gain a deeper knowledge of the VBA code in Chapter 3, I recommend reading *Microsoft Access 2010 VBA Programming Inside Out* from Microsoft Press (2011).

For a quick reference to techniques for rapidly achieving productivity increases with more general Access functionality, rather than reading an in-depth discussion of the topics, I recommend you read *Microsoft Access 2013 Plain & Simple* from Microsoft Press (2013).

For an in-depth look at Access 2013 in both the context of desktop and web apps, I recommend *Microsoft Access 2013 Inside Out* from Microsoft Press. This Microsoft Access book has a great amount of content that will supplement this book in providing an ideal reference text for an Access developer.

Who should read this book

This book is written for two types of readers. It's written for experienced Access developers who want to understand the detailed design choices they are making when creating a web app, and it's also written for readers who are starting to develop web apps and want to better understand how to develop an Access web app using Office 365.

Organization of this book

This book is divided into three parts. In Part I, "Working with Office 365 and Access web apps," I introduce Office 365 and the Access web app development environment. I also look at issues related to taking an existing desktop database and converting the data it contains into a web app. After reading the first part of the book, you should have the necessary overall understanding to plan in detail how you will move existing data into a web app or start creating a web app with new data in the cloud.

In Part II, "Designing Access web apps," I dive into the details of how to construct a web app. This coverage includes designing tables, queries, and views. I also introduce data macro programming, which is essential to fitting together the different components of the web app to construct a completed application.

In Part III, "Extending Access web apps," I start with a case study illustrating how to create a public-facing web app and manage the public-facing, web app security. Then I look behind the scenes at Azure SQL to get a better understanding of how our web app works with data, queries, and data-macro programming. I also look at linking other technologies—such as PowerPivot, Visual Studio 2013, and SQL Server Reporting Services (SSRS)—to the back-end data in Azure SQL. In a final section, I introduce developing and working with the new Apps for Office technology.

Following is a brief description of each chapter.

In Chapter 1, "Finding your way around Office 365," I describe how to work with Office 365. I take you through concepts such as sites, OneDrive, security, themes, and all the other basic features you need to understand before creating a web app.

In Chapter 2, "Finding your way around Access 2013," I help you get comfortable with the new GUI interface you will use to design Access 2013 apps. I provide an overview of how all the components in a web app fit together.

In Chapter 3, "Converting a desktop database to a web app," I discuss taking an existing desktop database and converting the database to a web app. I show you all the issues to avoid and how to best resolve problems. Toward the end of this chapter, I include examples showing VBA code, and I also make the assumption that you are familiar with the Access desktop database experience. This chapter is written for experienced Access developers who need to tackle more demanding problems with converting existing applications.

In Chapter 4, "Creating a blank web app and using templates," I go back to the basic ideas of a web app and show how to construct a blank web app, add tables, and create relationships between tables.

In Chapter 5, "Displaying data in views," I give you a look at how to create and manage the basic components for interacting with data, including the list details, datasheet, blank and summary views. Then I provide a systematic examination of the available controls in each view.

In Chapter 6, "Creating data sources by using queries," I show you how to take advantage of using queries in your web app, including working with calculations and parameters.

In Chapter 7, "Programming a web app by using macros," I look in detail at writing both UI and data macros. I also delve deeper into SQL Azure to see how the data macros get implemented as stored procedures and triggers.

In Chapter 8, "Managing security and a public-facing web app," I look at a number of great features for making your web app available to anonymous users and configuring security for external users.

In Chapter 9, "Looking under the hood at Microsoft Azure SQL Database," I provide a more detailed look at working with Azure SQL and guiding you through the process of using the SQL Server Management Studio (SSMS) to connect to and manage your web app.

In Chapter 10, "Other techniques for reporting," I look at how to extend support for your web app using PowerPivot, Visual Studio 2013, and SSRS.

In Chapter 11, "Using Apps for Office with Access," I introduce the new features for integrating Apps for Office in your web apps.

Conventions and features in this book

This book presents information using the following conventions, which are designed to make the information readable and easy to follow:

- Boxed elements with labels such as "Note" provide additional information or alternative methods for completing a step successfully.

- Text that you type (apart from code blocks) appears in bold.

- A plus sign (+) between two key names means that you must press those keys at the same time. For example, "Press Alt+Tab" means that you hold down the Alt key while you press the Tab key.

- A vertical bar between two or more menu items (for example, File | Close) means that you should select the first menu or menu item, then the next, and so on.

System requirements

You will need the following hardware and software to complete the practice exercises in this book:

- Windows 7 or Windows 8.

- Office 365 subscription that includes Office 365 ProPlus. (Access 2013 is required for all chapters, and in Chapter 10 Excel 2013 is required.)

- Visual Studio 2013 standard edition for some examples in Chapters 10 and 11.

- SQL Server 2012 Express Edition (or newer edition), with SQL Server Management Studio 2012 Express or newer for Chapter 9.

- SQL Server 2012 with Advanced Services (developer, standard, or newer edition) for SSRS examples in Chapter 10.

- SQL Server Business Development Studio (obtained with SQL Server 2008 or 2008R2 express or higher edition) for SSRS examples in Chapter 10.

- A computer or device that has a 1.6-GHz or faster processor (2 GHz recommended).

- 1 GB (32 bit) or 2 GB (64 bit) RAM. (Add 512 MB if running in a virtual machine or SQL Server Express Editions, and add more for advanced SQL Server editions.)

- 5400-RPM hard disk drive.

- Internet connection to download software or chapter examples

Depending on your Windows configuration, you might require Local Administrator rights to install or configure Visual Studio 2013 and SQL Server 2012 products.

Downloads: Companion content

Most of the chapters in this book include companion content that let you interactively try out new material learned in the main text. All sample web apps, can be downloaded from the following page:

> http://aka.ms/AccessApps/files

Follow the instructions to download the AccessApps_667686_CompanionContent.zip file.

Installing the companion content

Follow these steps to install the companion content on your computer or device so that you can use them with the exercises in this book:

- Unzip the AccessApps_667686_CompanionContent.zip file that you downloaded from the book's website (the contents of which should be extracted to your desktop or another appropriate location).

Using the companion content

The folder created by the ExtendAccess.zip file contains the following subfolders:

- **Chapter2**   This folder contains the desktop database NorthwindRestructuredData.accdb which is used as a source of data when you create your NorthwindData web app.

- **Chapter3**   This folder contains the desktop databases Chapter3_ReKeyedTables.accdb, Chapter3_TablesToConvert.accdb, ConvertAttachments.accdb, and NorthwindReportsChangeToExternalWriter.accdb.

- **Chapter6** This folder contains the completed web app for Chapters 2, 3, 4, 5, and 6. The web app NorthwindData_Completed.app can be uploaded to Office 365 as described in Chapter 1 in the section "Uploading a web app package."

- **Chapter7** This folder contains the desktop database NorthwindRestructuredMacros.accdb, which is used as a source of data when you create your NorthwindRestructuredMacros web app. The web apps NorthwindRestructuredMacrosCompleted.app and Projects with Printable Sales Orders - MultiUser.app contain the completed examples and can be uploaded to Office 365 as described in Chapter 1 in the section "Uploading a web app package."

- **Chapter8** This folder contains the sample web app UKAUG_PublicWebSite. app and can be uploaded to Office 365 as described in Chapter 1 in the section "Uploading a web app package."

- **Chapter9** This folder contains the desktop databases DSNManagement. accdb, NorthwindADOX.accdb, and NorthwindDAO.accdb, and the script files ListRelationships.sql and ScriptOutDesign.sql.

- **Chapter10** This folder contains the desktop database NorthwindReportsForSSRS.accdb and a folder named SSRSWebAppReports that contains the SSRSWebAppReports.sln Visual Studio project with the converted SSRS report Invoice.rdl.

Note To follow along with the examples in Chapter 9, you will need a copy of Microsoft SQL Server 2012. (The Express edition can be used.) For parts of Chapter 10 and Chapter 11, you will need a copy of Microsoft Visual Studio 2013 (the minimum Standard edition with any current service packs).

For the section in Chapter 10 on SSRS, you will need a Developer or Standard edition of SQL Server 2012 with Advanced Services. (The Express edition cannot be used.) You also will need the SQL Server Business Development Studio (available as part of a SQL Server 2008 or 2008R2 installation). The Express edition can be used to obtain this feature).

Acknowledgments

I'd like to thank Jeff Conrad at Microsoft for performing the technical review of the book and for his invaluable guidance in helping to clarify explanations in the text. My thanks also to Kevin Bell for his assistance through many discussions on newer product features. Thanks also to other members of the Access Team at Microsoft for taking the time to help on several technical issues.

My thanks to the staff at Microsoft Press, including Devon Musgrave and Rosemary Caperton for editorial guidance. Thanks also to Roger LeBlanc for his diligent copy-editing and Steve Sagman for editorial and production management. Thanks also to Kenyon Brown for instigating the work that has resulted in this text.

My final thanks is to my wife, Pamela, for her understanding and patience with me as I undertook the writing.

Errata, updates, & book support

We've made every effort to ensure the accuracy of this book and its companion content. You can access updates to this book—in the form of a list of submitted errata and their related corrections—at:

http://aka.ms/AccessApps/errata

If you discover an error that is not already listed, please submit it to us at the same page.

If you need additional support, email Microsoft Press Book Support at mspinput@microsoft.com.

Please note that product support for Microsoft software and hardware is not offered through the previous addresses. For help with Microsoft software or hardware, go to *http://support.microsoft.com*.

Free ebooks from Microsoft Press

From technical overviews to in-depth information on special topics, the free ebooks from Microsoft Press cover a wide range of topics. These ebooks are available in PDF, EPUB, and Mobi for Kindle formats, ready for you to download at:

http://aka.ms/mspressfree

Check back often to see what is new!

We want to hear from you

At Microsoft Press, your satisfaction is our top priority, and your feedback our most valuable asset. Please tell us what you think of this book at:

http://aka.ms/tellpress

We know you're busy, so we've kept it short with just a few questions. Your answers go directly to the editors at Microsoft Press. (No personal information will be requested.) Thanks in advance for your input!

Stay in touch

Let's keep the conversation going! We're on Twitter: *http://twitter.com/MicrosoftPress*

Finding your way around Office 365

This chapter looks at features in Microsoft Office 365 you can use for developing Access web apps. Although this information focuses on describing Office 365, if you have an on-premises Microsoft SharePoint 2013 Server with Access Services, you can use that as an alternative to having an Office 365 environment. When working on-premises in this way, you should interpret all references to Microsoft Azure SQL Database as referring to your on-premises Microsoft SQL Server 2012 product, and you should interpret references to Office 365 as referring to your SharePoint 2013 Server.

All the screen shots in this chapter were taken in Microsoft Windows 8. If you are using an earlier version of Windows, you won't find required programs that get installed on your machine on the Windows Start page as shown in these screen shots; instead, they will be available through the Windows Start menu.

Tip If you are working with Windows 8, you might find it easier to create a new account rather than using the built-in Administrator account. The built-in account has limitations in terms of opening a browser and, often, in displaying other files, such as PDF documents.

Office 365 subscriptions

Office 365 features Microsoft's latest public cloud productivity services and apps. The services are available by subscription. There are several types of subscriptions available; you need to purchase an appropriate type of subscription for your required number of user licenses. Figure 1-1 shows the Office 365 elements.

FIGURE 1-1 Elements of Office 365. (Graphic reproduced courtesy of Microsoft Office Ignite team.)

At the core of Office 365 are the following three services:

- **Exchange Online**, for managing email
- **SharePoint Online**, for document and site management
- **Lync Online**, for communications

In addition to the core services, a subscription can include additional services, such as the following:

- **Office 365 ProPlus**, featuring the latest Office Professional Desktop products, including Access

- **Project Online**, providing online project management tools

- **Visio Pro for Office 365**, design tools for visual presentations

> **Tip** For a detailed comparison of which Office Professional products are available with different subscriptions, visit *http://technet.microsoft.com/en-us/library/jj819251.aspx*. In addition to checking out TechNet, visit *http://community.office365.com* or *http://www.officeignite.com* for further Office 365 resources.

You should refer to the currently available subscriptions online for details of each type of subscription; this book does not provide a detailed list of all available subscriptions (because such information can become outdated). You need an Office 365 subscription that includes Access 2013 (part of Office Professional) or, alternatively, a desktop copy of Access 2013 and an Office 365 subscription against which you can use it. The information in this book assumes you purchased an Office 365 subscription that includes Access 2013.

Figure 1-2 shows a number of the key benefits offered by Office 365.

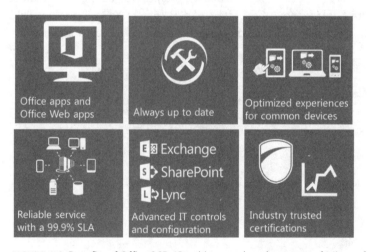

FIGURE 1-2 Benefits of Office 365. (Graphic reproduced courtesy of Microsoft Office Ignite team.)

With a subscription that includes Office 365 ProPlus, each user is allowed five installs of the desktop Office software. Key Office 365 features are shown in Figure 1-3.

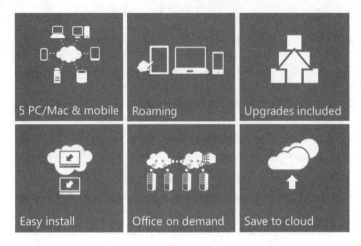

FIGURE 1-3 Key features of Office 365 ProPlus. (Graphic reproduced courtesy of Microsoft Office Ignite team.)

In Figure 1-4, you can see a global map showing the data centers (at the time of this writing) that contain your data. See *http://office.microsoft.com/en-us/business/office-365-business-transparency-FX103046257.aspx* for the latest details about the location of data centers. You will also find links to related information and help on complying with regulatory requirements at that location.

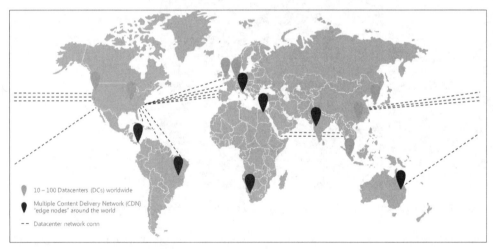

FIGURE 1-4 Microsoft's Office 365 Global Footprint. (Graphic reproduced courtesy of Microsoft Office Ignite team.)

All the screen shots in this chapter use a combination of an Office Small Business Premium subscription and an Enterprise Office 365 subscription. (I will point out any key differences between the two subscriptions in relation to the areas I cover in this chapter.) You might find minor differences in my screens compared to your own subscription.

In Chapter 9, "Looking under the hood at Microsoft Azure SQL Database," you will see that when you create a web app in Office 365, this automatically creates the data structures in a Microsoft Azure SQL Database.

Office products in a browser

Access is different from the other Office products when operated in a browser. For example, with a product such as Excel or Word, if you use the browser to work with a spreadsheet, you can change the design of the spreadsheet in the browser window. However, in a browser, Office products operate with reduced functionality compared to the desktop versions of those products. These Office products also include a separate desktop version of each product.

Working with an Access web app in a browser is called the *runtime experience*. You cannot change the design of a web app while working in the browser. To change the design of a web app, you must download it into a local copy of Access on your desktop, where you can then change the design. To make any design changes, you first need to install the desktop version of Access on your local machine as described in the next section.

A great feature of working with the new web app desktop interface to develop your application is that when you create or change objects in a web app, they are automatically saved to Office 365 (or saved when you click the Save button). So there is no need to publish your work; everything happens dynamically. In Chapter 2, "Finding your way around Access 2013," you will see in detail how to work with the new Access web app design interface.

Getting started with Office 365

Figure 1-5 shows a schematic map of the key elements of Office 365 explored in this chapter.

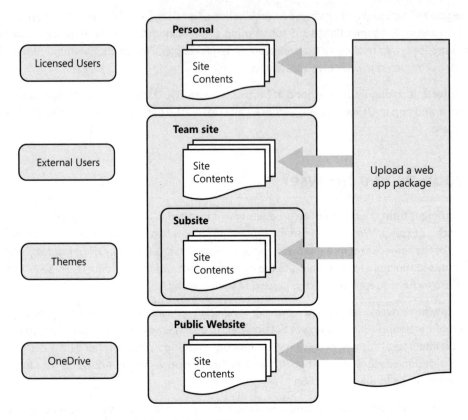

FIGURE 1-5 Key elements for focus in Office 365.

Following is a brief description of each of these key elements:

- **Licensed Users** With Office 365, you can create multiple user accounts and assign users different permissions. Each user must have an Office 365 license.

- **External Users** Documents and sites or subsites can be shared with external users who are not licensed users. These users will need to obtain a free Windows Live logon to use your site.

- **Themes** You can apply a theme to change the appearance of your site or subsite. The theme will then apply to any web app in the site or subsite.

- **OneDrive** You can use OneDrive for general file storage but not to create a runtime web app.

- **Personal** This is a private area where you can create web apps.

- **Team Site** This is a shared area for creating web apps.

- **Public Website** This is a public area for creating web apps.

- **Subsite** These are additional areas contained within a site for creating web apps and documents. Subsites can have a unique theme and permissions for users.

- **Site Contents** This is a list of available apps, web apps, and documents available in the site or subsite.

The first step in using Office 365 is to sign in to your account. You can also select the check box to keep you signed in, as shown in Figure 1-6.

FIGURE 1-6 Sign in to Office 365.

Team site, personal site, and public site

Office 365 has three areas where you can publish and display your web apps. The first area is called *Team Site*; this area is where you can place an application when you want to share it with other users. The second area is *Public Site*, which will be covered in Chapter 8, "Managing security and a public-facing web app." The third area is called *Personal*; it provides a private area where you can keep applications that are solely for your own use. In this section, you'll see how to locate the Team Site and Personal Site areas, where you will later create web apps. Figure 1-7 shows the screen displayed when you select the Sites menu option on the main menu at the top of the screen.

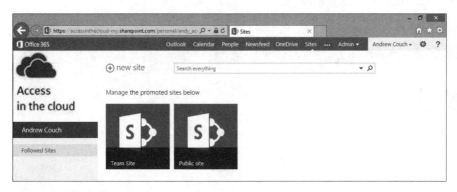

FIGURE 1-7 Displaying your sites.

> **Tip** The Public Site provides you with an area for displaying a public-facing website, for which you can also arrange to map your own domain names.

If you click the Team Site icon, you will be taken to the Team Site page. Click the Site Contents link on the left of the screen, as shown in Figure 1-8. This is where you will later see your web apps.

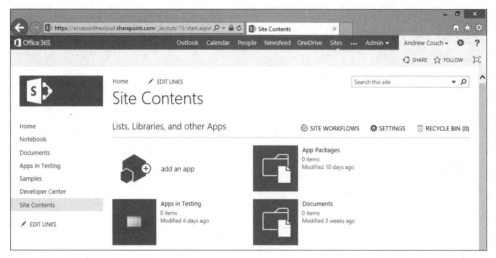

FIGURE 1-8 Site Contents page for Team Site.

> **Tip** If you are using the Small Business Premium subscription, you will not see the Apps In Testing, Samples, or Developer Center items on the left menu in Figure 1-8, nor will you see the Apps In Testing folder on the Site Contents page; these are not essential features for what follows in this book and are available in an Enterprise subscription.

Click your name near the top-right corner of the menu. Doing so drops down the selections About Me and Sign Out. Choose About Me, as shown in Figure 1-9.

FIGURE 1-9 About Me selection for displaying your Personal Site.

Selecting Apps from the menu on the left will display your applications, as shown in Figure 1-10. This is your Personal Site, the second main area where you can create a web app.

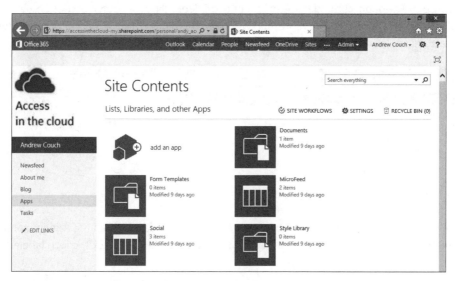

FIGURE 1-10 Site Contents page for Personal Site.

There is no direct-transfer feature for moving a web app between Team Site and Personal Site (or more generally, between any two sites). However, because you can save a web app as a package (discussed later) and then subsequently upload it and make it available in either of these areas, you can effectively move an app between the different locations by using packages.

> **Tip** Behind the scenes, SharePoint has created two site collections. The sites in each collection are your Personal Site and Team Site. Later in this chapter, you will see how to create additional subsites in a collection; you can also create new site collections if you are using an Enterprise account. You can think of a *site collection* as content used by a significant part of a large business, such as the finance or production departments, and think of the *sites* as representing collaborative groups or projects within each business area.

Installing Office Professional

In an Enterprise subscription, clicking the Admin menu (or, depending on your subscription, selecting Office 365 from the drop-down menu if present) will take you to the Office 365 Admin center. From the dashboard, click the link shown in Figure 1-11 to download the latest version of Office.

FIGURE 1-11 Downloading Office Professional from an Enterprise subscription.

If you have a Small Business Premium subscription, choosing Office 365 from the Admin menu will take you to the screen shown in Figure 1-12. On the right of the screen, click the icon labeled Software.

FIGURE 1-12 Downloading Office Professional from a Small Business Premium subscription.

With Small Business Premium, you will then see the Get Started With Software screen, at the bottom of which is a button labeled Start Now. After you click that button, you'll see a screen with three options, as shown in Figure 1-13. Select option 1, Set Up Your Software.

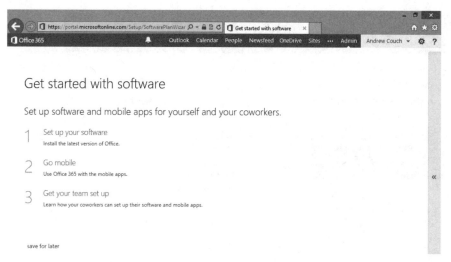

FIGURE 1-13 Getting started with software.

In both an Enterprise and Small Business Premium subscription, you next select your language and click the Install button shown in Figure 1-14. The default option is to install the 32-bit version. Clicking the Advanced link gives you a choice between 32-bit and 64-bit versions of the software.

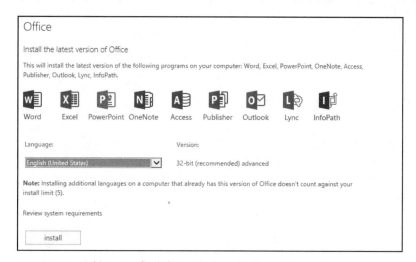

FIGURE 1-14 Making your final choices before installing Office Professional.

Click the Run option, as shown in Figure 1-15.

FIGURE 1-15 Running the install file.

Click Yes in the User Account Control pop-up window shown in Figure 1-16.

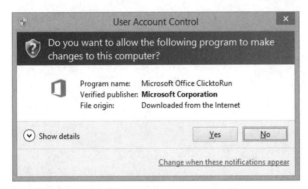

FIGURE 1-16 Acknowledging permissions for User Access Control.

You will also find it worthwhile to click the Sign In button shown in Figure 1-17 after Office has been installed.

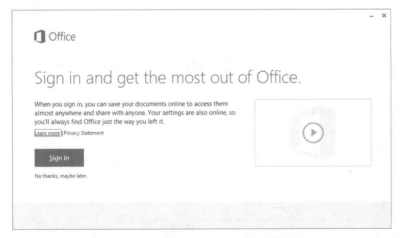

FIGURE 1-17 Sign in, and get the most out of Office.

At the Sign In prompt shown in Figure 1-18, enter the sign-in details for your Office 365 account. It is also worthwhile to select the Keep Me Signed In check box, shown in Figure 1-18.

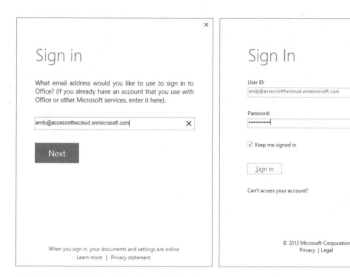

FIGURE 1-18 Entering the sign-in details to your account.

Among the Windows desktop tiles, you will now see the Office applications that have been installed on your machine, as shown in Figure 1-19.

FIGURE 1-19 Office 365 tiles on the Start screen in Windows 8.

OneDrive and OneDrive For Business 2013

After installing Office, you will see a link on the start menu to OneDrive For Business 2013. This is the same link you will see in the Office 365 site in a web browser called OneDrive; in the browser windows, *OneDrive* is an abbreviation for *OneDrive For Business 2013*.

Note In some screen shots, you might see the older term SkyDrive. You should read this as meaning *OneDrive*.

OneDrive For Business 2013 is similar to OneDrive (you might already have used the free Windows OneDrive version provided with a Windows Live account, to store documents in the cloud), except that it gives you much better control of security and how documents are managed and shared. In Office 365, clicking the OneDrive menu item will take you to OneDrive For Business 2013, as shown in Figure 1-20.

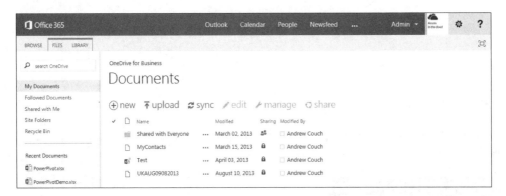

FIGURE 1-20 *OneDrive For Business 2013 when viewed in a browser.*

After visiting OneDrive in the browser window, click the OneDrive For Business 2013 Windows 8 tile. (You will not be able to link to this using the standard OneDrive tile on the Windows start menu shown in Figure 1-19.) This will then display the synchronization options shown in Figure 1-21.

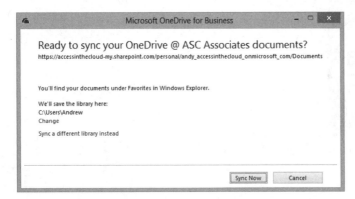

FIGURE 1-21 Sync a folder to OneDrive For Business 2013.

When synchronization is completed, in File Explorer you will see a mapping to OneDrive For Business 2013 as shown in Figure 1-22, this shows the same content as displayed in Figure 1.20 with the OneDrive displayed in the browser window. (The window title will display the text OneDrive.)

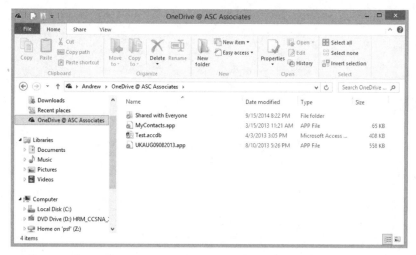

FIGURE 1-22 OneDrive For Business 2013 mapped to a drive on the desktop.

 Tip You can store desktop database files on OneDrive For Business 2013 and directly open the files from this location by using Access. You cannot publish a web app to OneDrive For Business 2013, but you could save backup copies of your web app as packages on OneDrive For Business 2013.

Start Access from the desktop tile, as shown in Figure 1-19.

When Access opens, you should find that you are already signed in, as shown in Figure 1-23. If you are not signed in, this is a good time to sign in to avoid subsequent requests to sign in when you undertake other activities in Access. Click Open Other Files.

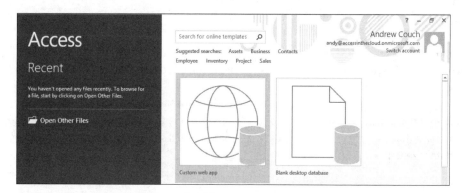

FIGURE 1-23 Starting Access for the first time.

As shown in Figure 1-24, both Sites (shown as Sites - ASC Associates) and the OneDrive For Business 2013 (shown as OneDrive - ASC Associates in the figure) and shown under Recent Folders.

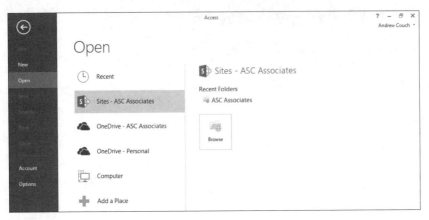

FIGURE 1-24 Where to open files related to your Office 365 site.

If you select OneDrive under the Recent Folders section, you will see the File Explorer window displayed in Figure 1-25, we have used the left side menu to scroll up and locate the OneDrive.

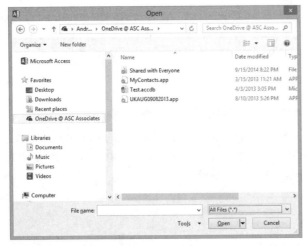

FIGURE 1-25 A view of OneDrive For Business 2013 as seen from inside Access.

In summary, you can use OneDrive For Business 2013 both to save backup copies of a web app (when saved as a package, as will be described in a later section in this chapter) and to save and use a desktop database (for example, a reporting database, which you'll see later in Chapter 3, "Converting a desktop database to a web app").

Tip You might also have noticed a tile on the Windows 8 start menu named OneDrive, which I suggested that you do not use. You can use this to link to a OneDrive page, but *not* to the OneDrive For Business 2013 site used in this book; you should already have a link for OneDrive For Business 2013 in your Recent Files area.

If you look back at Figure 1-24, below the Open title you will see an icon labeled OneDrive - Personal; you can use this, but it is a different type of OneDrive—it is the same type of OneDrive you can use from the Windows 8 Start screen. You can't link your OneDrive For Business 2013 through this option—and you don't need to, because you will have already mapped it into File Explorer, and it will also be available inside Access.

For example, if you had another OneDrive containing data, you could use the OneDrive Personal icon to link to that OneDrive. If you then try to open a desktop database saved to a traditional OneDrive page, you will find that you will be prompted to save the database as a local file before it can be opened. This illustrates another difference between OneDrive and OneDrive For Business 2013, because you can directly open an Access database from OneDrive For Business 2013.

In Figure 1-26, you can see the screen displayed when you click the OneDrive - Personal icon.

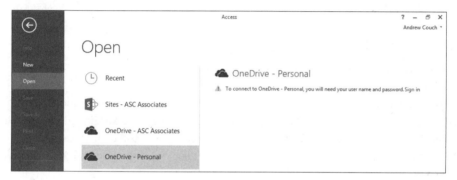

FIGURE 1-26 Connecting Access to OneDrive.

In Figure 1-27, you can see that you linked to a standard OneDrive page. Note that the credentials used for this are different from those used in the Office 365, because this is a separate OneDrive page that is not connected with Office 365 (not a OneDrive For Business 2013 page).

FIGURE 1-27 Access linked to a OneDrive page.

Looking back at Figure 1-24, you can also browse into the contents of your Team Site from inside Access. If you click on the recent folder for Team Site and click Browse, you will see contents similar to Figure 1-28..

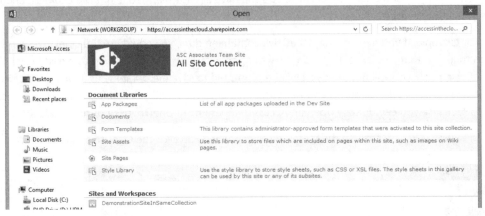

FIGURE 1-28 Browsing the contents of Team Site from inside Access.

When attempting to browse to Team Site, you might receive the error message shown in Figure 1-29. If so, you should open your browser and ensure that the Keep Me Signed In option is selected. Then close and reopen the browser window, and retry the operation in Access. (You should find that the site has already been added to the trusted sites list in your browser, but depending on your browser, you might want to check this.)

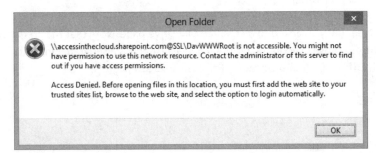

FIGURE 1-29 Open Folder error message when attempting to browse to Team Site.

Creating a web app using a template

This section explores how to create a web app using one of the built-in template applications. I chose a template here to demonstrate the basics of interacting with a web app, saving a web app as a package, and uploading a web app package to distribute an application to other sites or to different areas in your site.

When you start Access and want to create a new database or web app, you will see the screen shown previously in Figure 1-23. You can create the following four types of applications from the available icons:

- **Custom web app**   This will create a blank web app in Office 365, which you can then use to create an application starting from scratch.

- **Blank desktop database**   This creates a blank desktop database on your computer, which you can then use to create a traditional desktop Access database.

- **Web app template**   These and other named items are templates for creating a predefined web app in Office 365, such as Contacts.

- **Desktop template**   These and other named items prefixed with the word *Desktop* create a desktop Access database based on templates, such as Desktop contacts (these are further down the list and not shown in Figure 1-30).

Click the Contacts template shown in Figure 1-30.

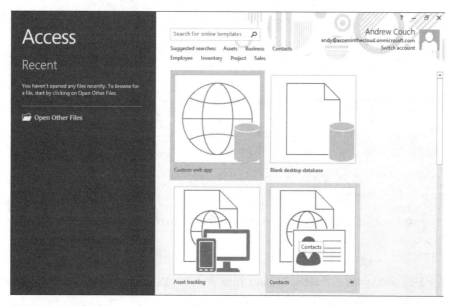

FIGURE 1-30 Selecting a web app template.

You'll see the dialog shown in Figure 1-31. There are several points to note here. First, you need to enter a name for your application, and then you need to decide where you want to place the application. Notice that when the dialog opens, the personal area is selected by default. You might prefer to use the shared Team Site choice. (Review the section "Team Site, personal site, and public site" earlier in this chapter for more details about how you would subsequently locate your app in the Office 365 menus.)

Note For this example, select Team Site so that your experience will more closely reflect the remaining screens in this section.

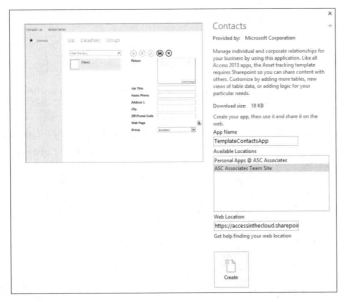

FIGURE 1-31 Choosing the location in which to create the web app.

Choosing Personal Apps in this example uses the following URL: *https://accessinthecloud-my.sharepoint.com/personal/andy_accessinthecloud_onmicrosoft_com.*

Choosing the Team Site in this example uses the following URL: *https://accessinthecloud.sharepoint.com/.*

You also have the option to directly type in a URL—which is useful when you want to create the web app in a subsite.

Tip Figure 1-31 shows the Get Help Finding Your Web Location hyperlink, which provides further assistance in finding your web location.

After deciding on a location (again, you should select Team Site to more closely follow the remaining screens in this section), provide a name for your web app and click the Create button.

After you create the web app, it will be displayed in the desktop design environment, as shown in Figure 1-32.

FIGURE 1-32 The web app as seen in the desktop design environment.

If you click the Launch App icon on the Home tab, you will see the web app displayed in a browser window; this is called the *runtime experience*. In subsequent chapters, you will spend a lot of time looking at and working with this interface and exploring all the features, but for the moment, ignore the details of how you work with the interface.

If you now go to your Team Site, you will see the web app you created in the Office 365 site, as shown in Figure 1-33.

Tip You will need to select Site Contents and scroll down the page to see the icon shown in the figure.

From Team Site, you can also click the application name that appears under the Recent item on the left side of the page; this area is shown but not selected in Figure 1-33.

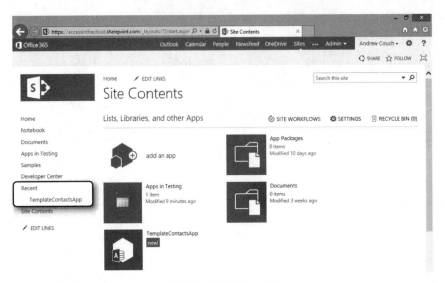

FIGURE 1-33 The web app as seen in Office 365, in Team Site.

> **Tip** In an Enterprise Office 365 subscription, you will notice that the web app is shown as an icon in the Site Contents window and is also listed in the Apps In Testing folder. Using this folder, which also appears as a menu item on the left area of the screen, makes it easier to see all your available web apps.

If you click the application icon or the link on the left of the screen, you will see the application displayed in a web browser window, as shown in Figure 1-34.

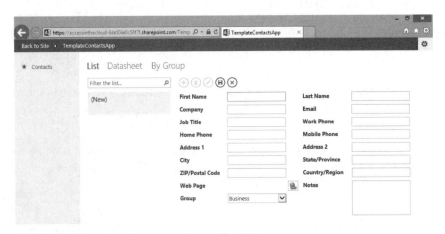

FIGURE 1-34 Displaying the web app from Office 365.

In summary, you can now see that you can launch a web app in two ways: either into a browser window while you are working on the design inside Access or by going to the appropriate site or subsite in Office 365 and clicking the web app.

Opening a web app with Access

If you have followed along, you should still have Access open displaying your web app. Close Access, and then open the web app from Team Site in a browser window as described in the previous task.

Because your web app is saved dynamically in Office 365, it is very easy to go to a different machine (as long as that machine also has Access 2013 installed) and continue working on your application design. Alternatively, you might find that after a period of time you can't easily locate the link in the recent files in Access for an application you worked on a long time ago. In that case, you can use the following method to continue working on the application design. Here's how to resume working on an application that doesn't appear in the Recent list.

With the web app displayed in the browser window as shown in Figure 1-35, click the Settings drop-down icon at the top right of the browser window, and select Customize In Access.

FIGURE 1-35 Preparing to download a web app from Office 365 to Access.

At the bottom of the browser window, you will see the pop-up window shown in Figure 1-36. This pop-up window gives you the options to directly open the web app, save a link to the web app, or cancel the operation.

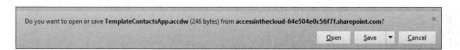

FIGURE 1-36 Allowing the browser to download the web app.

Click the Open option, and then click OK in response to the prompt shown in Figure 1-37. The prompt asks you to confirm that you are opening content from the Internet or intranet and has a check box that, when selected, will stop the message from being displayed when you next attempt this operation.

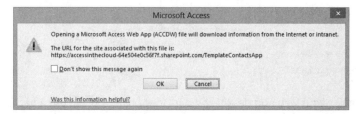

FIGURE 1-37 The confirmation message after downloading the web app.

Note that the method I am showing here is not the method you would normally use to continue working on the design of a web app. Instead, I show a method for working on a web app someone else has created, a web app that's on a different machine, or a web app you can no longer easily find from your desktop. You need to do this only once; subsequently, when you start Access and use the links on your recent files list, you will continue working on the web app.

Saving a web app as a package

In preparing this book, I wanted to create sample applications that readers could upload to their own sites. This exercise looks at how you can prepare a web app package similar to the ones I created. If you have not opened the web app in Access as previously described, start Access now, and click your Recent file list as shown in Figure 1-38.

FIGURE 1-38 Opening a web app in Access from the Recent file list, if the app is not already open.

With your web app open in the Access desktop design tool, click the File menu. (This will display Access application information and management options; this view is often referred to as *backstage*.) Click the Save As option on the left, and then click the Save Database As icon, as shown in Figure 1-39. Click on the Save As Snapshot button to save your web app.

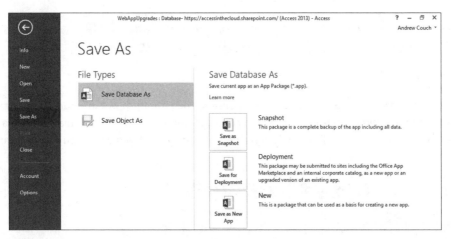

FIGURE 1-39 Saving the web app as a package.

A *package* is a file that contains your web app design and data (optional). You can use a package as a way to create a backup of a design before undertaking further design changes or as a way to distribute an application for use on other sites. Figure 1-39 allows the web app to be saved using three different techniques: Snapshot, Deployment, and New. The Deployment option is discussed in more detail in Chapter 2, in the section "Upgrading and deploying a web app."

> **Tip** Be aware that if you make a snapshot backup and later choose to replace an existing web app with the snapshot backup, this will replace both the design and the data. If you choose to create a new package without data, you will have a web app that, when uploaded, does not contain any data. You also can use the deployment options to upgrade a web app, which I will discuss in Chapter 2.

When saving a snapshot you will see a prompt to enter a title for the package and a comment in the popup indicating that all data will be saved. If you had chosen the Save as New App option then you would see the prompt shown in Figure 1-40 where you provide a title for your package, and decide whether to include data.

FIGURE 1-40 Naming the package and choosing whether to include data.

Select a location to save your application package. You have the option to select a location on your local computer, but because you have a OneDrive For Business 2013 site, it is useful to save the package to OneDrive For Business 2013, as shown in Figure 1-41. (Using this location means that if you are working on a different device, you can easily locate your saved packages.)

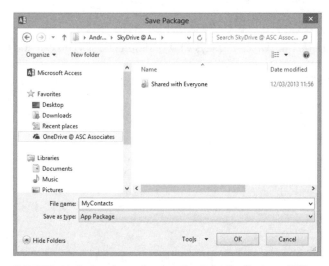

FIGURE 1-41 Saving the package to OneDrive For Business 2013.

Uploading a web app package

In this section, you will see how to upload an app package to Office 365. You can upload the app package to the same Office 365 Team Site where you created it, to your Personal Site, or to a subsite. (Subsites are discussed later in this chapter.) You can also use this technique to load the web app onto a different Office 365 site.

Note that the procedure shown here is not the only way to upload an app package—the technique described here is called "side-loading" a web app. At the end of this section, you'll see an alternative method of uploading an app; however, the method shown here should be available in all subscriptions.

From your Team Site, click the Site Contents menu shown on the right of the screen in Figure 1-42, and then click the Add An App button. The following sequences of screen shots were captured using a Small Business Premium subscription.

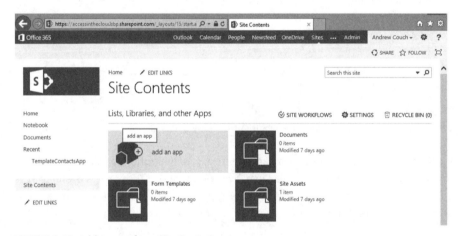

FIGURE 1-42 Add an app from Site Contents.

You'll see the screen shown in Figure 1-43, which displays a list of different apps you can add to your site.

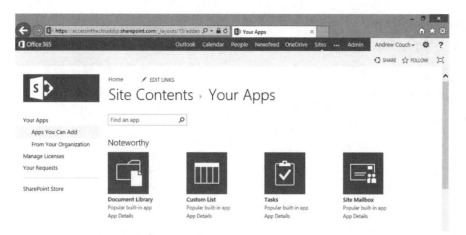

FIGURE 1-43 Apps you can add.

At the bottom of the screen, as shown in Figure 1-44, there is an arrow button next to the text "1 – 16" that allows you to page to the next page of apps. Click that button, and then repeat that process, clicking through any subsequent pages until you reach a page that includes the Access App option.

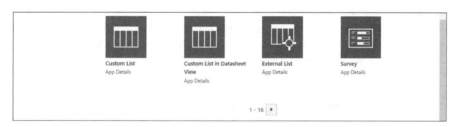

FIGURE 1-44 Scrolling down the Your Apps page.

> **Tip** In Figure 1-43, on the left, if you click Your Apps, a list of all the apps you can add will be displayed. Next to the title caption that reads All Your Apps, you will see two links: Newest (which sort the apps by date, and is the default) and Name (which sorts the apps by name). Selecting Name will bring Access near or at the top of the list; this saves you from needing to page and scroll through lists of your apps, as previously described.

After locating the page with the Access App button, click that button. You'll then see the window shown in Figure 1-45. (You can see the Access App button in the background of the figure.) You use this window to either create a blank Access app or upload an existing Access app package. Click the Or Upload An Access App Package link.

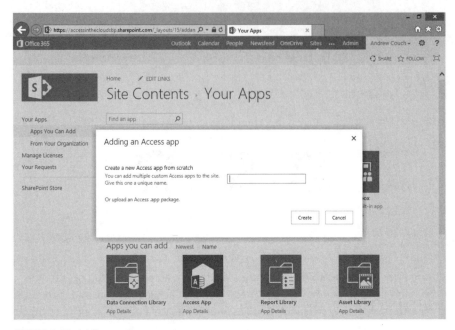

FIGURE 1-45 Adding an Access app.

You can then use the Browse button shown in Figure 1-46 to locate the app package to upload (which you saved in the last section to OneDrive For Business 2013), or you can load the file from an alternative location. Click the Create button after you locate the file.

FIGURE 1-46 Uploading an Access app from a file.

Figure 1-47 shows the screen displayed when you browse to locate the app package stored in OneDrive For Business 2013.

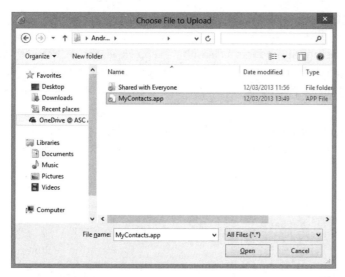

FIGURE 1-47 Selecting the package from OneDrive For Business 2013.

You will then see the screen shown in Figure 1-48, which displays your newly uploaded app. (You might need to wait a few minutes until the app has been uploaded.)

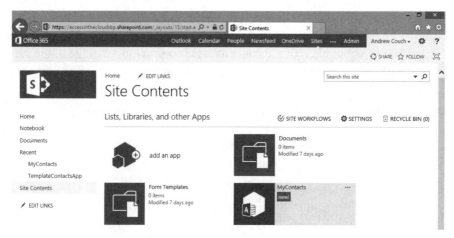

FIGURE 1-48 Site Contents after uploading an app.

If you prefer to upload an app to your personal site, you will not see a menu item called Site Contents; instead, you will see an item called Apps on the left menu. Selecting that item takes you through a similar set of steps.

Editing a web app package

When you save a web app as a package, it produces a file with the .app file extension. However, the file has the same format as a .zip file. You can change the file extension as shown in Figure 1-49 to a .zip file. You can then browse inside the package and view or alter the contents of the package.

 Caution Care should be taken if you decide to make any manual alterations to the app package. If you modify, delete, or add items incorrectly, the package might no longer function; a backup copy should always be created before making any changes to a package.

FIGURE 1-49 Changing the app package file extension to a .zip file.

 Tip To display a custom icon in Office 365 for your web app, create a 96-by-96-pixel .png graphic image, and save that file with the name **accessapp.png**. Add that file to the .zip file for the app package (replacing the default file named accessapp.png in the package).

Figure 1-50 displays the contents of the package created earlier in this chapter.

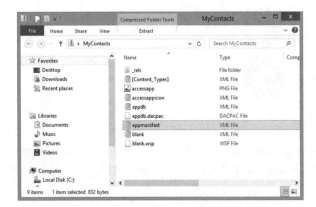

FIGURE 1-50 Looking inside the app package when viewed as a .zip file.

The appmanifest.xml file can be opened in Notepad. It contains information about your package, which you can change. For example, the file contains a tag that describes the supported languages for the app, which in our system is *en-GB*.

```
<SupportedLanguages>en-GB</SupportedLanguages>
```

Using Notepad, you could edit the contents of this tag to include support for other languages, as in the following example:

```
<SupportedLanguages>en-US;en-GB</SupportedLanguages>
```

After changing the contents of the file, save the file to another location, such as your desktop, and then copy the file into the .zip file, replacing the existing file.

> **Note** After updating the app manifest file, you need to change the package file extension from .zip back to .app. Because it is a known file type and because the default folder settings hide known file types, you might need to display the folder options by using the Options icon shown in Figure 1-51.

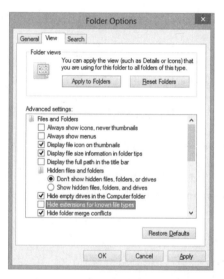

FIGURE 1-51 Locating folder options for OneDrive For Business 2013.

Figure 1-52 highlights the folder option Hide Extensions For Known File Types.

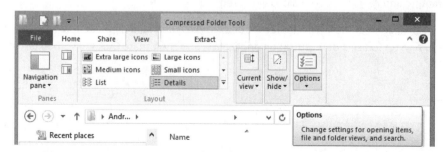

FIGURE 1-52 Making file extensions for known file types visible.

Tip To learn more about SharePoint app manifest files, visit the page "Explore the app manifest and the package of an app for SharePoint" at *http://msdn.microsoft.com/en-us/ library/fp179918.aspx.*

Displaying a web app in a browser

In earlier sections of this chapter, you saw how to upload a web app into Office 365 so that you can then open the app in a browser window. After the app is open in the browser, you also saw the option to download the app into a local copy of Access, which then allows you to work on the design of the app and also provides an option to save the app as a package (Figure 1-53).

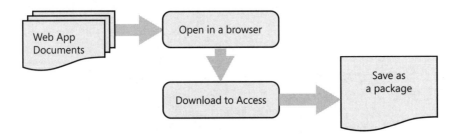

FIGURE 1-53 Schematic showing how the web app can be downloaded and saved.

After opening an app in Access, a number of additional desktop features are available for quickly reviewing changes you make to the design in a browser window. You will investigate these features in Chapter 2.

Sharing a web app with external users

With Office 365, you can share content with other people who are not registered users of your site or subsite; these people are referred to as *external users*. There are also facilities you can use to manage sharing by granting and revoking permissions when required.

This feature is managed at the Team Site level. For example, you could create a new Team Site to allow people to sign up to use a demonstration application and then share that site with external users.

When displaying your Team Site, clicking the cogs icon at the top right of Team Site page displays a list of settings options, as shown in Figure 1-54. Selecting the Shared With option displays further information on sharing.

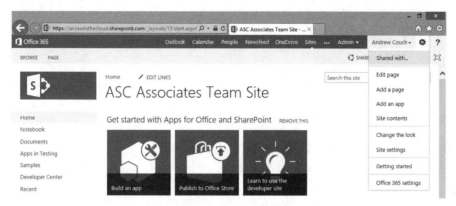

FIGURE 1-54 The settings menu for managing a Team Site.

The Shared With information is shown in Figure 1-55. Click the Invite People link at the lower left of the screen.

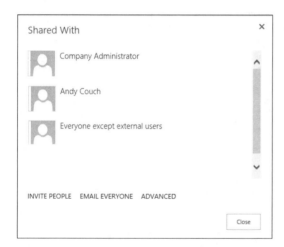

FIGURE 1-55 Shared With pop-up window.

The related pop-up window, shown in Figure 1-56, allows you to enter email addresses and an invitation message. At the bottom of the screen, you can assign permissions for the Team Site.

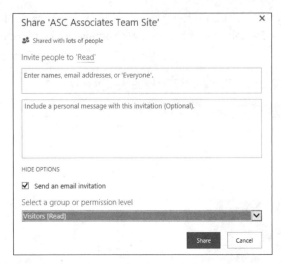

FIGURE 1-56 Invite People pop-up window.

External users will then receive an email with a link. When they click the link, they will need a Microsoft sign-in account to use your Team Site. (There is also a link on the sign-in page to create an account if they do not already have one; these Windows Live accounts are free.) You are allowed a maximum of 500 or 10,000 external users depending on your Office 365 subscription.

In Figure 1-57, the default choices available for the Select A Group Or Permissions Level are as follows:

- Excel Services Viewers [View Only]

- Members [Edit]

- Owners [Full Control]

- Visitors [Read]

Following the name of each group, the permissions are listed in square brackets. The available permissions for a group are as follows:

- Full Control

- Design

- Edit

- Contribute

- Read

- View Only

- Create New Subsites

Tip The default selection for the permission level of Visitors allows users to view but not edit data in the web app. Selecting Members allows users to edit the data in the web app, and it also shows a Settings icon that allows them to download the database and customize it in Access. If you either change the Visitor group permissions to include Contribute permissions or create a new group with Contribute permissions, users in that group can edit the data in a browser interface but will not see the Settings icon (which would allow them to download and customize the web app). To change permissions for an existing group (for example, Visitors), select the check box next to Visitors (visible in Figure 1-60), and then click Edit User Permissions on the ribbon.

Looking again at the Shared With pop-up window in Figure 1-55, if you clicked Advanced at the lower right of the screen, you will see the Permissions webpage shown in Figure 1-57. On this page, click any of the group links—for example, Visitors.

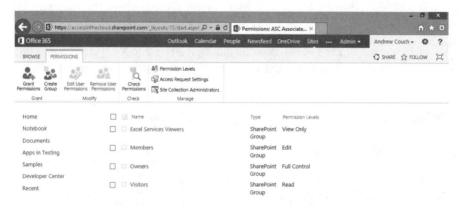

FIGURE 1-57 Managing SharePoint Group permissions on the Team Site.

This will then display the screen shown in Figure 1-58. You can select groups on the left, and then you can select individuals from the resulting list. For operations such as removing a user, select the user and then click the Actions drop-down menu for a list of available actions.

FIGURE 1-58 Managing people and groups in a Team Site.

Creating sites and subsites

The terms *site* and *subsite* in the Office 365 interface both refer to creating a SharePoint subsite.

> **Note** For a more detailed explanation of these terms, read the following section, "Creating site collections," where a distinction is drawn between these terms for users with an Enterprise subscription. In this section, the terms *site* and *subsite* mean the same thing.

As described in the last section, you use a site to manage external users. Later you will see that you can also use a site to apply a theme. When you start working with Office 365, a SharePoint Collection is created behind the scenes, and both your Team Site and Personal Site are created in two separate site collections.

To provide support for more precise management of security, for changing the visual presentation of a web app using different themes, and as a general method of organizing Office 365, you might want to create additional subsites.

To create a new site, on your site's menu, click the plus sign (+) next to New Site. This will open a pop-up window where you can start a new site. Provide a name for the new site, and click Create, as shown in Figure 1-59.

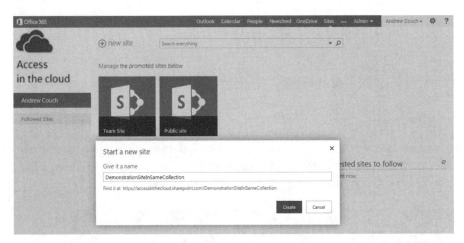

FIGURE 1-59 Adding a new subsite.

After SharePoint creates the new subsite, SharePoint navigates you to the Home page of the subsite, as shown in Figure 1-60.

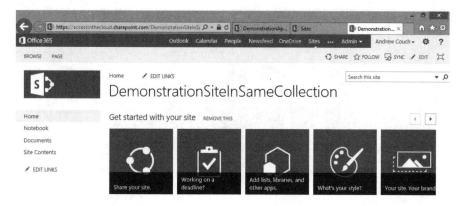

FIGURE 1-60 New site page.

I will now describe how you can promote your site. This feature is available in an Enterprise subscription. As shown in Figure 1-61, copy the URL link for the newly created site to the clipboard.

FIGURE 1-61 Copying the site URL and then promoting a new site on the sites page.

In Figure 1-61, above the list of site icons is a Manage hyperlink. When you click this link, you can manage and promote the new site and create a new icon on your site's menu for accessing the newly created site. Click the Manage link.

In the Add A Promoted Site pop-up window shown in Figure 1-62, enter a title for your site (in our example, I entered SubSite Example for the title) and paste into the link location the URL you copied to the clipboard in the previous step. There are additional boxes (all optional) where you can add a description of the site and provide a URL pointing to an image to use as a background for your site.

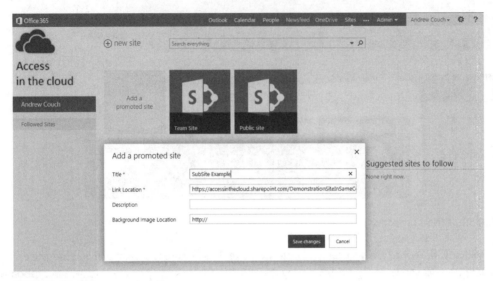

FIGURE 1-62 Add a promoted site.

After adding the new promoted site, click the link marked Click Here To Stop Editing, as shown in Figure 1-63.

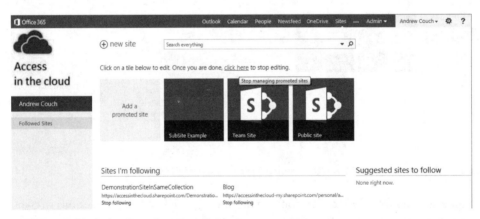

FIGURE 1-63 Displaying the new promoted site.

After you create additional subsites, you might want to create more complex settings for the site. First, you'll see how to delete a site, because it is very easy to create extra sites when you are experimenting with a technology and then later want to remove those early experiments.

Select your site from the site's menu, click the cogs icon at the top right, and select Site Settings, as shown in Figure 1-64.

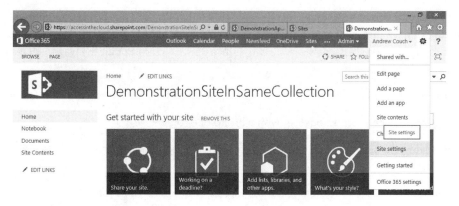

FIGURE 1-64 Displaying Site Settings.

The Site Settings menu shown in Figure 1-65 has an option under Site Actions to delete the site. (You can delete this site if desired because you will not be making any further use of it.)

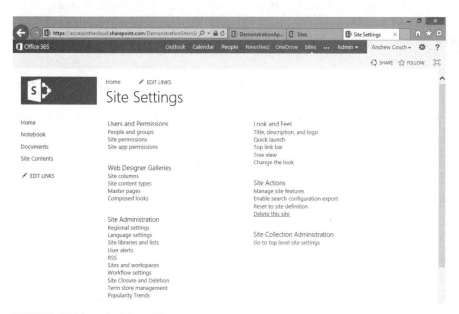

FIGURE 1-65 Managing site settings.

Creating site collections (Enterprise subscription)

At the heart of SharePoint is the concept of a site collection. Typically, a site collection groups together sites that have something in common. This section focuses on using site collections based on functionality. Visit "Overview of site collections and sites in SharePoint 2013" at *http://technet.microsoft.com/en-gb/library/cc262410.aspx* for a more in-depth study of these features.

This section demonstrates techniques that are available only with the Enterprise subscriptions—but even if you do not have that level of subscription, you might find that a quick read-through helps you understand more of the features available with Office 365, which can point the way to increased scalability on larger applications.

With Office 365 Enterprise, you can create new site collections focused on the following features:

- **Team Site** A place to work together with a group of people.

- **Blog** A site for a person or team to post ideas, observations, and expertise that site visitors can comment on.

- **Developer Site** A site for developers to build, test, and publish apps for Office.

- **Project Site** A site for managing and collaborating on a project. This site template brings all status, communication, and artifacts relevant to the project into one place.

- **Community Site** A place where community members discuss topics of common interest. Members can browse and discover relevant content by exploring categories and sorting discussions, by popularity or by viewing only posts that have a "best" reply. Members gain reputation points by participating in the community, such as starting discussions and replying to them, liking posts, and specifying best replies.

Without exploring all the details of the site collections architecture, the simple way to think of this concept is that when you create a new site collection, you specify a top-level site with a function as defined in the preceding list. Then within the collection, you can create a number of subsites that have the same characteristics as the top-level site.

It is beyond the scope of this book to delve into the different types of site collections you can create, but you should find this section informative in gaining a better understanding of what is happening under the hood or to help you get started using Enterprise features in Office 365.

Creating a new site collection with a top-level Team Site automatically creates a Team Site and allows you to create further subsites in this new collection. The advantage of creating a new site collection rather than adding a subsite to your default site collection is that it allows for more flexible administration for enterprise businesses, and because each new site collection involves generating a new content database, it provides for improved scalability.

> **Tip** You can think of a site collection as a business unit, and think of a subsite as a project or application used by a team of people within that business unit.

Early in this chapter, you saw how to locate your Personal Site and Team Site. These are both examples of Site Collections. You can see the URLs for the two collections in Figure 1-66, which was displayed by clicking the Admin drop-down menu and then selecting SharePoint. The site collection that ends with *sharepoint.com* contains your Team Site, and the site collection that ends with *-my.sharepoint.com* contains the personal sites for each user.

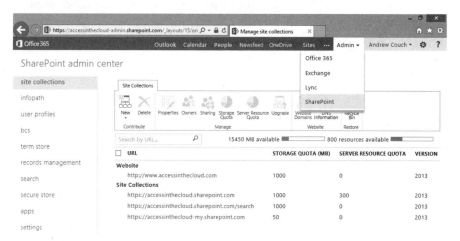

FIGURE 1-66 Displaying the SharePoint site collections.

With an Office 365 Enterprise subscription, you can create additional site collections. Figure 1-67 shows the result if you click the New drop-down menu on the ribbon and then select Private Site Collection. (The Public Website option is disabled because you can have only one public website, and this site was automatically created for you when the subscription was provisioned.)

FIGURE 1-67 Creating a new site collection.

You use the next pop-up window, shown in Figure 1-68, to enter a name and URL for the new site and site collection (you are naming both the collection and the initial site, which is always present in a site collection) and to choose a template for the sites in the site collection.

> **Tip**   If you are using an Office 365 developer subscription available through the Microsoft Developer Network (MSDN), your default site collection will be provisioned using the Developer Template. For most other subscriptions, you will have a default site collection provisioned using the Team Site template. With an Enterprise subscription, you can create an additional site collection based on the Developer template if you required the Apps In Testing feature described earlier in the chapter.

FIGURE 1-68 Displaying the New Site Collection pop-up window.

By scrolling further down the page, you can see the options to specify an administrator and storage quota, as shown in Figure 1-69. On that screen, clicking OK will create the new site collection.

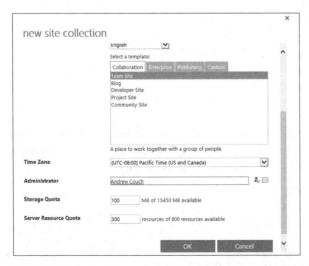

FIGURE 1-69 Assigning an administrator and creating the site collection.

You will then see your new site collection listed together with the URL, as shown in Figure 1-70.

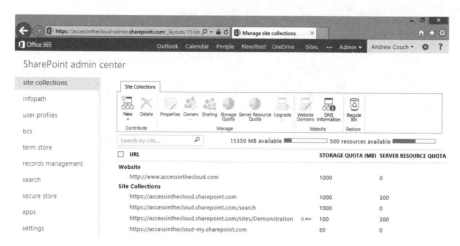

FIGURE 1-70 Displaying the new site collection.

After creating your new site collection, which will contain a new site, you might want to promote it in your list of sites. If you don't do this, you need to use the explicit URL to display the site.

Tip After you create a new subsite, it will be added on your Sites page to the Sites I'm Following list. You can also find the site by looking in your Team Site in the site contents on the lower part of the page, which displays a list of subsites.

On the Sites page, click the Manage link shown in Figure 1-71.

FIGURE 1-71 Promoting the new site in the Sites page menu window.

In the Add A Promoted Site screen, complete the Title and Link Location fields for your site, as shown in Figure 1-72, and then click Save Changes.

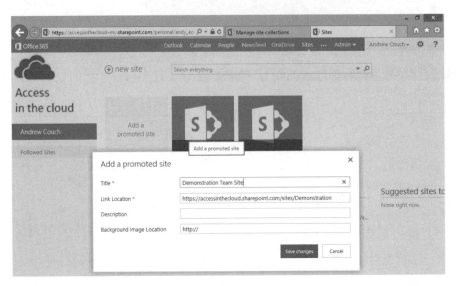

FIGURE 1-72 Adding a promoted site.

Your new site, which you just created in a new site collection, will now be displayed as shown in Figure 1-73. Make sure that you click the Click Here link above the site icons to finish your Promote Sites edit session.

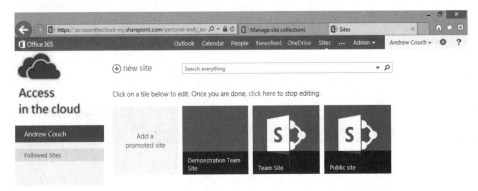

FIGURE 1-73 Displaying the new promoted site.

 Tip There are two points worth noting in Figure 1-70. First, the collection my.sharepoint. com contains the personal sites for all users, although the user details are not exposed in the interface. Second, when using other subscriptions, you may not be able to explicitly display the site collections, but under the hood, you will have separate collections for your Team Site and its subsites and personal sites (for each user).

Applying a theme

An Access 2013 web app has limited formatting features, because any theme you apply to your site will be applied automatically to all the web apps in that site. So rather than your theme being defined within a web app, it is inherited from the SharePoint site where it resides.

Tip If you want to apply a different theme to a web app but leave the main site theme unchanged, you can create a subsite and place the web app in that subsite, to which you then apply the theme you want for the web app.

While viewing your site or subsite, click the Settings icon, as shown in Figure 1-74, and select Change The Look.

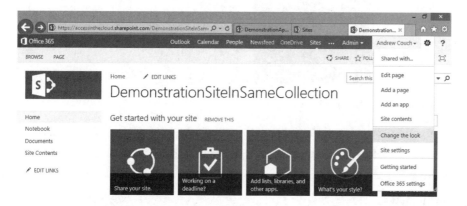

FIGURE 1-74 Change the look of a site.

Tip In Figure 1-74, you can also see a tile titled What's Your Style?, which can be used to change the site theme, rather than using the option on the Settings menu.

Selecting Change The Look displays a number of themes, as shown in Figure 1-75.

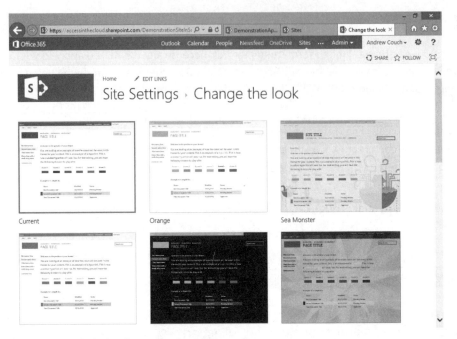

Current   Orange   Sea Monster

FIGURE 1-75 Displaying themes for the subsite or site.

Selecting a theme then displays the screen shown in Figure 1-76. On the left side of the screen are drop-down selections for changing the colors, site layout, and fonts, and an area for defining the background image.

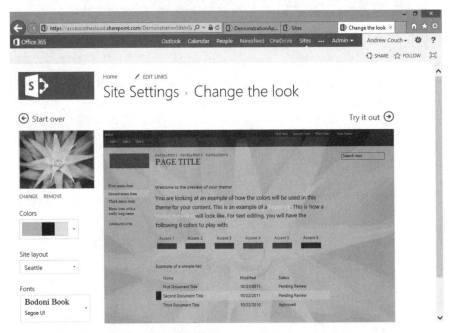

FIGURE 1-76 Selecting a theme for your site.

Clicking the Try It Out link on the top right of the screen lets you preview the site layout, as shown in Figure 1-77.

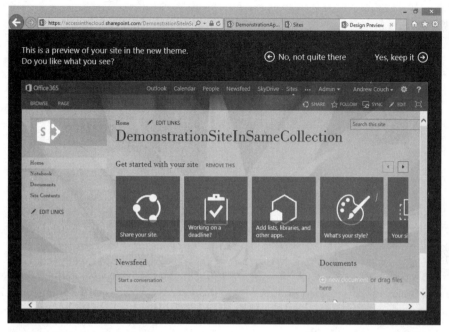

FIGURE 1-77 Trying out a theme.

At this point, you can either return to make additional selections for the theme or use the appropriate links above the sample window, which are marked No, Not Quite There and Yes, Keep It. Any Access web apps you place in the subsite will then use the current choice of theme.

Document storage and libraries

Office 365 can store documents in SharePoint lists, and a web app can have read-only links to these lists. This provides a technique for storing documents outside of the web app but still having links to these documents from within the web app.

Access desktop databases can contain documents in either an OLE Object data type or an Attachment data type. These data types are not supported in a web app, which instead supports a new Image data type for storing .jpeg, .png, .gif, .jpe, or .jfif image files. For documents, you could extract the documents from a desktop database and place them in a SharePoint list, which you can then link to from the web app. Chapter 3 discusses the topic of extracting documents.

Here's the process of linking to documents. For this example, you start by uploading some sample documents to your Team Site as shown in Figure 1-78. To do that, click the New Document link and browse to locate a file to upload.

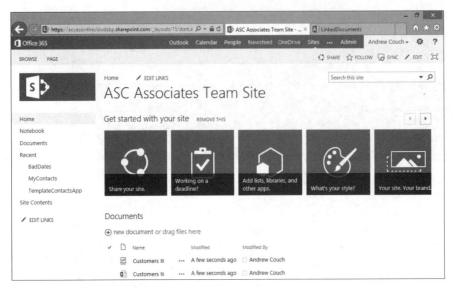

FIGURE 1-78 Uploading documents to Team Site.

Returning to the web app created earlier in Figure 1-32, clicking the Table icon on the ribbon will display the Add Tables screen shown in Figure 1-79. On this screen, you can click the SharePoint List link at the lower center.

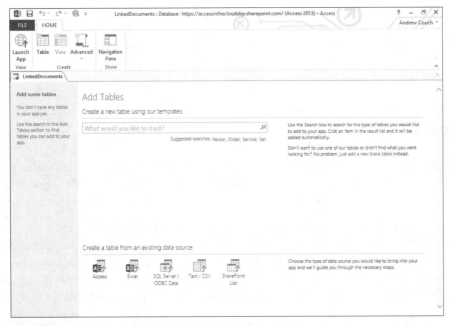

FIGURE 1-79 Creating a link to a SharePoint List.

At the bottom of this screen, below the title Create A Table From An Existing Data Source, are icons for Access, Excel, SQL Server/ODBC Data, Text/CSV, and SharePoint List.

In Figure 1-80, enter the URL for your SharePoint site, accept the default selection Link To The Data Source By Creating A Linked Table, and then click Next.

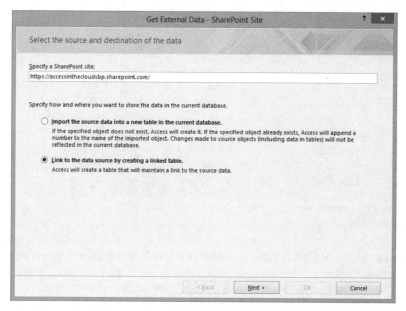

FIGURE 1-80 Specifying the SharePoint site URL.

Tip If you cannot remember the URL of your site, here are two easy ways to obtain it: Start creating a new custom web app as shown previously in Figure 1-31, and then copy the web location to the clipboard; alternatively, hover the mouse over the recent folders shown previously in Figure 1-24 to display the site URL.

Using the next screen, shown in Figure 1-81, you can select a list. Select the Documents list, and then click OK.

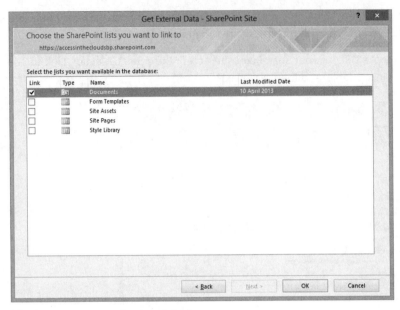

FIGURE 1-81 Selecting the SharePoint list.

The next screen, shown in Figure 1-82, requires you to click the Trust It button to create the link.

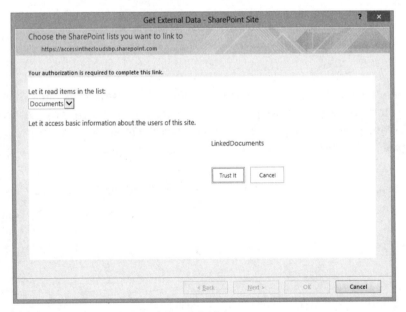

FIGURE 1-82 Trusting the linked SharePoint list.

Completing this process creates a linked table in your web app and two associated views for displaying the data, titled List and Datasheet, as shown in Figure 1-83. Click the Launch App icon located at the far left on the Home ribbon.

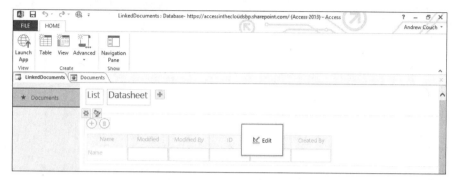

FIGURE 1-83 Displaying the linked SharePoint table in a web app.

The launched app will then display the resulting data, as shown in Figure 1-84. The documents are shown as hyperlinks (in the field next to the caption Name), and clicking a document will prompt the user to allow the document to be downloaded and opened with an appropriate application.

FIGURE 1-84 Displaying the linked content in a browser window.

Next to the Filter The List text box visible in Figure 1-84, you will notice that the icons for adding and editing records are grayed out. They are disabled because the SharePoint lists are read only. This set of icons is called the *action bar* and will be discussed in more detail in Chapter 2.

Microsoft Azure SQL Database, Office 365, and Access

At this point, it is worthwhile to introduce an overview of how all the technologies used in conjunction with a web app can eventually be linked together. Figure 1-85 shows the interrelation between three technologies: Access, Office 365, and Microsoft Azure SQL Database.

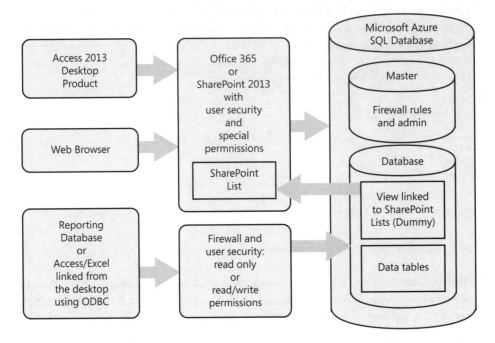

FIGURE 1-85 A roadmap of how Access, Office 365, and Microsoft Azure SQL Database are related.

In a web app, data is not held inside an Access database; instead, it is held in a Microsoft Azure SQL Database. Microsoft Azure SQL Database is a cloud offering of the familiar on-premises SQL Server. Keeping the data there means that your web app can benefit from the great scalability features of Microsoft Azure SQL Database. Chapter 9 looks at the structure of a Microsoft Azure SQL Database in more detail.

The Access 2013 desktop product, shown in the top left of Figure 1-85, links into Office 365, the Office 365 environment, and then saves all the Access design objects from the web app and maintains the underlying database in Azure. Each web app has its own Azure SQL Database instance.

The Azure SQL Database is protected by a firewall; Access 2013 allows you to open up that firewall to allow linking from external applications. If you want to use only the browser interface with built-in features, you do not need to do this. You can create a desktop reporting database or add links to any other desktop database, which—rather than going through Office 365—connect directly to the database tables in Azure. This is shown in the bottom left of Figure 1-85, where you can see that both read only and read/write permissions are available.

In Figure 1-85, you can also see links from within the Azure SQL Database to SharePoint document lists in Office 365. I mentioned earlier that this provides a method for linking from the web app to documents that cannot be stored directly inside the database.

Figure 1-86 shows an overview of how security relates to Office 365 and Azure SQL Database. In the top left of the screen, you can see that browser users interact by logging in to Office 365, while the lower part of the screen shows how an external application can use either the read or read/write Access control to connect directly to Azure SQL Database.

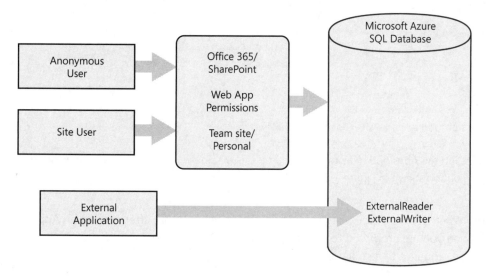

FIGURE 1-86 How security relates to the back-end data in Azure SQL Database.

App Catalog

The App Catalog is sometimes also known as the *Corporate Catalog*. Each subscription has a single App Catalog, and you will see how this now has an important role to play with respect to Microsoft Office 2013 Service Pack 1 features. When you are upgrading a web app. the different versions of the web app are held in the App Catalog. This is described in Chapter 2. Another topic relates to where an app for Access is stored, which is described in Chapter 11, "Using apps for Office with Access."

The App Catalog is a document library, where information is held relating to the applications you have made available for the subscription.

Tip For a small business or small business premium subscription, the option to display the App Catalog is not provided through any menus. However, changing the URL from *https://mycompany.sharepoint.com/SitePages/Home.aspx* to **https://mycompany.sharepoint.com/sites/AppCatalog** will display the App Catalog.

With an Enterprise subscription, you can use the SharePoint menu shown in Figure 1-87 to locate the menu system for the App Catalog.

FIGURE 1-87 Displaying the SharePoint menu choice.

Selecting the Apps option from the menu on the left side will display a screen showing the App Catalog option shown in Figure 1-88.

Tip When using a developer subscription, you might find that after clicking on App Catalog you are prompted to create the App Catalog. This process involves following a simple sequence of instructions.

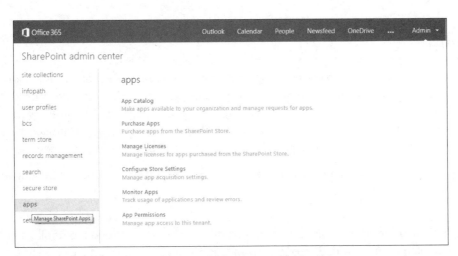

FIGURE 1-88 Selecting the apps menu to display the App Catalog link.

Clicking on the App Catalog link displays the App Catalog, an example of which is shown in Figure 1-89. You get to this by selecting the Apps For SharePoint menu item on the left and then clicking on the New App link to upload an existing web app into the App Catalog. The reason for doing this is to make the web app available to other sites.

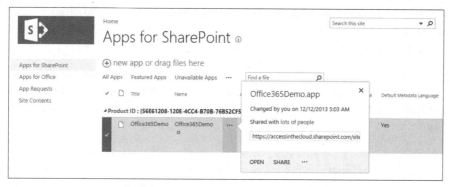

FIGURE 1-89 Adding an app to the App Catalog.

If you click on the ellipses button next to app name, a window is displayed with details of the app. This window has a link to share the app. Sharing the app with everybody means that when you go to a site and add an app as described earlier in the chapter, the app you just shared will be listed in the Apps From Your Organization section, as shown in Figure 1-90.

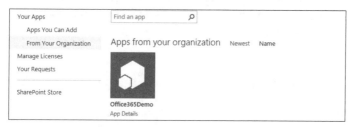

FIGURE 1-90 Adding an app from a site, after sharing the app through the App Catalog.

Summary

Because there is so much new to learn when developing Access web apps, in this chapter I focused on providing you with an overview of the features and concepts you need to learn to begin creating your own web apps.

You started by looking at the Office 365 subscriptions and its components, and I described how to get started with Office 365. Although you can change subscriptions, you'll find it is easier to start out with a subscription best-suited to your needs.

I then introduced the important topic of the different locations where you can construct web apps, either in Personal Site or Team Site. I also mentioned Public Site, which is more fully described in Chapter 8. Later in this chapter, I also described how to expand on the idea of a Team Site by creating your own subsites and, with an Enterprise subscription, how you can go one step further by creating your own site collections.

The idea of a site is important, and you saw how security for both licensed and external users can be managed at the site level. I also demonstrated how a site can be themed, which is important because a web app inherits many of the presentation features from the site theme.

To get you started with the process of creating a web app, I demonstrated how to create a web app based on a template. Then you looked at how both the data and the design of a web app can be downloaded and saved as a package. You saw how packages can be edited and how to upload a package to a site.

When it comes to document storage, you saw the role played by OneDrive For Business 2013 as a location for storing your packages and other files, and you looked at the general document features in Office 365, which you can use to link your web app to display documents stored on your site.

Finally, I indicated how an Access web app is related to both SharePoint in Office 365 and to Microsoft Azure SQL Databases, where your web app data is stored. In later chapters, I will make many references to where the data is stored and indicate how the web app features are related to the capabilities of SQL Database.

Now that you have mastered the capabilities of Office 365 and can find your way around the product, in Chapter 2 I will provide you with the knowledge you need to understand the key capabilities and features of an Access web app.

Finding your way around Access 2013

This chapter provides an overview of how to work with the Access design interface when constructing a web app and also highlights the main features of a web app.

You'll work through the process of creating a custom web app and then import data from the *NorthwindRestructuredData.accdb* sample database.

A new way of building applications

This section provides an overview of the main components used in web apps. First, you'll look at the basic ideas behind the table selector and view selector in the desktop design tool, and then, in the next section, you'll create a custom web app in step-by-step fashion that you can use to interact with the features discussed here.

Figure 2-1 shows a web app as it looks in the desktop design tool. The vertical table selector on the left displays a list of table captions, one for each table in the web app. When you select a table, a view selector appears to the right of the table caption, toward the top of the screen, showing a list of available views for the table.

View ── ┐   ┌── View selector

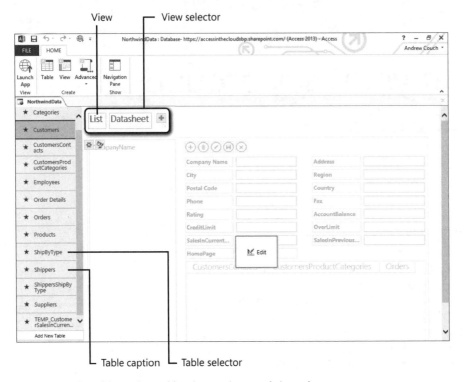

┌── Table caption   └── Table selector

FIGURE 2-1 The table caption, table selector, views, and view selector.

In a web app, tables and queries cannot be directly displayed in a browser window; instead, a user interacts with the data using *views*. (A view is similar to a form found in a desktop Access database.)

The table selector is the first key item you need to understand in a web app. When you create a table, it will appear listed as a table caption in the table selector.

You can change table captions in the following ways:

- Edit the caption manually. Changing the caption does not change the name of the underlying table.

- You can change the order in which the table captions appear in the table selector.

- You can hide a table caption from view when a user looks at the table selector in his browser.

 Caution You can also delete a caption, but doing so also deletes the associated table and any related views on the view selector.

- The icons displayed with each table caption can be changed individually by selecting from a list of icons.

- You can Lock or Unlock a table. Locking the table prevents data in the table being modified.

The table selector is a side menu through which users interact with your application. You can hide everything in the table selector and use only pop-up views in an application, but most applications use the table selector as the main menu.

When you create a table, two views will automatically appear on the view selector. The view selector is a horizontal list of different ways to present your data. By default, you will see a view titled List (which is also called the *List Details view*) and a second view, titled Datasheet. If you create a table using one of the template tables (as discussed in detail in Chapter 4, "Creating a blank web app and using templates"), you might also see an additional default view called Summary. These are called *default views* because Access creates them automatically.

Here are some important points to consider in relation to the view selector:

- You can edit the title or caption for a view. Doing so does not change the underlying name for the view object. A view can also be deleted and duplicated (copied to the same table caption or a different table caption, or copied to become a standalone view).

- From the design interface, you can use the Open In Browser action to quickly display the view in a browser window.

- You can add new views. There are four basic types to choose from: Datasheet, List, Blank, and Summary. You can also reorder views in the view selector.

- Summary views are read-only presentations of summarized data.

- Datasheet, Summary, and List Views display data either from the associated table (on the table selector) or from a query result that includes data from that table. Later you will see that you can work beyond this limitation by organizing unrelated views on a common table caption.

- You can create blank views that display data associated with a table caption and display data from any table in your design. These views take more effort to construct.

- If you do not manually edit the default Datasheet and List views, when new fields are added to a table, these views will be automatically updated to include the new fields. However, if you edit these views, they will no longer update automatically.

- You can open a view as a pop-up window. When you open a List view (which consists of two parts, a List control and Detail area) as a pop-up window using the Popup View property of a control—such as the related items control (RELIC)—the List control is automatically hidden. If you use the OpenPopup macro to open the view, both the list and the detailed area are displayed.

- You can create a Standalone view that is not associated with a table caption; this type of view can be duplicated from your normal views associated with a table selector. The Standalone views are then always opened as pop-up windows by using macros.

If you click the Launch App icon on the home ribbon, the web app design will be displayed in a browser window. This is called the *runtime experience*, which is shown in Figure 2-2. A user can navigate the application by selecting a table caption in the table selector and then selecting a view from the view selector.

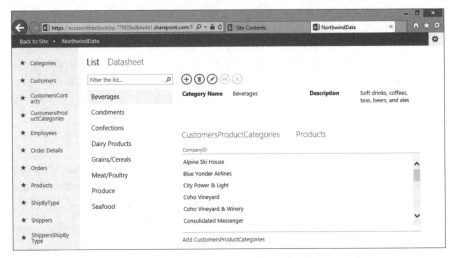

FIGURE 2-2 The runtime experience displaying the web app in a browser window.

Figure 2-3 shows an overview of some of the key objects in a web app and how these objects relate to tables and views.

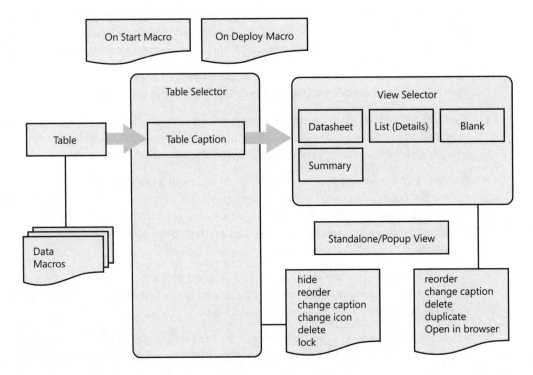

FIGURE 2-3 Overview of key components in a web app.

When the application starts in a web browser, if you have provided an On Start macro it will execute to perform any setup operations. The table selector is displayed, and the first view for the first table caption is displayed. As a user makes different choices on the table selector, the view selector for the selected table caption is displayed, and the first view in the view selector is displayed.

As users interact with certain controls (discussed later in this chapter), further views will be displayed in pop-up windows. Users need to close these pop-up windows in the same sequence that they were opened. This natural pop-up capability is a powerful feature of the interface.

Create a custom web app

Chapter 1, "Finding your way around Office 365," showed how to create a simple web app based on a template application. In this chapter, you'll start by creating a blank custom web app. On the New menu in the backstage (File menu), select the Custom Web App icon, shown in Figure 2-4.

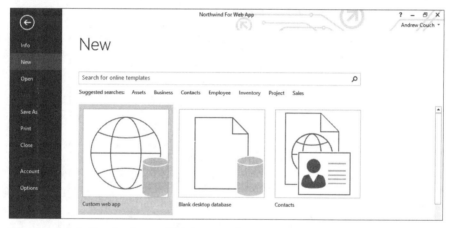

FIGURE 2-4 Selecting the Custom Web App template.

> **Tip** Although you can choose from a number of templates for creating both desktop and web app databases, there is also a new feature in a web app that allows individual or groups of tables to be added to an existing web app. This will be discussed in Chapter 4.

In the custom web app pop-up window shown in Figure 2-5, enter a name for your app, select a location in which to create the web app (note that the default is the Personal Apps location), and then click the Create button.

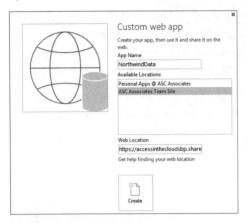

FIGURE 2-5 Selecting the web location.

After creating the web app, the Add Tables screen is displayed, as shown in Figure 2-6. You will use the Add Tables screen in the next section to import data.

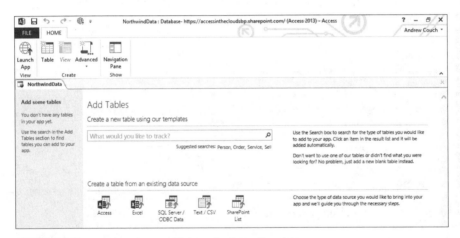

FIGURE 2-6 The empty web app with icons for importing data.

Importing data from Access

In this section, you will import data from the sample database *NorthwindRestructuredData.accdb*. (See the Introduction to this book for details about how to download the sample data files.)

As shown in Figure 2-6, at the bottom of the screen, click the Access icon to start the Get External Data wizard, shown in Figure 2-7. Browse to locate the *NorthwindRestructuredData.accdb* sample database, and then click OK.

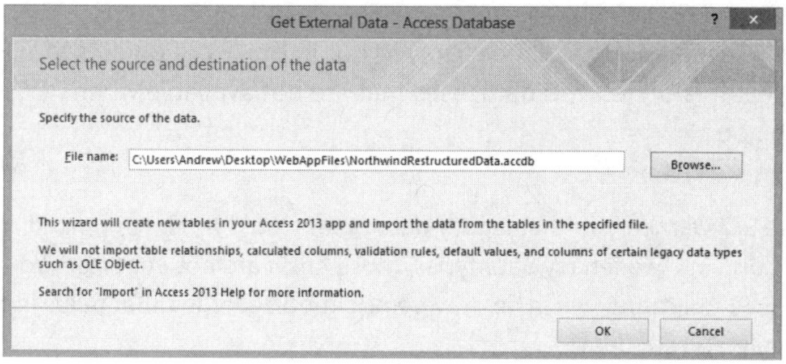

FIGURE 2-7 Selecting a desktop database.

You can see some text in Figure 2-7 explaining that the following desktop database features will not be imported. (Conversion will be discussed in detail in Chapter 3, "Converting a desktop database to a web app.")

- **Table relationships** These are either converted to lookups or ignored.

- **Calculated columns** Data in the calculation gets saved as a new field of the appropriate type.

- **Validation rules** Field and table rules are not imported.

- **Default values** These are not imported.

- **Legacy data type columns** These include OLE objects and attachments, and they are not imported.

In Figure 2-8, you can see the Import Objects pop-up window. This window shows fewer choices than are available when importing between desktop databases. In addition to selecting which tables to import, you can use other options in the dialog to choose whether relationships are processed and whether to import data in addition to table structures. Select all the tables (keeping the default options shown in the figure), and click OK.

FIGURE 2-8 Importing tables, data, and relationships.

Tip You might wonder why several options appear grayed out in the list of objects to import. These are legacy features of desktop databases that are not available when importing data into a web app.

As mentioned earlier, Figure 2-7 warned you that legacy data types would not be imported. Because the sample database contains two legacy data types, those fields are not imported. You'll see a warning (as shown in Figure 2-9) indicating which fields were not imported; the other fields in these tables were imported and populated with data.

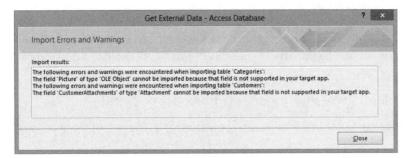

FIGURE 2-9 Warning about unsupported data types.

Using the navigation pane

The navigation pane is a simple, searchable list of all the design objects in your web app. In Figure 2-10, you will see that in addition to displaying the new table selector, you can display the more traditional navigation pane by clicking the Navigation Pane icon on the right on the home ribbon. This icon acts as a toggle button for hiding and displaying the navigation pane. You can also use the shutter bar on the top right of the navigation pane to close the window. On the right of the table selector are two icons, one showing a cogs symbol and the other showing a paintbrush. These are called *charms*, and each charm displays a drop-down menu of choices when clicked.

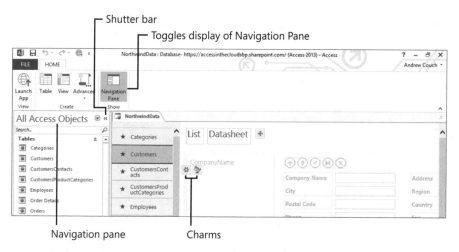

Shutter bar

Toggles display of Navigation Pane

Navigation pane

Charms

FIGURE 2-10 Displaying the navigation pane.

The desktop design interface provides a familiar look and feel that resembles the UI you see when working with traditional desktop databases, although there are quite a few differences. You will probably find that the table selector and ribbons are the most natural methods for working on a design. When working on table selector or other design objects, you normally can click a charm such as settings/actions or right-click an object, which will then display a drop-down menu for one of possibly several associated actions.

 Tip The navigation pane is essential when you work with standalone views, macros, or queries.

Working with tables, lookups, and relationships

In Chapter 4, you'll see detailed steps for inspecting the design of objects in the web app. In this section, however, you will see only what the results look like so that you can get an overview of some differences between a web app and desktop database.

Inside the sample desktop database you used earlier for importing data, tables are tied together with relationships, such as those shown in Figure 2-11.

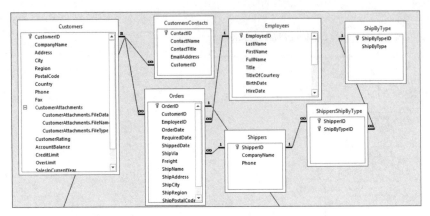

FIGURE 2-11 Relationship diagram from a desktop database.

In addition to having defined relationships in the desktop database, you can also have lookups defined. An example of a lookup is shown in Figure 2-12.

Field Name	Data Type	Description (Optional)
OrderID	AutoNumber	Unique order number.
CustomerID	Number	
EmployeeID	Number	Same entry as in Employees table.
OrderDate	Date/Time	
RequiredDate	Date/Time	
ShippedDate	Date/Time	
ShipVia	Number	Same as Shipper ID in Shippers table.
Freight	Currency	
ShipName	Short Text	Name of person or company to receive the shipment.
ShipAddress	Short Text	Street address only -- no post-office box allowed.

Field Properties

General | Lookup

Display Control	Combo Box
Row Source Type	Table/Query
Row Source	SELECT Employees.EmployeeID, [LastName] & ", " & [FirstName] AS Name FROM Emplo
Bound Column	1
Column Count	2

FIGURE 2-12 A lookup defined in a desktop database.

For the imported data, if you display the web app in a browser by clicking the Launch App icon on the ribbon, you can see in Figure 2-13 that the web app does understand how data in the different tables are related. This figure shows the related items control (RELIC) and has automatically produced a tabbed area on the screen to display related items from several associated tables.

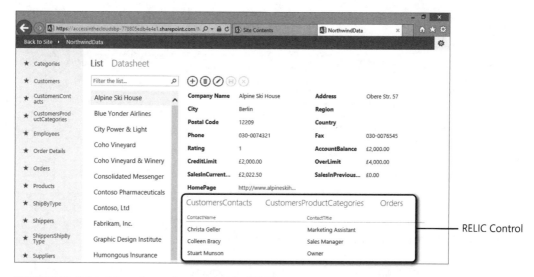

FIGURE 2-13 Related items in a web app using the RELIC.

Figure 2-14 illustrates another way to display related information. The desktop database did not have a lookup for the customer in the *CustomersContacts* table, but the web app is displaying a lookup using the new autocomplete control. As you type into this control while editing the record, it provides assistance with looking up a related value.

FIGURE 2-14 The autocomplete control assisting when editing data.

If you examine the design of the web app table, you will see that a new lookup was created based on the relationship between tables, as shown in Figure 2-15. (Click to highlight the field *CustomerID*, and then click the Modify Lookups icon on the Design tab.)

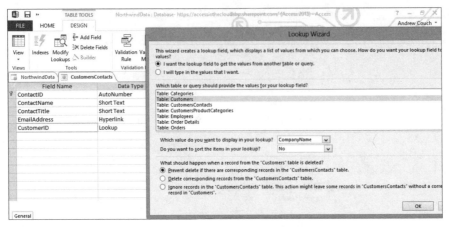

FIGURE 2-15 Web app table design showing a new lookup for related data.

In summary, a desktop database can contain relationships (which often enforce data-checking rules called *referential integrity*) and can also have lookups defined in a table structure to provide assistance when completing information (so that users can choose the appropriate value from either a list box or combo box filled with the related data).

A web app does not show lookups and referential integrity separately; instead, it has its own special new type of lookup that combines those two ideas. You can present related information using several techniques, including displaying lists of related records and using controls that assist users when selecting data.

> **Tip** You must have relationships defined in your data *before* importing it into a web app; otherwise, you will miss out on many great features of a web app. The process in which the web app does all the hard work for you—automatically creating views and displaying related information—is often referred to as *scaffolding*. Everything you see in this chapter (apart from the Web Browser control and subview described toward the end of the chapter) was created automatically by Access—no design effort was required!

Displaying data in a browser

When you are working in the desktop design interface for a web app, you will be working with the design of views and other objects, not the data that is displayed using the views. To see the data displayed, you need to launch the web app in a browser window. Access has a special icon on the ribbon to do that and also some shortcuts you can use when working with a design object to quickly display that design object in a browser.

Figure 2-16 summarizes the methods you can use from within the desktop design interface and browser window to display data.

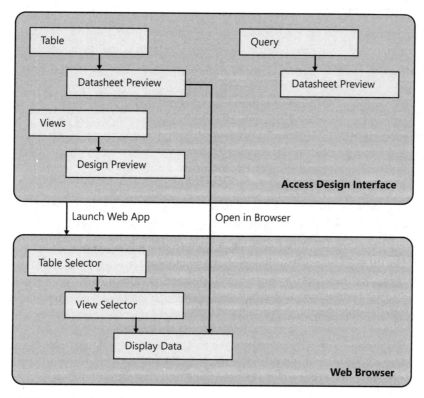

FIGURE 2-16 Roadmap showing how to display data using a web app.

From the table selector, click to select a table, click the Settings/Actions charm to see a drop-down list of actions, and then choose View Data, as shown in Figure 2-17.

FIGURE 2-17 Using the actions menu of a table caption to open a table in datasheet preview.

This displays the data inside the desktop interface using a special preview datasheet, as shown in Figure 2-18.

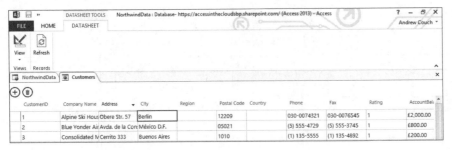

FIGURE 2-18 Data from a table displayed in the datasheet preview.

 Warning Be very careful not to confuse the *datasheet view* (which is a type of view and a real object) with the *datasheet preview* (which is not visible as an object in the application—it is solely a design-time feature for previewing data).

In Chapter 6, "Creating data sources by using queries," when you look at queries, you will see that you can also display a query in a datasheet preview inside the design interface. You can't directly display queries in a browser; they are always used with a view, where the view shows the data from the query.

These two examples are the only situations where you see data displayed in the design interface within Access. A view needs to be displayed in a browser window to interact with the data.

In Figure 2-17, shown previously, you can see the Launch App icon on the left side of the ribbon. As you have seen, clicking the Launch App icon opens the app in the browser window, displaying the first view for the first table in the table selector.

To help you improve your productivity when working in the design interface, if you click any view and then select the Settings/Action charm for that view, you will see an option to Open In Browser, as shown in Figure 2-19. Choosing that option opens the view in a browser window, which saves you the time you would otherwise need to spend navigating to the view in the browser by using the table and view selectors to display the view.

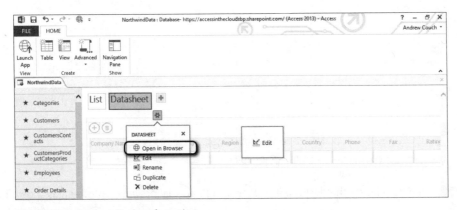

FIGURE 2-19 Settings/Actions for a view.

Warning You probably already noticed the large Edit button in the center of the screen. This button is used to edit the view, not the table. In the design interface, when you click a view, you will see that view presented in what is called *design preview* on the screen. Clicking the Edit button takes you into the design for that view.

After saving any changes, you can also switch between your design interface and a browser window and refresh the browser window to quickly display changes you are making to the views in the design tool.

Working with different views

A view consists of controls that display data. Figure 2-20 shows a schematic layout for a List view (also called a List Details view). The view contains a List control and Filter box on the left and an individual detail control in the center. Other controls can also be added to this view. The view has two events, *On Load* and *On Current*, to which you can attach macro code. Individual controls have combinations of *On Click* and *After Update* events to which you can also attach macro code. The Action bar elements support *On Click* events for custom buttons, which I discuss in Chapter 7, "Programming a web app by using macros."

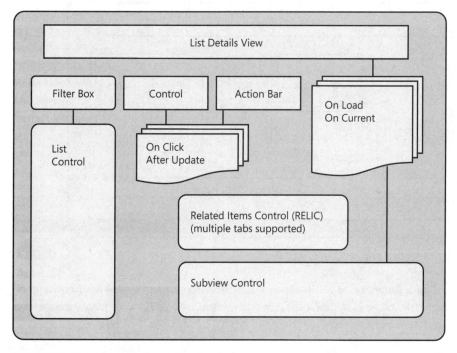

FIGURE 2-20 Main components in a List Details view.

Two controls of particular importance are the RELIC and the Subview control (discussed later in this chapter). The RELIC can be multitabbed and show related information. It also has a special pop-up feature: when you click a data item, an additional pop-up view displays more detail about the related record.

The List control provides a list of matched results and has an associated Filter Box control for filtering the data shown in the list.

> **Tip** I mentioned earlier that opening a List view using the pop-up property on the RELIC will automatically hide the normal list portion of the view and show only details. This is important because it explains how Access can automatically make use of views, both to display as a List view associated with a table caption and to display details when you drill through by using the RELIC.

Figure 2-20 also provides a good description of what can be constructed in a blank view if you ignore the List control and Filter box on the left side of the picture.

A Datasheet view has a different structure. (See Figure 2-21.) You can add controls to the tabulated datasheet or add buttons to the Action bar.

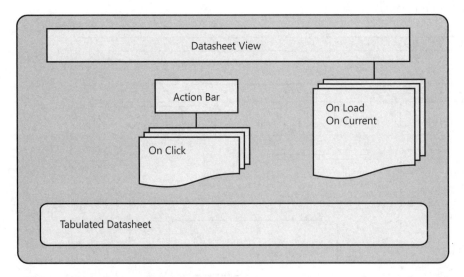

FIGURE 2-21 Main components in a Datasheet view.

The layout for a Summary view is shown in Figure 2-22. This type of view is read-only and different from the other types of views in that it has a special control for displaying summary details. Notice that it does not have an Action bar.

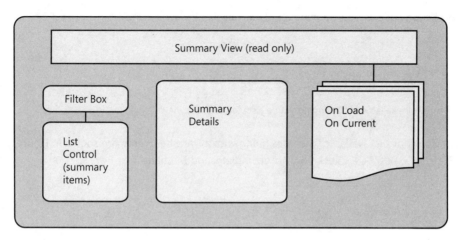

FIGURE 2-22 Main components in a Summary view.

Controls available in a view

Chapter 5, "Displaying data in views," provides more detailed information about working with the more complex controls in views. This section provides an overview of the view controls. Figure 2-23 lists the different controls you can use in constructing views. The specific set of controls available varies according to the type of view.

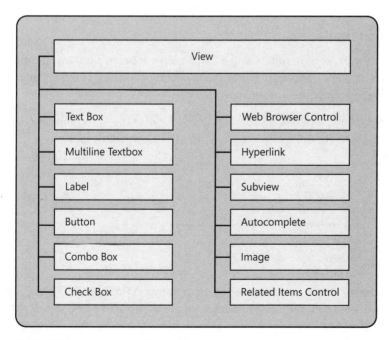

FIGURE 2-23 Controls available for designing views.

The controls available when designing a List view or Blank view are shown in Figure 2-24.

FIGURE 2-24 Controls available for designing with a List view or Blank view.

The following controls, available when designing with a Datasheet view, are shown in Figure 2-25: Text Box, Button, Combo Box, Check Box, Autocomplete, and Multiline Text Box.

FIGURE 2-25 Controls available for designing with a Datasheet view.

 Tip A Summary view does not have any available controls you can add in design view.

The remainder of this section takes a more in-depth look at the more sophisticated controls, which you probably have not used previously. You'll also explore the Action bar and the List control, which are controls that do not appear in the toolbox but get added to a view when the view is created (if appropriate for the type of view).

Autocomplete control

There is a potential performance problem when using a Combo Box control in a browser to present a long list of choices. The Autocomplete control performs a similar function but is both richer in features and better optimized to improve performance.

In Figure 2-26, when not editing a record, if you hover the cursor over the Autocomplete control next to the CustomerID label, the control is displayed as a hyperlink along with a tooltip.

FIGURE 2-26 Hovering over an Autocomplete control.

If you now click the hyperlink, a pop-up window appears, as shown in Figure 2-27. This pop-up window is the List view associated with the *Customers* table (where the list part of the view is not displayed). At this point, you could click on any related items or other Autocomplete controls in the pop-up window to open yet another pop-up window. This process can repeat to a depth of around eight windows. To get back to the original view, you need to step back through the screens by closing the individual windows.

FIGURE 2-27 A pop-up window showing related information for the Autocomplete control.

Close the pop-up window, and then click the Edit icon on the Action bar (the button marked with a pencil symbol). If you clear the contents of the Company Name field and start typing as shown in Figure 2-28, the control will display a drop-down list of matched choices. Notice also that at the bottom of the list is a choice marked <Add A New Item>. The matching process here is against any records that contain the characters you enter.

FIGURE 2-28 Matching records as you type into an Autocomplete control.

> **Tip** The Autocomplete control will display up to a maximum of eight items with each search. Note also that a combo box is limited to displaying a maximum of 500 entries, so for a large number of related records, the Autocomplete control is a better choice of control. It is also the control that Access uses when creating your default views and linking to display data from other tables. (Combo boxes are used when an explicit value list lookup is provided.)

Related items control

The related items control (RELIC) is designed to display related information for a record. For example, it can show a list of child records in a one-to-many relationship. It also can be used to drill-down to open a related view displaying even more detailed information. This control is limited to displaying a maximum of four fields in each tab. It also has an option you can use to add an additional aggregate calculation over one of the four fields (depending on the field data type). By using this control, you can add tabs to display data from other related tables. Earlier in this chapter, in Figure 2-13, you saw an example of how the RELIC can display data from related tables. Figure 2-29 shows what the RELIC looks like when working in the design tool to specify the field information for displaying data in the control.

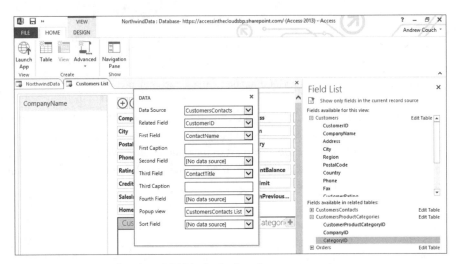

FIGURE 2-29 Data options for a RELIC in the Design view.

Subview control

A Subview control is like a SubForm in a desktop database; the control lets you embed one view inside another view and gives you better control of the layout. It is not limited to just four fields, but constructing it involves more work than creating a simple RELIC, and the Subview control does not have the built-in drill-down capability of the RELIC. In Chapter 5, I will describe both the RELIC and Subview controls in more detail. In Figure 2-30, you can see an example of a subview with a horizontal scroll bar, illustrating how more than four fields can be displayed by using the control.

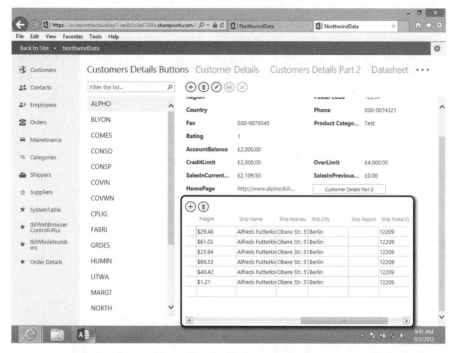

FIGURE 2-30 Subview shown with scrollbars in the browser window.

Action bar

You already saw the Action bar displayed on several screens. For a Datasheet view, the Action bar contains a reduced set of icons—Delete and Add. For a List view or Blank view, the Action bar has icons for Add, Delete, Edit, Save, and Cancel; the icons that will be available depend on whether you are currently editing a record. The Summary view does not support an Action bar.

> **Tip** You can add your own icons to the Action bar. You can also delete existing icons, but they cannot be added back after they've been deleted. You might prefer to use macro code to hide a built-in button icon. If you later want to make a copy of the view, you can optionally make the hidden buttons available on the copy.

List control

On the left side of a List view or Summary view, you will see a List control; this control cannot be deleted from the view and cannot be added to any other type of view. (The List control and associated filter box are automatically present when a List or Summary view is created.) This control has more clever features than you might think, so it needs a bit of explaining. Figure 2-31 shows the UI after some text has been typed in and the Enter key has been pressed to filter the results.

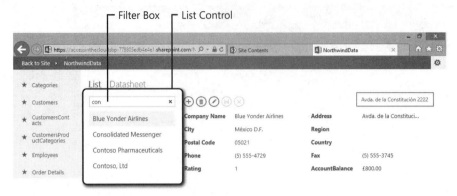

FIGURE 2-31 Searching using the List control.

Notice that the first record matched to the pattern "con" does not appear as part of the company name *Blue Yonder Airlines*. This record is matched because the filter acts to search on all fields, and the address field for the first record contains the word *Constitución*.

As an example of the more advanced search, you can reduce which fields are searched by entering the field name, a colon, and then the search criteria, as shown in Figure 2-32.

FIGURE 2-32 Searching a specific field using the List control.

> **Tip** Additional search techniques include adding a space between words to search on multiple AND criteria, or embedding a string in double quotes to include spaces in the pattern.

Hyperlink control

The Hyperlink control acts as a hyperlink when viewing data. When editing a record, clicking the icon next to the control will display a pop-up window for editing the hyperlink, as shown in Figure 2-33.

FIGURE 2-33 Edit Hyperlink pop-up window.

Multiline Text Box control

The multiline text box is a text box that is fixed to display more than one line of text. The cursor navigation means that pressing the Enter key inserts a new line when editing data in the control. An example of a multiline text box is shown at the lower right in Figure 2-34.

FIGURE 2-34 Multiline Text Box control.

Web Browser control

The Web Browser control is a little disappointing, because much of the functionality is available only with an on-premises version of SharePoint 2013. If you try to use it to link to a URL in Office 365, you will often see a message similar to that in Figure 2-35.

FIGURE 2-35 Attempting to display nonsecure data in the web browser control.

> **Tip** If you try to use a link to a document on your Office 365 site—for example, linking to a spreadsheet document or .pdf file, with something like the following link: *https://accessinthecloudsbp.sharepoint.com/Shared%20Documents/ Customers.xlsx?Web=1*—you will get an error indicating that the content cannot be displayed in a frame.

Overview of macro programming and data macros

This section introduces the new macro programming environment for attaching code to a web app. Before examining in detail at what macro programming looks like in Chapter 7, it is useful to have an overall picture of where you can add macros in a web app and gain an understanding of the terms used to refer to macros. Figure 2-36 provides an overview of how macros fit into the environment and how other related objects can be associated with macros. Note that the On Deploy macro is not shown in this diagram; this is discussed in Chapter 7.

There are two distinct types of macros: *user interface macros*, which execute in the browser, and *data macros*, which execute in the Microsoft Azure SQL Database. Each type of macro has a different set of macro commands.

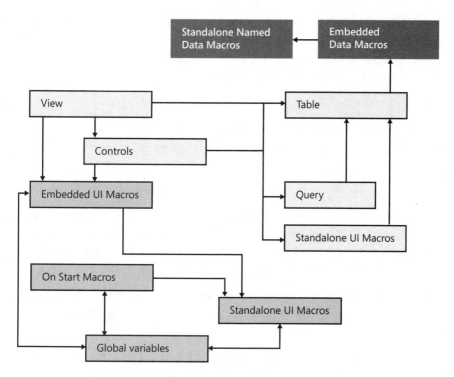

FIGURE 2-36 Overview of where macro code can be located in an application.

Macros can be embedded in an object, or they can be standalone. A standalone macro can be used by other macros; a macro that is embedded cannot be directly used by another macro or referenced from another user interface object. In Figure 2-36, I do not show all the possible ways in which macros can interact with each other; that will be discussed in Chapter 7.

Macro code can be placed in the On Start macro, embedded in a view or table or embedded as a standalone item accessible through the navigation pane:

- **On Start**   This is a special macro. You can have only one *On Start* macro, and this macro is associated with the app itself and not a specific view. You use this macro to perform setup activities. It executes whenever the associated web app is refreshed. The macro has the user interface set of macro commands and can also execute other standalone UI macros.

- **Views**   Inside a view, you can attach macros that execute in response to events, such as when a view is loaded or a button is clicked. These are referred to as *embedded user interface macros*, or sometime as *UI macros*. These macros can also execute standalone UI macros.

- **Tables**   Data macros are different from UI macros, because they have special actions that can execute only in a data macro. An *embedded data macro* is attached to the table design. Data macros execute when data in the table changes. These macros can also execute standalone named data macros.

- **Navigation pane**   You can view standalone macros (both UI and named data macros) in the navigation pane in the Macro section. These macros can be called from other places where you can write macros. Often, these standalone macros contain sequences of steps you might want to run from more than one part of your application.

It is also useful to consider the following list of basic macro features:

- **Trace table**   A macro tracing table can record the actions of data macros. This capability is particularly useful when investigating why a data macro does not act as anticipated.

- **Parameters**   Data values can be both passed into and received back as a return value from standalone macros; this allows you to write general-purpose code.

- **Global variables**   UI macro variables are global variables and hold values that are available in other UI macros on different views—for example, holding values for a user's preferences. These variables are not available inside data macro code, but they can be passed from a UI macro as a parameter to a standalone data macro.)

- **Execution scope**   This is where you most likely need to take care when writing macro code when using certain macro commands, because your code can refer only to objects that are in scope.

- **Syntax**   When you refer to objects, you often can use both a formal method of reference and a shorthand notation (involving less formal syntax). Establishing the full formal syntax clearly in your mind by using it in your code (and avoiding shorthand references) will save you time over the long run by helping make your code error free.

Upgrading and deploying a web app

Before Service Pack 1, the only techniques available for upgrading or changing applications were editing the live application or, as described in Chapter 1, saving the web app as a package, modifying it (by restoring on a test system, changing, testing, and then saving again as a package), and then uploading it to replace a live system. The problem was that unless the web app contained static data, when it was replaced any changes made to data would be lost; the application and the data cannot be split apart and changed independently.

Both this lack of a good upgrade path and concerns from developers who wanted to protect their designs from changes if made available in the Office Store, has led to a number of new features being added.

Before I describe some scenarios for upgrading a web app, I need to discuss three new features: locking a table, locking an application, and the On Deploy Data Macro.

Each table now supports a new action, as shown in Figure 2-37, which enables a table to be either locked or unlocked.

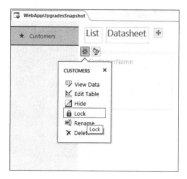

FIGURE 2-37 Locking a table.

Once locked, the data in the table becomes read-only for all users (including the developer). Later, when we look at upgrade scenarios, you will see that locked tables always replace existing tables, both in terms of structure and data (a technique referred to as *rip and replace*). Candidates for these tables could be static data lists or tables used for managing your system.

> **Tip** Although a locked table is read-only, you can change the data either by using data macro code or through an external Open Database Connectivity (ODBC) link to the table.

A second new feature is available when saving an application as a package: an option to lock the application. This option is shown in Figure 2-38. This feature applies only when using the deployment option. (It does not apply when saving as a snapshot or new web app.)

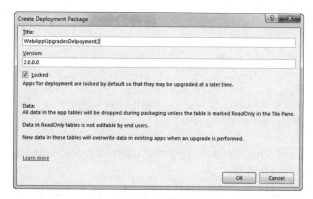

FIGURE 2-38 Setting the Locked property when saving an application as a package.

The main idea of a locked application is to protect your design and prevent others from altering your design. Once an application is locked, the following rules apply:

- The Customize In Access option is no longer available in the runtime environment, protecting your design against being opened with a copy of Access.

- External data links using ODBC are no longer available. This means you cannot create a desktop database linked to the web app or use PowerPivot or any other techniques to connect to the web app data using external tools. (The reason for this is because you need to be able to customize a web app in Access to find out the Azure SQL Database credentials).

- No option for repackaging to create a backup exists. Because the Customize In Access link is removed, you cannot create another package to back up a system.

- The process of locking an application could be used by a developer who wants to put an application into the Office Store but protect the design. To make the design available for others to change, the application should be left unlocked.

 Caution There is no mechanism for unlocking the web app or extracting data from the web app once it has been locked.

Another new feature is the On Deploy Macro. This is a special macro that is executed only once, when an upgrade is applied to a web app. The macro is executed after the tables, queries and other such items have been upgraded (and schema changes have been applied). This macro is similar to a standalone data macro (but without input parameters or return values), and it is listed on the Advanced menu in the design desktop, as shown in Figure 2-39.

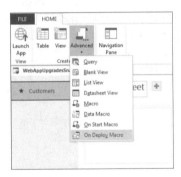

FIGURE 2-39 The On Deploy Macro selected from the Advanced menu.

The macro will execute when a web app is upgraded or first installed, and it can also be executed on demand from other user interfaces or data macros.

The macro is executed after any schema changes have been applied and can be used to manipulate data that is required as part of an upgrade. You will see examples of using this macro in Chapter 7, in the "On Deploy macro" section.

Caution If you delete a column, because the ODM executes after schema changes, the data in that column will be lost. If you rename a column, the data will also be lost, because the rename is implemented as a DROP column and then an ADD column. So when you are renaming a column, you could create the new column and, in the ODM, copy the data to the new column. Then, when upgrading the next version, you could delete the column before preparing the upgrade package.

The process of changing version numbers is, in part, a manual process in which you need to edit the app package. In Chapter 1, I demonstrated how to edit the appmanifest.xml file, which contains a version-number tag.

Caution There is no mechanism for preventing an application from being upgraded and skipping over a previous version-number upgrade. This means the ODM might need to be designed to allow for skipping version upgrades. To do this, you could add your own version-number table to the web app to control which sections of the ODM are executed. Referring back to my point regarding renaming a field that contained data, there could be a loss of data if a field was renamed in V2 and deleted in V3. Then, when applying V4, the schema changes would mean that because in V3 the field was dropped, the V2 code to move data into the renamed field would fail.

There are two new packaging options, so in total there are three options, as shown in Figure 2-40.

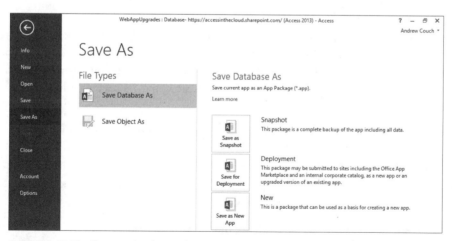

FIGURE 2-40 The three packaging options: Save As Snapshot, Save For Deployment, and Save As New App.

Before I discuss the deployment and upgrading process of each option, I need to explain the significance of globally unique identifiers (GUIDs) and version numbers. In the appmanifest.xml file, there are two attributes: one is called the GUID and the other is the version number. The combination of these needs to be unique when a web app package is uploaded to your Office 365 subscription.

If you need to use the same tenant for production, test, and development, because the GUID and version number combination needs to be unique on the tenant (subscription), you will need to edit your appmanifest.xml file before starting development and testing. You could use a naming convention such as 1.1.0.0 to indicate testing, and 1.1.0.1 to indicate final deployment. Then, for the next version, 1.2.0.0 indicates the next test version and 1.2.0.1 indicates the next live deployment version.

Here is an explanation of the three packaging options shown in Figure 2-40:

- **Save As New App** This option creates a new package with a new GUID. The version number is always set to 1.0.0.0, and the application title is not saved. This is a great method to use when you want to start a completely new branch of development for your product or application. You have an option to include data. (Application locking does not apply.) A package created with the New option should not be deployed to the Office Store or App Catalog because it is not upgradeable. The New package option is also useful for simple, single-user development, where you want backups, you are the only system user, and you do not need any upgrade features.

- **Save As Snapshot** This option uses the current version number and generates an image containing all the data. It uses the current version number (which you probably want to edit in the appmanifest.xml file). This packaging option uses the same GUID and version number. Data is always included. (Application locking does not apply.) A package created with the Snapshot option should not be deployed to the Office Store or App Catalog because it would overwrite data in an existing installation. A Snapshot package can act as a backup of an upgradeable system or as a point from which to start developing an upgrade for an existing system and retaining live data for testing.

- **Save For Deployment** This packaging option is the standard mechanism for deploying upgrades and upgradeable systems. It retains the GUIDs, and only data in locked tables are included (which saves you the effort of emptying out test data). It includes an option to lock the application. Applying an upgrade will change the title and version number to match the values in the package. This is the format to use if you are deploying to the Office Store or App Catalog.

If you want to take advantage of the versioning and upgrade features, you need to upload the application to the App Catalog. If you directly upload a web app to a site (a process known as *side-loading*), the versioning mechanism will not be applied. However, as you will see later in this section, you can make use of side-loading to speed up the development cycle. For the moment, to avoid any possible confusion, forget all about side-loading.

To take advantage of the new versioning and upgrading features, you need to start your web app in the App Catalog.

A typical development scenario involves a bespoke developer or in-house developer creating a web app (single system) and needing to maintain the application. Here is how such a scenario should play out:

- Once the application is developed, start by creating a deployment package. This package must be uploaded to the App Catalog (and it will be version 1.0.0.1).

- Deploy the application to the production site.

- Leave the application unlocked, and manage the security with Microsoft SharePoint by using Contribute permissions for users (to prevent users from editing the design). When you use this approach of leaving the application unlocked, the external data features are available (for example, to be used with a desktop reporting database). If the application was locked, the external data features would not be available.

- As new versions are required, the developer can open the app in Access, create a package using the Snapshot option, edit the version number by cracking open the package (version 2.0.0.0), and then upload that to a test site.

- After completing development and testing, create a new package using the Deployment option, edit the package version number (making it version 2.0.0.1), and upload the package to the App Catalog.

This upgrade will then automatically be available for individual sites to manually apply it.

Once your web application is ready for deployment as a live system, save a deployment package of your web app and proceed to the App Catalog. (See the "App Catalog" section of Chapter 1 for details about how to locate the App Catalog). Figure 2-41 shows the Apps For SharePoint page of the App Catalog. From the menu on the left, select Apps For SharePoint and then click on the New App button.

FIGURE 2-41 Adding a new app for SharePoint to the App Catalog.

Clicking the New App button will display the window shown in Figure 2-42, where you can enter a path in the Choose A File text box or browse to locate your web app deployment package. (You will also see an optional text box for entering version comments.) After locating the file, click the OK button.

FIGURE 2-42 Locating the web app file to upload.

Clicking OK uploads the web app and displays the window shown in Figure 2-43, which can be used to adjust the web app properties.

FIGURE 2-43 Saving the details of the uploaded web app.

After you save any changes to the properties, the newly uploaded web app will be listed in the Apps For SharePoint screen shown in Figure 2-44. The two most important properties are the version number, which shows as 1.0.0.0 in the App Version column, and the unique GUID, which appears in the Product ID column.

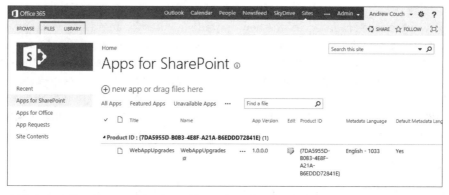

FIGURE 2-44 Resulting entry for the web app after it is uploaded.

Next, proceed to the site where you intend to make the web app available, go to your site contents page, and click on the Add An App button, as shown in Figure 2-45.

FIGURE 2-45 Adding an app from the Site Contents page in a Team Site.

After selecting to add an app, you will be taken to the Your Apps menu shown in Figure 2-46. This is the area where you previously created blank web apps. But in this case, click on the From Your Organization item in the menu on the left. In the center pane, you should then see the web app that was uploaded into the App Catalog. Click on the web app to complete the process of creating the live system.

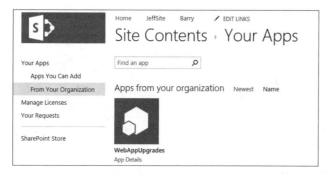

FIGURE 2-46 Selecting the web app that was previously uploaded to the App Catalog.

> **Tip** If you want to take advantage of the new upgrade features for an existing web app, you need to customize the existing web app in Access and create a new Snapshot package. Then replace the existing application by uploading the new Snapshot package into the App Catalog. Then, on the web app site, delete the old web app and create a new one based on the available web app in the App Catalog. You can then move forward using the new deployment features for managing upgrades to the application. I recommend that you run through all the steps with a test application before attempting this with a valued existing web app.

The next step is to create a development site and a development copy of the web app. You want to have a web app in the development area that has the same unique Product ID (GUID), but it must have a different version number (because the GUID and version number combination in a tenant need to be unique).

Start by opening your live system in the browser window and selecting the Customize In Access option as shown in Figure 2-47.

FIGURE 2-47 Opening the live web app and selecting Customize In Access.

After opening the web app in Access, from the file menu choose Save As, and then select Save As Snapshot as shown in Figure 2-48.

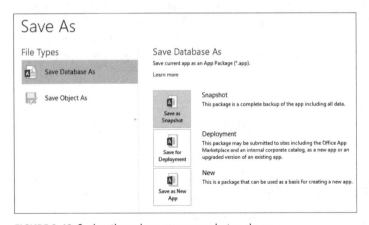

FIGURE 2-48 Saving the web app as a snapshot package.

After saving your file, change the file extension from *.app* to *.zip* as shown in Figure 2-49. This process of editing a package was also described more fully in Chapter 1 in the "Editing a web app package" section.

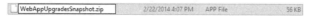

FIGURE 2-49 Changing the file extension of the package to a .zip file.

Use Notepad to edit the appmanifest.xml file so that the *Version* attribute is 1.0.0.1, as shown in Figure 2-50. Note you will need to save a copy of the file and then drag and drop the file into the .zip file to replace the existing appmanifest.xml. Be sure to check that you successfully edited the file; otherwise, it will fail to upload.

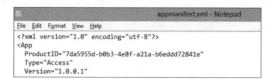

FIGURE 2-50 Editing the version number attribute from 1.0.0.0 to 1.0.0.1 in the appmanifest.xml file.

After editing the appmanifest.xml, rename the web app snapshot file, changing the file extension from *.zip* back to *.app*.

Create a new subsite for your development work. Then, in Site Contents, choose to add an app. (Refer back to Chapter 1, Figure 1-42 for detailed steps.) In Figure 2-51, the Access App button was clicked to add an Access app. Next, upload the snapshot package into your development site.

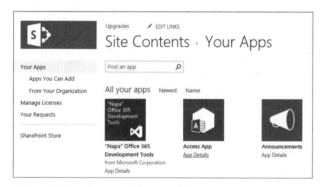

FIGURE 2-51 Uploading (side-loading) the new web app to your developer site.

Once the package is uploaded, click on the app to display the web app in a browser window and then click Customize In Access. (Refer back to Chapter 1, Figures 1-33 through 1-35 for detailed steps.) In Figure 2-52, with the Customers table in design view, a new additional field (CustomerAddress) has been added to our existing Customers table as an example of preparing an upgrade to the design of a web app.

WebAppUpgradesSnapshot | Customers

Field Name	Data Type
ID	AutoNumber
CustomerName	Short Text
CustomerAddress	Short Text

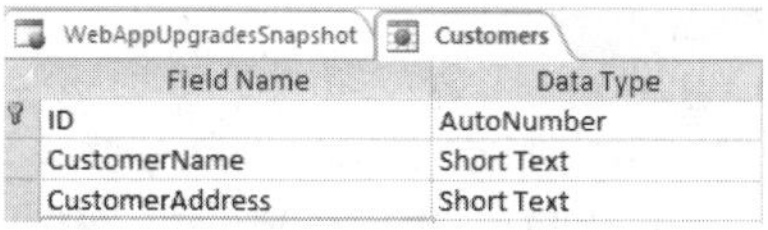

FIGURE 2-52 Making a structural design change by adding a new field to a table.

Caution If you delete a field, data in that field will be lost during the upgrade. This also applies if you rename a field, because a rename is equivalent to deleting the field and then adding back the field. In Chapter 7, in the "On Deploy macro" section, I discuss the relationship between the macro and schema changes.

After you complete your design changes, return to the file menu and, from the Save As menu, choose Save Database As, and then click the Save For Deployment button, as shown in Figure 2-53.

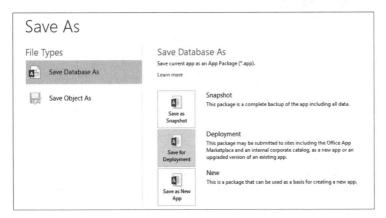

FIGURE 2-53 Creating the deployment package for the new version of the web app.

After you click Save For Deployment, the window shown in Figure 2-54 is displayed. In this screen, I changed the version number to 2.0.0.0 and renamed the deployment package as *webAppUpgradesDeploymentV2*.

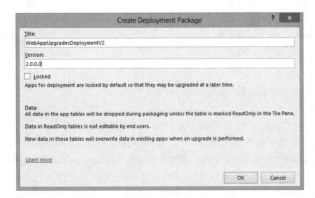

FIGURE 2-54 Changing the version number to 2.0.0.0 when creating the deployment package.

After creating the package, repeat the steps described in Figures 2-41, 2-42, and 2-43 to upload the deployment package to the App Catalog. This results in the App Catalog shown in Figure 2-55. Notice that the product IDs for both the original web app and the upgrade have the same GUID, but the App Version attributes are different.

Tip If you want to go exploring into the depths of the deployment feature, you could make a copy of the deployment package and rename the file extension to *.zip*, and if you have SQL Server 2012 installed, you can double-click on a file called *appdb.dacpac*, extract the contents, and move them to a temporary directory. Inside the extracted dacpac is a file called *model.sql* containing information for creating a new database. This process is not documented, and you should attempt it only with a copy of the package.

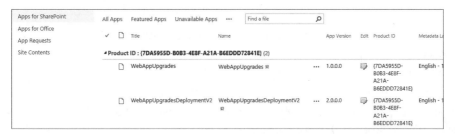

FIGURE 2-55 The new deployment package after it is uploaded to the App Catalog.

Next, proceed to your live site and locate the live web app. Clicking on the ellipses button on the icon from the Site Contents menu will display the window shown in Figure 2-56. Click on the About button.

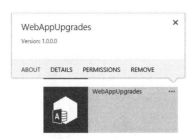

FIGURE 2-56 Displaying the ABOUT link for the web app in the live system site.

This displays the screen shown in Figure 2-57. Clicking on the GET IT button will start the web app upgrade process.

FIGURE 2-57 Using the Get It button to upgrade the live web app.

The upgrade process can take a significant amount of time to process, during which the web app is shown as displayed in Figure 2-58, indicating the upgrade is in progress.

FIGURE 2-58 The notification shown while you wait for the web app to complete the upgrade process.

Tip During the upgrade process, a new Azure SQL Database will be created and upgraded. If the upgrade is successful, the existing Azure SQL Database is removed and the new database is renamed.

After the upgrade is completed, you should see that the new field has been added to the table and all the existing data in the live web app has been preserved.

Figure 2-59 shows a roadmap summarizing the following upgrade steps:

1. Create a snapshot, and upload the snapshot to the App Catalog.

2. In the live site, create a web app based on the web app in the App Catalog.

3. Create a snapshot based on the live web app, manually edit the version number, and upload the app to your developer site.

4. After making design changes in the developer site, create a deployment package and upload it to the App Catalog.

5. From the live site, upgrade the web app.

Once this approach to upgrading the web app is in place, you can just repeat steps 4 and 5 to deliver future upgrades to the web app. You will also have a record in the App Catalog of the upgrades.

You could also use other variations of this approach. In Figure 2-59, you start in step 1 with a Snapshot package (which obviously contains data and assumes you are putting an existing web app with data under the version control). You could start with V1 as a deployment package—in which case, it would not contain any data.

Tip You could start with an app package that contains only reference tables that hold data that can be edited. To do this, you lock all the reference tables and then create a deployment package, V1, which erases all the data in any other tables. Then, as a final step, create another deployment package, V2, which when used to upgrade V1 unlocks all the previously locked tables.

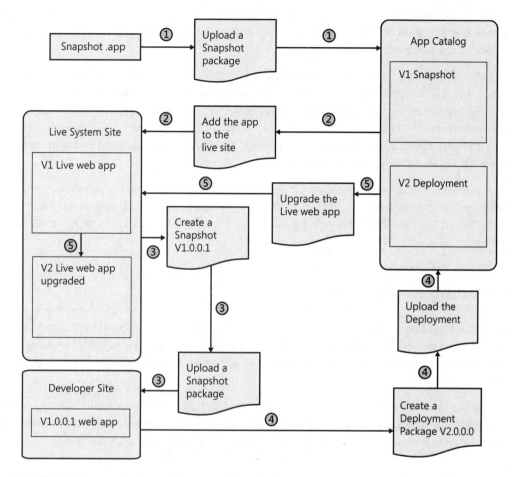

FIGURE 2-59 Steps required to perform upgrades using the App Catalog.

A web app also has an internal "Is Edited" flag, which is set if the design of the web app is changed by a user. If this happens, a subsequent version upgrade will fail. This result can be prevented by limiting user permissions to prevent users from editing the web app design. If you need to get around the problem, you have to create a new snapshot, upload that into the App Catalog, and then replace the live web app, after which you can apply the new upgrade.

A software company wanting to use the Office Store and protect its code in a web app could proceed as follows:

- Start by creating a deployment.

- Publish the web app to the Microsoft Office Store.

- Periodically create a deployment and update the application in the Microsoft Store.

The only caveat for a software company wishing to pursue this approach of locking the web app is that it could not allow clients to use external tools to supplement the features of a web app without unlocking the application.

Behind the scenes, inside a web app package is something called the *DACPAC*. This is a great example of the cross-sharing of technology in a web app, where Access exploits and uses existing product features without re-inventing the wheel. In SQL Server terminology, *DAC* stands for *data-tier applications* and *DACPAC* refers to the packaging of this feature into a portable component. The key idea is to package up a SQL Database into a package that can be both deployed and upgraded, and this is the key technology used with app packages.

If you want to look behind the scenes at the contents of a DACPAC, you can download from *http://msdn.microsoft.com/en-us/data/hh297027* the Microsoft SQL Server Development Tools for Visual Studio 2010 and 2012. This includes a tool for comparing DACPACs to see what the net changes will be.

Side-loading a web app

Using the App Catalog as described in the previous section is not the only method of upgrading a web app. The process of uploading a web app directly to a site or subsite is called *side-loading* a web app, and you can use this method to upgrade a web app to a new version. This process is discussed in more detail in Chapter 7.

The two distinct methods of upgrading—using the App Catalog and side-loading an upgrade—cannot be mixed. However, by creating a snapshot from a web app created using either approach and then removing the existing web app, you can move from using one approach to the other.

Designing and commissioning with existing data

If you are designing a web app based on using data from an existing desktop database, you will likely experience a time lapse between when you get your snapshot of data and start development and when you are ready to go live. The process of moving from a system containing test data to loading the system with live data is sometimes referred to as *commissioning a system*.

You cannot directly empty all the data and then repopulate the data in a web app without using the upgrade feature.

You start by creating an empty web app and importing the existing desktop data. (In Chapter 3, I discuss converting existing data in more detail.) Then you develop your new web application.

Once you are ready to go live, you create a deployment package for the newly developed web app, identified as *Version 2*.

Next, create a new empty web app and import the latest data, which will be used to commission the new web app. Then delete all the views and any other design objects in the newly created web app.

Now create a snapshot of the new web app that only contains data, and edit the contents of the package, changing the *ProductID (GUID)* in the appmanifest.xml file. This means you will have a Version 1.0.0.0 snapshot and a Version 2.0.0.0 deployment package, both with the same ProductID.

Then either use the side-loading approach or the App Catalog approach to upload the snapshot. Then apply the upgrade.

This process is shown schematically in Figure 2-60.

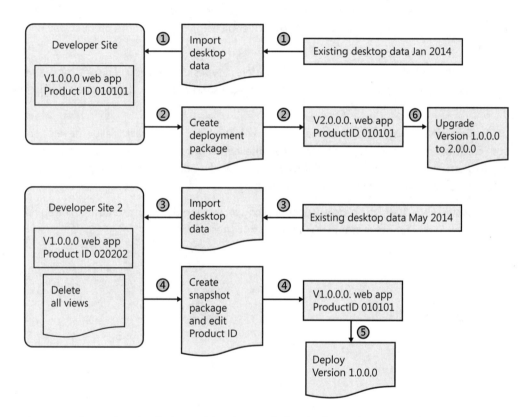

FIGURE 2-60 Steps when developing and then later replacing the data with a new set of data.

Summary

This chapter provided a tour of the new Access web app design environment, starting with the table and view selectors that provide the basic components for navigating within an application. You saw how to construct a blank custom web app, and then you examined how you can import existing Access desktop database tables into the web app. You saw how a web app can make use of relationships and lookups when using the RELIC to automatically construct views of your data that display related information on a single screen.

The navigation pane provides an alternative method to the table selector for app navigation in your designs. You saw several techniques for switching from the design view of your application to viewing results in a browser window; this knowledge will help you work more productively on your design.

Toward the end of this chapter, you saw the different types of views you can construct as well as an overview of the new web app controls. I then provided a short overview of how macro programming fits into the development process.

The final part of this chapter examined how new features in Service Pack 1 allow developers to both construct mechanisms for protecting their intellectual property rights (by locking an application and preventing the code from being downloaded and modified), and also support the software design life cycle with great new deployment options.

In Chapter 3, you'll see the process for converting an existing desktop database to a web app and start to look in greater detail at underlying data structures.

Converting a desktop database to a web app

In this chapter:

In this chapter, I will start by providing some simple examples of how to approach the conversion of basic table structures and relationships between tables, from a desktop database to a web app. In addition, I will show a number of techniques that will help you make a smoother transition of converting your database to a web app.

You will also find one or two screen shots that show the underlying Microsoft Azure SQL Database structures when viewed using the SQL Server Management Studio (SSMS). SSMS is discussed in more detail in Chapter 9, "Looking under the hood at the Microsoft Azure SQL Database."

In this chapter, you will need the Chapter3 sample database, as described in the book's Introduction.

Tables and primary key fields

To follow through the examples in these sections, create a new web app called TablesToConvert. You will be importing data from the sample Microsoft Access desktop database Chapter3_TablesToConvert.accdb. If you need to see examples of creating a blank database and importing tables, look back at Chapter 2, "Finding your way around Access."

You should find that your table names and field names are preserved when imported into a web app. However, there are restrictions on the use of special characters or reserved words for table and field names.

> **Tip** Both table and field names can be up to 64 characters long and can include spaces. But they cannot contain any special characters, such as / \ % * ? & # . , [ ] { }. In our experience #, ?, and % are sometimes encountered in databases.

The sample database contains a table called *ABad#TableName?*, which has special characters in the table and field names. If you try to import that table, you will find that the table will import correctly, but when a special character is encountered in a field or table name, it gets replaced with an underscore character. Another interesting feature of this table is that it had an AutoNumber field but no primary key, and the web app changed the existing AutoNumber field into the primary key. To display the resulting table design, click on the Settings/Action charm shown in Figure 3-1, and then click Edit Table from the list of available actions, which will display the table in design view.

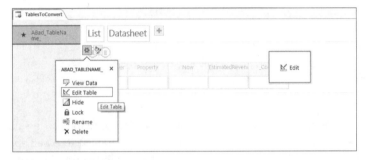

FIGURE 3-1 Switching a table into design view.

In Figure 3-2, you can see how special characters in field names have been replaced with an underscore character, and AutoNumber has been assigned as the primary key.

FIGURE 3-2 Editing a web app table in design view.

> **Tip** If you have a field called *Count?* and another field called *Count#*, the table will fail to import because the web app will try to create two fields, both called *Count_*. You need to rename one of the fields before importing the data.

In undertaking these exercises, if you need to return to this stage to import another table, clicking on the Table icon shown in Figure 3-3 will return you to the Add Tables screen, where you can import more tables from the sample databases.

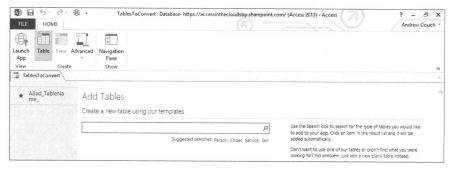

FIGURE 3-3 Displaying the Add Tables screen.

Another sample table, called APrimarykeyAndAutonumber, has both a primary key field and an AutoNumber field that is not the primary key. If you import that table, you will find that the web app switches the primary key from the existing Short Text field to the AutoNumber field.

 Caution You can create tables in an Access desktop database that include an AutoNumber field that is not the primary key and where the field contains duplicate values. This circumstance occurs if you use a Make Table query to create a table from two related tables and include an AutoNumber field from one side of a relationship. To get around this problem, you need to change the existing AutoNumber field to a Number data type field before importing the table into the web app.

In a desktop database, a table can have different choices of data types used as the primary key. The most popular choices are numeric, AutoNumber, and text key fields. A table also can have a primary key formed by a combination of more than one field, as long as the combined values of those fields are unique.

In a web app, each table needs to have an AutoNumber field for the primary key, and keys consisting of more than one field are not supported.

This means that if your table does not have a single AutoNumber field as the primary key, after conversion it will have a new primary key called *ID*, which is an AutoNumber.

Tip If you already have a field called *ID* in your table and a new AutoNumber needs to be added, Access will append a number to the word *ID* to produce a unique name—for example, ID1.

In the sample database, you have a table called CustomerData, which has the design structure shown in Figure 3-4. Note in these images that not all fields are displayed in each image.

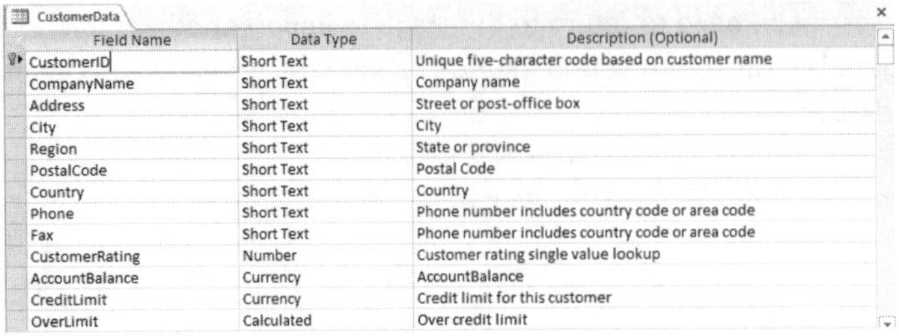

CustomerData

Field Name	Data Type	Description (Optional)
CustomerID	Short Text	Unique five-character code based on customer name
CompanyName	Short Text	Company name
Address	Short Text	Street or post-office box
City	Short Text	City
Region	Short Text	State or province
PostalCode	Short Text	Postal Code
Country	Short Text	Country
Phone	Short Text	Phone number includes country code or area code
Fax	Short Text	Phone number includes country code or area code
CustomerRating	Number	Customer rating single value lookup
AccountBalance	Currency	AccountBalance
CreditLimit	Currency	Credit limit for this customer
OverLimit	Calculated	Over credit limit

FIGURE 3-4 Desktop table design showing the Short Text primary key.

After importing the desktop table into the web app and viewing the design of the table, you see the new ID primary key that was added, together with the old CustomerID field, as shown in Figure 3-5.

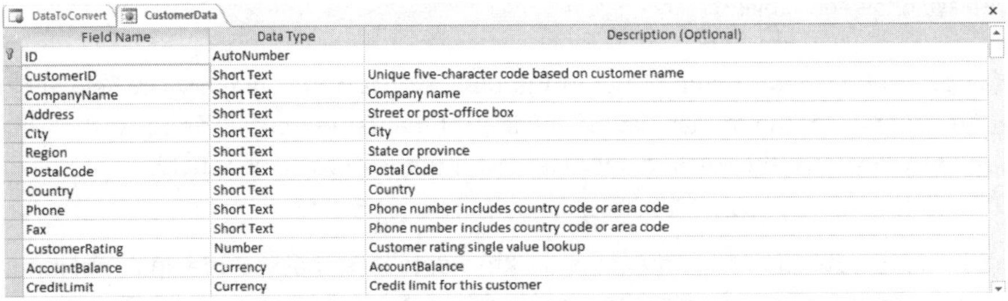

DataToConvert | CustomerData

Field Name	Data Type	Description (Optional)
ID	AutoNumber	
CustomerID	Short Text	Unique five-character code based on customer name
CompanyName	Short Text	Company name
Address	Short Text	Street or post-office box
City	Short Text	City
Region	Short Text	State or province
PostalCode	Short Text	Postal Code
Country	Short Text	Country
Phone	Short Text	Phone number includes country code or area code
Fax	Short Text	Phone number includes country code or area code
CustomerRating	Number	Customer rating single value lookup
AccountBalance	Currency	AccountBalance
CreditLimit	Currency	Credit limit for this customer

FIGURE 3-5 Table imported into a web app with the new ID primary key field.

> **Tip** Access names key fields *ID* to produce a key that is not language specific. In design view in a web app, you can change the name of the key field to be more meaningful.

The second area of consideration with regard to changes Access has made to a primary key in a table is how that affects any foreign keys you defined that have lookups or relationships against them.

Relationships and lookups

In a desktop database, you have two distinct ideas when it comes to linking data in different tables. You can have a relationship between the two tables, a lookup between the two tables, or both.

A lookup provides assistance when you type in data by displaying a list of choices for you.

A relationship can either act as a guide to linking the tables together or enforce referential integrity to perform rule-checking. Rule-checking prevents tables from having inconsistent values for foreign keys because they are referencing primary keys that no longer exist. It also has options to cascade a delete or an update. A cascading delete is used to delete any related records if the parent record is deleted (subject to not violating any other rule-checking). Less often used is a cascading update, which updates the foreign-key values in another table if the primary-key values are changed.

> **Tip** Access desktop databases are unusual in allowing a link between two tables on a relationship diagram that does not enforce referential integrity, and also in allowing a default join to be specified on the diagram. Most other databases do not support these features. Remember that our data will be held in the Microsoft Azure SQL Database, which does not support these two ideas.

To investigate what happens when importing tables using different combinations of relationships, I set up four different pairs of tables. You can try importing these tables from the sample database to examine the results:

- **tblParent, tblParentChild** You have a lookup from the child to its parent table and a relationship with referential integrity.

- **tblParentNoLookup, tblParentNoLookupChild** You have only a relationship with referential integrity.

- **tblParentNoRel, tblParentNoRelChild** You have only a lookup from the child to the parent table.

- **tblParentLinkOnly, tblParentLinkOnlyChild** You have only a relationship, which does not enforce referential integrity.

Figure 3-6 displays the relationships as defined in the desktop database.

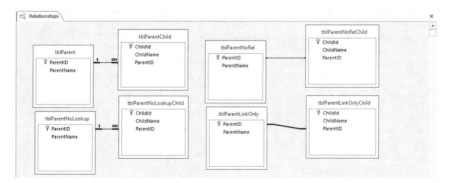

FIGURE 3-6 Relationships between four sets of tables to be imported into a web app.

A web app does not have a separate area for viewing relationships. (In Chapter 9, I will discuss techniques for extracting the information to construct a diagram.) The idea of a relationship and lookup has been mixed together in a web app to provide a new type of lookup that can enforce rule-checking.

The result of importing the eight tables is that a lookup will be created from the child table looking back to the parent table in all cases except in the last pair of tables: tblParentLinkOnly, tblParentLinkOnlyChild:

- **tblParent, tblParentChild**   You have a lookup from the child table to the parent table and a relationship with referential integrity. This creates a lookup with a Prevent Delete restriction on the parent records. This results in a real database-level relationship.

- **tblParentNoLookup, tblParentNoLookupChild**   You have only a relationship with referential integrity. This creates a lookup with a Prevent Delete restriction on the parent records. This results in a real database-level relationship.

- **tblParentNoRel, tblParentNoRelChild**   You have only a lookup from the child table to the parent table. This creates a lookup but does not enforce a relationship in the database.

- **tblParentLinkOnly, tblParentLinkOnlyChild**   You have only a relationship link, which does not enforce referential integrity. (With Access desktop databases, you can create links on the database diagram that do not enforce referential integrity. These are not true relationships.) This does not create a lookup.

You can view the lookups by right-clicking on the table selector and selecting edit table, and then moving to the lookup field and clicking Modify Lookups on the design ribbon. The result is shown in Figure 3-7.

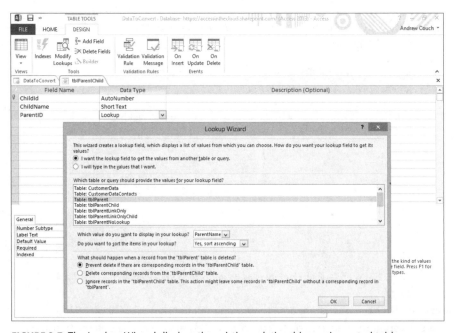

FIGURE 3-7 The Lookup Wizard displays the existing relationships on imported tables.

If you examine the database held in the Microsoft Azure SQL Database (which you look at in Chapter 9), you see that when the lookup is defined as shown in Figure 3-7 with either of the first two options at the bottom of Lookup Wizard (the choice to Prevent or Delete), a foreign-key relationship is created in the Microsoft Azure SQL Database tblParentChild, as shown in Figure 3-8. If the third option in Figure 3-7 is selected, no foreign-key relationship is created.

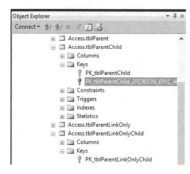

FIGURE 3-8 Relationships are created depending on the Lookup Wizard choices.

> **Tip** You can see that Access makes a great attempt at translating the lookups. If the lookup is supported with a relationship with referential integrity (R.I.), a real relationship is created; however, if it is simply a lookup without R.I., a simple lookup is created, which does not generate anything in the back-end Microsoft Azure SQL Database. This suggests you should not focus your efforts on lookups, but make sure that you have relationships with R.I. before importing data.
>
> The new lookup feature is split between information being held inside the back-end database when R.I applies and other information related to the U.I held within Access Services (the service for the web app design).

If you return now to the relationships in the sample desktop database for this chapter, you can see the relationship shown in Figure 3-9. If you import these two tables into the web app, you'll see that the relationship is not imported. If you want to try this and have been following along, here's what you need to do. In the web app, if you already have the CustomerData table but not the CustomerDataContacts table, you need to delete the CustomerData table—because if you import in-dividual tables, relationships do not get imported. But you will find that even when you import these two tables with a relationship at the same time, the relationship will not be imported.

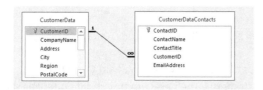

FIGURE 3-9 Desktop database relationship between the two example tables.

After importing the two tables, you will see that when the table CustomerData is imported, it receives a new primary key ID, because the existing primary key, *CustomerID*, is of a Short Text data type, which is not supported in the web app.

So what happens to the foreign key CustomerID in the related table CustomerDataContacts? The answer is you now have a problem: although the table will be imported, the relationships will not create a lookup, and going forward the data between the two tables will not be related.

At this point, if you decide to experiment and import the tables CustomerData and CustomerDataContacts, delete the tables by highlighting them in the table selector and then click on the Settings/Actions charm (or right-click on the table caption) and select Delete.

The only sensible action here is to restructure your tables before importing the data, create a new primary key in the CustomerData table, create a new foreign-key field in CustomerDataContacts, and then use the old fields to run an update query to populate the new foreign key. It would also be a good idea after doing this to delete the old primary and foreign keys.

You can now follow through the steps or look at the new sample database to see the results. To do this, create a new database called Chapter3_ReyKeyedTables.accdb and then import the tables CustomerData and CustomerDataContacts. Then delete the existing relationship between the two tables.

Next add a new primary key field. Add a new field CustID to CustomerData, and select an AutoNumber data type. (See Figure 3-10.) Then save the table.

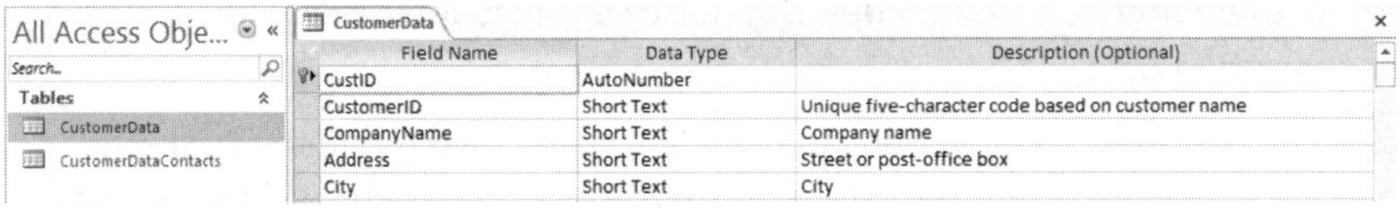

FIGURE 3-10 The new CustID AutoNumber field added to the table CustomerData.

Next you need to create a new foreign key. Add a new field CustID to the CustomerDataContacts table, selecting a Number, Long Integer data type. (See Figure 3-11.) Save the table.

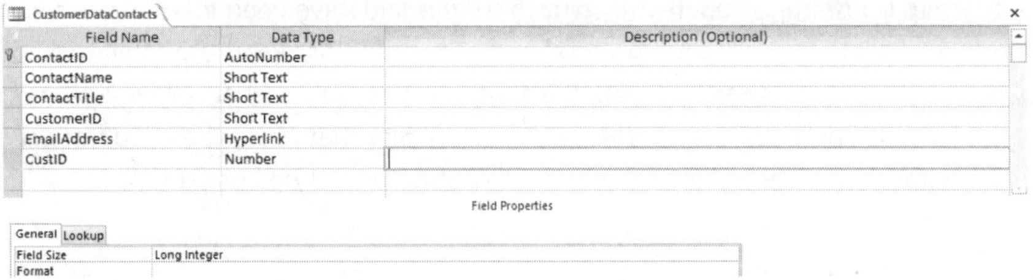

FIGURE 3-11 The new CustID Number Long Integer field added to the table CustomerDataContacts.

Update the new foreign key by creating an update query to update the field CustID in CustomerDataContacts, using the linking field CustomerID. Then execute this update query as shown in Figure 3-12. (You will need to first delete the relationship in the query grid linking the tables on CustID, and then add a new link based on the old CustomerID fields.)

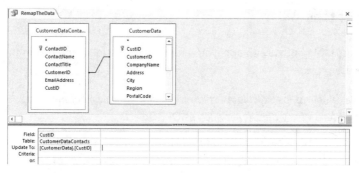

FIGURE 3-12 The update query for populating the new foreign key.

After running this query, you can create a new relationship between the two tables, based on the new primary and foreign keys.

Create a new relationship. Using drag and drop on the relationship diagram, create a new relationship based on the CustID field in each table that enforces referential integrity. (See Figure 3-13.)

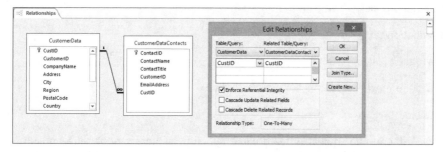

FIGURE 3-13 Creating the new relationship based on the new primary and foreign keys.

You don't need to create any new lookups, because Access will do that for you on the basis of the relationship that enforces referential integrity.

After this, you can delete the old CustomerID field in both the tables and import the two tables into your web app.

After completing this, you can delete the old tables CustomerData and CustomerDataContacts in your web app, and try re-importing the new tables to see how this has corrected the previously described import problems.

> **Tip** After working through this and the last section, you should see the importance of ensuring that all your tables have AutoNumber primary keys, and that you re-map any foreign keys and create appropriate relationships by enforcing R.I. between your tables before importing the data into the web app.

Table and field properties

When you are importing Access tables into a web app, you might notice the following text in the Get External Data – Access Database popup:

We will not import table relationships, calculated columns, validation rules, default values and columns of certain legacy data types such as OLE Objects.

In this and later sections, you will see what this limitation means and learn techniques for working around these limitations. The first part of this warning is not always true. It states "...not import table relationships...", but as you saw in the previous section, table relationships are imported as long as those are proper relationships that include referential integrity. For a simple link between two tables (without referential integrity), the statement holds true. Relationships are also not imported if the relationship is between field data types that are not supported—for example, a relationship between two short text data types or a relationship based on multiple fields in the keys.

In this section, I want to focus on what happens to basic field properties and table-validation properties. The most common properties for you to define that are not imported are as follows:

- Table validation rule

- Table validation text

- Field validation rule

- Field validation text

- Default value

- Input Mask (there is no equivalent feature in a web app, so these cannot be re-applied)

- Format

It will help at this point to compare and contrast the available properties for a field in a desktop database with those of a web app. Figure 3-14 shows properties for a typical field—in this case, a currency field.

FIGURE 3-14 Desktop database properties for a currency field.

Figure 3-15 shows the same properties for this field after the table is imported into a web app. The list is familiar, but reduced, and it does not include a separate lookup tab because lookups are handled in a different way in a web app.

| CreditLimit | Currency | Credit limit for this customer |
| OverLimit | Currency | Over credit limit |

Field Properties

General	
Currency Symbol	$
Label Text	
Default Value	
Validation Rule	
Validation Text	
Required	No
Indexed	No

FIGURE 3-15 Web app properties for a currency field.

A quick glance at this list shows that although not all the properties have been translated, there are still the options to create values for some properties that were not translated.

> **Tip** One reason why Access has not translated all the properties is that a desktop database offers extreme flexibility in defining some properties to use custom Visual Basic for Applications (VBA) functions. It is preferable to have a higher success with importing the tables than to ensure that every property is translated.

You will find that although the properties we discussed are not translated, it is useful to construct some program code to extract the values from your desktop database to have a list of the values. You can then work through that list to implement the values where possible in the new web app.

Figure 3-16 shows a form in the sample database Chapter3_TablesToConvert.accdb that searches your tables and fields and populates a table called LostProperties with the results.

> **Tip** If you want to explore this example and other sample files, you need to trust the sample databases as you come to use them and enable macro/VBA code to execute using the Trust Center.

FIGURE 3-16 Sample form for identifying table and field properties.

Figure 3-17 shows the results of clicking the Create List Of Table And Field Properties button, which displays a list of the table and field properties. After converting a database, you can use this as a working list to check through and re-create any missing defaults or validation rules in the web app.

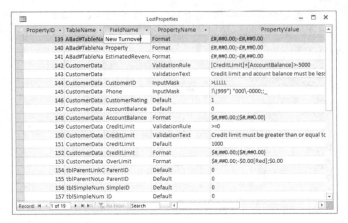

FIGURE 3-17 Results of identifying field and table properties.

The form uses the following VBA code to scan through the tables and then the fields in each table:

```
Private Sub cmdLostProperties_Click()
' Creates a list of properties which will not be converted
Dim db As Database
Dim rst As Recordset
Dim tdef As TableDef
Dim fld As Field
Dim prop As Property
' Empty the results table
CurrentDb.Execute "DELETE * FROM LostProperties"
Set db = CurrentDb
Set rst = db.OpenRecordset("LostProperties", dbOpenDynaset)
' search all the tables
For Each tdef In db.TableDefs
    If InStr(tdef.Name, "MSys") = 0 And (tdef.Name <> "LostProperties") Then
        If tdef.ValidationRule <> "" Then
            rst.AddNew
            rst!TableName = tdef.Name
            rst!Propertyname = "ValidationRule"
            rst!PropertyValue = tdef.ValidationRule
            rst.Update
        End If
        If tdef.ValidationText <> "" Then
            rst.AddNew
            rst!TableName = tdef.Name
            rst!Propertyname = "ValidationText"
            rst!PropertyValue = tdef.ValidationText
            rst.Update
        End If
        ' Search all the fields in the table
        For Each fld In tdef.Fields
            If fld.ValidationRule <> "" Then
                rst.AddNew
                rst!TableName = tdef.Name
                rst!FieldName = fld.Name
                rst!Propertyname = "ValidationRule"
                rst!PropertyValue = fld.ValidationRule
```

```
        rst.Update
    End If
    If fld.ValidationText <> "" Then
        rst.AddNew
        rst!TableName = tdef.Name
        rst!FieldName = fld.Name
        rst!Propertyname = "ValidationText"
        rst!PropertyValue = fld.ValidationText
        rst.Update
    End If
    If fld.DefaultValue <> "" Then
        rst.AddNew
        rst!TableName = tdef.Name
        rst!FieldName = fld.Name
        rst!Propertyname = "Default"
        rst!PropertyValue = fld.DefaultValue
        rst.Update
    End If
    ' Not every field has these properties

On Error Resume Next ' ignore potential errors
    If fld.Properties("InputMask") <> "" Then
        If Err = 0 Then
            rst.AddNew
            rst!TableName = tdef.Name
            rst!FieldName = fld.Name
            rst!Propertyname = "InputMask"
            rst!PropertyValue = fld.Properties("InputMask")
            rst.Update
        End If
        Err.Clear
    End If
    If fld.Properties("Format") <> "" Then
        If Err = 0 Then
            rst.AddNew
            rst!TableName = tdef.Name
            rst!FieldName = fld.Name
            rst!Propertyname = "Format"
            rst!PropertyValue = fld.Properties("Format")
            rst.Update
        End If
        Err.Clear
    End If
    On Error GoTo 0 ' enable error handling
    Next
  End If
Next
MsgBox "Table LostProperties refreshed", vbInformation, "Processing Completed"
DoCmd.OpenTable "LostProperties"
End Sub
```

Tip You can import the table LostProperties and the frmLostProperties form in the sample database Chapter3_TablesToConvert.accdb into your own databases to perform the analysis described in this section on your own desktop database design.

Boolean data

Access has a Yes/No field, and that can be True or False, but because a web app doesn't migrate defaults, you might wonder what will happen when entering new data. The answer is that Access always assumes a Boolean is False unless otherwise stated. Once the data gets moved into the Microsoft Azure SQL Database, this then uses what is called a *bit field* for the Boolean, and the bit field can be True, False, or NULL. The good news is that a web app takes that into account and automatically creates a default to avoid the problem of having any null values before it loads your data.

```
ALTER TABLE [Access].[CustomerData] ADD
CONSTRAINT [DF_CustomerData_BA1CFB0C_CCB5_453D_A387_A55AAE5CF34C]
DEFAULT (CONVERT([bit],'False',0)) FOR [Archived]
GO
```

Adding this rule is a good idea because it means that Microsoft Azure SQL Database will have a default set to 0 for False when the data gets uploaded.

> **Note** If you specified a default of True in Access, because default properties are not translated, you could end up with an unanticipated default of False.

Value-based lookups

Although a web app supports value-based lookups, where you type in a list of choices, it supports only a single column of choices. This is different from a desktop database, where you can have both a value that is displayed to a user and a different value that is saved in the column.

For example, in the CustomerData table, you have a field called CustomerRating, which is a numeric field with a lookup Value List. The RowSource is (1;"Active";2;"Prospect";3;"Inactive"). After conversion, the lookup feature will not be persevered and the field will become a simple numeric data type holding the values 1, 2, or 3.

However, if you defined the RowSource as using only a single column—such as (1;2;3)—during the conversion, the field would have been changed to the new Lookup data type.

This means you should check any Value List lookups where the column count is more than 1 and change the RowSource to include only one column. Alternatively, you can create a separate table for holding the lookup values; this means you can continue to hold one value while displaying a second value.

Multi-value data

A desktop database supports multi-value data, which is a feature that is not supported in a web app. The following example, shown in Figure 3-18, shows a multi-value lookup that is based on a value list. The field has one column containing three possible values.

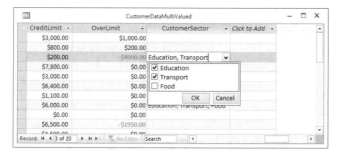

FIGURE 3-18 A typical multi-value field in a desktop database.

This example would import the multi-value field as a Long Text data type. The data shown in Figure 3-18 would be held as Education;Transport.

With multi-value fields, you can decide to create new tables to hold the multiple values before importing your database.

Importing different data types

In this section, you will see how the basic data types get mapped between a desktop database and a web app. Before I cover the details of some of the data types, take a look at a summary tabulating how the different data types are converted.

TABLE 3-1 Summary of how data types are converted

Desktop Data Type	Web App	Microsoft Azure SQL Database
AutoNumber	AutoNumber	Identity property on a long integer
Short Text (255), default 255	Short Text (4000), default 220	NVARCHAR(255)
Long Text	Long Text	NVARCHAR(MAX)
Number Long Integer	Number Whole number (no decimal places)	INT
Number Byte	Number Whole number (no decimal places)	INT
Number Single	Number Floating-point number (variable decimal places)	Float
Number Double	Number Floating-point number (variable decimal places)	Float
Number ReplicationID	Short Text (60)	NVARCHAR(60)

Desktop Data Type	Web App	Microsoft Azure SQL Database
Number Decimal	Number Floating-point number (variable decimal places)	Decimal(28,6)
	Number Date Fixed-point number (6 decimal places)	Decimal(28,6), default 0.0 is added
Yes/No	Yes/No	BIT (Not Null is also added, and a default 0 is added)
Currency	Currency	DECIMAL(28,6)
Hyperlink	Hyperlink	NVARCHAR(MAX)
Calculation	Varies depending on the type of calculation	
DateTime	Date with Time	DATETIME2(3)
	Date	DATE
	Time	TIME(3)
OLE Object	Not Supported	
Attachment	Not Supported	
	Image	VARBINARY(MAX)
	Lookup	

UNICODE and Microsoft Azure SQL Database

Short Text and Long Text are converted to Unicode data types. In Microsoft Azure SQL Database, a Short Text varying text field is called a VARCHAR, and a Long Text varying text field is called a VARCHAR(MAX), where *MAX* means the biggest amount of storage supported in the current version of the Microsoft Azure SQL Database.

In a web app, rather than using a VARCHAR, NVARCHAR is used. The *N* prefix means UNICODE, the ASCII character set for storing characters allows only up to 255 variations, and the data is stored in a computer byte. Because many languages have additional characters, ASCII is too restrictive. So the new standard is UNICODE, which uses more storage and allows for a greater range of characters. (Microsoft Azure SQL Database uses UCS-2, which requires 2 bytes of storage per character.)

A standard VARCHAR row in the Microsoft Azure SQL Database can store 8,000 characters, but because you are using NVARCHAR this explains why the Short Text field allows 4,000 characters.

Long Text (memo data)

In Access 2013 and the Access 2010, memo field data type has been renamed as *Long Text*. There are two features of Long Text in desktop databases that are not supported in web apps:

- **Rich Text**   The ability to have formatting embedded with the text

- **Append Only**   The ability to have a field that displays only the latest edits and maintains all previous values as a history for the field.

Calculated fields

Although a web app does support calculated fields, these are not translated during the import process. The existing calculated field will be converted to a text field showing the results of the calculation. You will need to re-create a new calculated field. You might want to delete these fields before performing an import.

Image data type

Although the new Image data type is stored as a VARBINARY(MAX) SQL data type, you are limited to storing a graphical image in a .gif, .jfif, .jpe, .jpeg, .jpg, or .png format. (The .bmp format is not supported.) The image size is limited to a maximum of 10 MB. (This is a restriction in the Access web app UI.)

> **Caution** If you try to be clever by storing an unsupported format in an Image data type (bearing in mind this is a VARBINARY(MAX) data type, which will allow the storage), which is possible by using a desktop database linked directly to the Microsoft Azure SQL Database back-end, you will have a serious problem if the web app tries to then display the column. So although you can store unsupported formats, this is not recommended.

Attachments and OLE objects

Before I can discuss strategies for managing attachments and OLE object data, I need to demonstrate how to construct direct connections to the Microsoft Azure SQL Database, which is described in the next section.

Reporting

Unfortunately, a web app does not have any features for generating reports or easily getting satisfactory screen prints. Until these features become available, all reporting is performed using a desktop reporting database. However, it is very easy to generate a set of linked tables, which can then be used with any existing reports or for creating new reports.

Chapter 9 explains more about the terminology you will see when generating a desktop reporting database. So to keep from repeating information, I will cover a minimum of terminology in this section.

Close any open web apps and desktop databases, and return to the web app called NorthwindData that you created in Chapter 2. Open the web app, and then using backstage (File menu), you will generate a web reporting database. Click on the Create Reports icon shown in Figure 3-19.

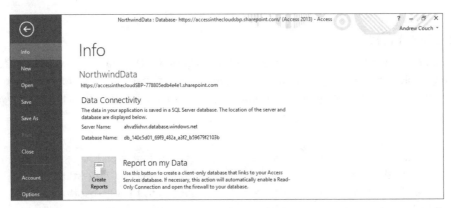

FIGURE 3-19 Backstage view showing the Create Reports icon.

In Figure 3-20, you are prompted to select a location for the file and enter a name for the reporting database.

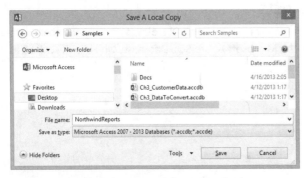

FIGURE 3-20 Prompt for creating a reporting database.

After you click the Save button, you see the sample reporting database with a table open displaying data, as shown in Figure 3-21.

FIGURE 3-21 Linked reporting tables.

Tip If you press Ctrl+G, switch to the Immediate window, type in the command **?currentdb.TableDefs("Customers").Connect**, and press Enter, the detailed connection string is displayed. (Note that your connection string will contain different codes than those shown here, which are unique to each individual database.)

```
ODBC;Description=AutoGenerated;DRIVER=SQL Server Native Client
11.0;SERVER=qp8my6zp2t.database.windows.net;
UID=db_4d16bb26_2807_4900_ad1e_20806e5265dc_ExternalReader@qp8my6zp2t;
PWD=r62Q%W8%>15pHBU;APP=Microsoft Office
15;DATABASE=db_4d16bb26_2807_4900_ad1e_20806e5265dc;
```

If you also try typing in **?currentdb.TableDefs("Customers").SourceTableName**, you will get `Access.Customers` as the `sourcetablename`. Chapter 9 explains this in more detail; a nice feature to notice is that the tables have all been named with the schema prefix *Access* removed from the linked table name. (SourceTableName is the true table name; TableName is the name being displayed for the linked table.)

By looking at the datasheet in Figure 3-21, you might think you can insert and edit data, but this is not allowed. If you try to save changes to a record, you will see the warning displayed in Figure 3-22.

FIGURE 3-22 Warning you receive when attempting to edit data in the reporting database.

To get a better understanding of the cryptic numbers in the connection string and the reason behind the failure of the update, return to backstage. Looking back at Figure 3-21, you can see the Server Name qp8my6zp2t.database.windows.net. (The end of this string .database.windows. net is common to Microsoft Azure SQL Database servers; the first part is unique to your subscription.) The database name db_4d16bb26_2807_4900_ad1e_20806e5265dc is unique for your web app. In Figure 3-23, the Manage icon was clicked in backstage to display options for managing connection information.

In Figure 3-23, you will observe that the options to enable use From My Location (your computer's IP address) and Enable Read-Only Connection have been activated as a result of your generating a reporting database.

FIGURE 3-23 Managing connections information.

If you decide that you want to make the reporting database available on any machine, at any IP address, click on From Any Location. If you click on View Read-Only Connection Information, the SQL Server Connection Information window will be displayed, as shown in Figure 3-24.

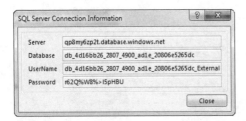

FIGURE 3-24 SQL Server Connection Information window.

If you look back at Figure 3-21, which shows the table connection, you will see how the details in Figure 3-24 have been incorporated into the connection string.

Tip The user name used in this section is ExternalReader. The user name used with a read-write connection is called ExternalWriter.

If you need more information about this type of direct connection, or you need to understand further ODBC driver requirements when using the reporting database on different machines, read through the "Creating an ODBC system DSN" section in Chapter 9.

References

In your reporting database, press Ctrl+G, or Alt+F11 to view the VBA code environment. In the VBA environment, click on the Tools, References option as shown in Figure 3-25.

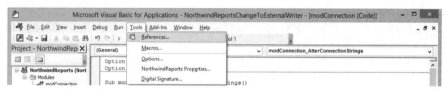

FIGURE 3-25 Displaying references in a VBA project.

This displays the references, as shown in Figure 3-26.

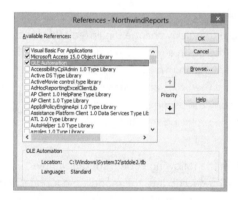

FIGURE 3-26 VBA project references.

You need to have a reference at least to the Microsoft Office 15.0 Access Database Engine Object Library, as shown in Figure 3-27, before you can do any real database programming. If you want to use Active Data Objects ADO, add it in an appropriate library. To add the library, scroll down the list of references until you locate the library. Pressing the M key will help you quickly move down the list. Select the reference, and click OK. You should find that the Microsoft Office 15.0 Access Database Engine Object Library was already added when the reporting database was created.

Tip Most VBA developers prefer to use Data Access Objects (DAO) rather than Active Data Objects (ADO). ADO is less integrated with Access than DAO. The advantage of using ADO is that it is a lightweight technology that delivers improved performance and has wider support for different data sources. It also offers a number of more sophisticated features when working with other types of data sources.

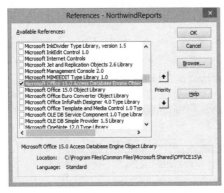

FIGURE 3-27 Adding a Microsoft Office 15.0 Access Database Engine Object Library reference.

Quick conversion to external writer

I will now show you a very neat trick, which you can use to quickly change the linked tables in the web app from using the ExternalReader to using ExternalWriter, with a minimum amount of effort. Ensure you are working in the web app database, and use the menu shown earlier in Figure 3-23. After clicking Manage, click on Enable Read-Write Connection and then click on View Read-Write Connection Information in the Manage options. You will need to copy the user name and password to Notepad to be able to later paste the details into the sample code replacing the string values assigned to the variables *strUID* and *strPWD*.

Make a copy of the reporting database, and paste in the following code from the sample database called NorthwindReportsChangeToExternalWriter.accdb into the module *modConnections* (remembering to replace the values in *strUID* and *strPWD* before running the code):

```
Sub modConnection_AlterConnectionStrings()
' run through the connection for the linked tables
' altering the connection strings
Dim db As Database
Dim tdef As Tabledef
Dim strCN As String
Dim posUIDStart As Long
Dim posDBStart As String
Dim strCNNew As String
Dim strUID As String
Dim strPWD As String
' ExternalWriter ID and Password
```

```
strUID = "db_140c5d01_69f9_482a_a3f2_b59679f2103b_ExternalWriter"
strPWD = "Fi&yJgz+SnaDGKu"
Set db = CurrentDb
For Each tdef In db.Tabledefs
    strCN = tdef.Connect
    If InStr(strCN, "ExternalReader") <> 0 Then
        posUIDStart = InStr(strCN, ";UID")
        ' slice out all characters in the string up to UID
        strCNNew = Left(strCN, posUIDStart)
        ' Now add the user ID and password
        strCNNew = strCNNew & ";UID=" & strUID & ";PWD=" & strPWD
        ' now slice back in the database name
        posDBStart = InStr(strCN, ";DATABASE")
        strCNNew = strCNNew & Mid(strCN, posDBStart, 255)
        ' alter the table definition and refresh the link
        tdef.Connect = strCNNew
        tdef.RefreshLink
    End If
Next
End Sub
```

After running this code, close and then re-open the database (to clear any authentication details from memory). Then return to the database window. You should then be able to directly edit the linked tables and save any changes you make to the data.

> **Tip** It is worth emphasizing just how much the technique described above will save you time compared to using the more advanced techniques I describe in Chapter 9 for creating ODBC connections.

Attachment and OLE data

A web app supports only the new Image data type, which you can use to upload an image up to 10 MB, in a .jpg, .jpeg, .png, .gif, .jpe, or .jfif format.

An Access desktop database supports Attachment data types (multi-value fields), which can include both graphic and other file types. It is possible to extract these files and directly move supported graphical formats into a table linked to the back-end Microsoft Azure SQL Database table, saving the graphic as a new Image data type.

You can also save files in their native format and upload those files to a SharePoint list. Then you can link data in an existing table using hyperlinks to the SharePoint documents, or alternatively (as described in Chapter 1, "Finding your way around Office 365") a web app can provide read-only links to a SharePoint list.

An OLE Data type presents a different challenge. The OLE Data type cannot be easily saved as a file (although you can find some code on the Internet to handle certain formats), because the data contains a complex header that is difficult to manage. But you can use the clipboard to copy and paste the data into a linked SharePoint list, or you can use a Microsoft Azure SQL Database table containing an image data type.

Uploading multiple files

If you extracted existing documents, these can be easily uploaded into a document list or folder in your Team Site. From your Team Site, click on the link New Document. In the list of choices displayed, select Upload Existing File, and then in the popup window shown in Figure 3-28 click Browse to locate the file or click Upload Files Using Windows Explorer instead. You might need to add your site to the trusted locations in Explorer before you can use the second option.

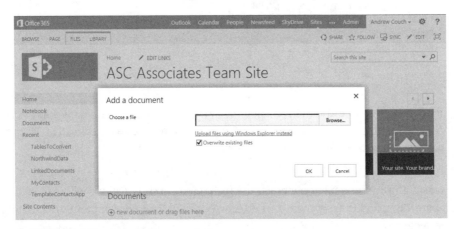

FIGURE 3-28 Add a document popup window.

This opens Windows Explorer, displaying your document list as shown in Figure 3-29. Files can then be selected when using the Browse option, or with the second option you can drag and drop files onto the browser window.

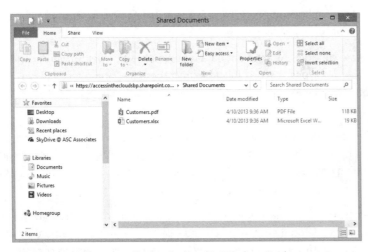

FIGURE 3-29 A document library displayed in Windows Explorer.

> **Tip** Rather than using the Windows Explorer option just described, you can use a general feature where you have both the browser window displaying your document list. When you open a Windows Explorer window, you can use drag and drop to upload files without using the New Document link.

Extracting attachment files

In this section, I will show sample VBA code for extracting documents from your desktop database tables, which can then be uploaded to a document list or, if the documents are in an appropriate graphical format, uploaded into Image data fields.

In March 2014, a new structural feature was rolled out in Office 365 for storing image data. Prior to this, image data was held in the same row as the main data record, but it was found that significant performance improvements could be achieved by holding the image data in a separate table. This means that under the hood when you create any table in a web app, a corresponding secondary hidden table called *tablename?Images* is also created. This secondary table lies dormant in anticipation of you adding an image field data type to your main table, in which case the images are stored in the secondary table.

If you open the sample database ConvertAttachments.accdb, you will see a linked table to the desktop database called CustomersDesktop, which contains the attachment data as shown in Figure 3-30. (You should use the Linked Table Manager to refresh this link to your local copy of the sample database NorthwindForWbAppRestructured.accdb. If you want to follow along with the example, ignore the linked tables called Customers and Customers?Images. We will be replacing that in the next section.)

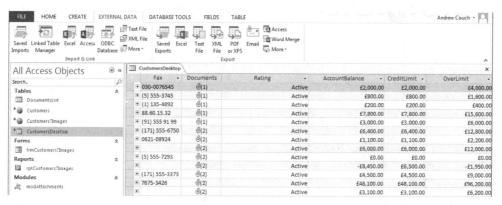

FIGURE 3-30 Sample table containing attachments.

To run the program, you need to create a folder called Docs in the same folder containing the sample database. At the top of the modAttachments module is the following code:

```
Sub modAttachments_Extract()
    strFilePath = CurrentProject.Path & "\Docs\"
    ' ensure directory has been created
    modAttachments_ExtractAttachments "CustomersDesktop", _
                                      "CustomerAttachments", _
                                      "CustomerID"
End Sub
```

The preceding code calls the following routine for extracting the attachment files:

```
Sub modAttachments_ExtractAttachments(strTablename As String, _
                                      strFieldName As String, _
                                      strKeyFieldName As String)
Dim db As Database
Dim doclistrst As Recordset2
Dim rst As Recordset2
Dim docrst As Recordset2
Dim fld2 As Field2
Dim strFileName As String
Set db = CurrentDb
CurrentDb.Execute "DELETE * FROM DocumentsList"
Set doclistrst = db.OpenRecordset("DocumentsList", dbOpenDynaset)
Set rst = db.OpenRecordset("SELECT " & strKeyFieldName & _
                           "," & strFieldName & _
                           " FROM " & strTablename)
' process each attachment field in the table
Do While Not rst.EOF
    ' Process all attachment documents
    Set docrst = rst.Fields(strFieldName).Value
    Do While Not docrst.EOF
        ' save the attachment file
        Set fld2 = docrst!FileData
        strFileName = strFilePath & docrst!FileName
        If Dir(strFileName) <> "" Then
            VBA.Kill strFileName
        End If
        fld2.SaveToFile strFileName
        If Err = 0 Then
            doclistrst.AddNew
            doclistrst!DocumentName = docrst!FileName
            doclistrst!DocumentFileType = docrst!FileType
            doclistrst!KeyFieldValue = rst(strKeyFieldName)
            doclistrst.Update
            Err.Clear
        End If
        docrst.MoveNext
    Loop
    rst.MoveNext
Loop
MsgBox "Extraction completed", vbInformation, "Finished"
End Sub
```

After running the code, the attachments will be extracted into the new Docs folder and the DocumentsList will be populated, as shown in Figure 3-31.

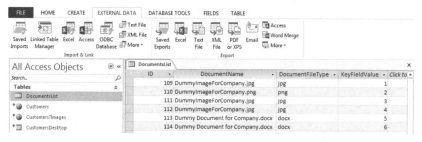

FIGURE 3-31 Table listing all the attachment files and key linking field values.

You can now use the technique I described in the preceding section to upload any documents that are not of the supported image data type to your Documents team site. The documents can be managed in a new folder on the site.

> **Tip** Before you convert your database, in the desktop database you could add a hyperlink field to the appropriate table—Customers, in our example—and run an update based on the data in the DocumentsList to create hyperlinks from your customer records to the attachments. If you had more than one attachment per table, you could use a similar technique, but using a separate table to hold multiple hyperlinks for each record.

Uploading image files

Following on from the last section, if you have attachments in an Image-compatible format (and you could consider converting any .bmp formats to .jpeg or .png formats), these could be directly uploaded into a new Image control in the web app.

In this example, I added a new column called CustomerImage (an Image data type) to the Customers Table, as shown in Figure 3-32, and I will demonstrate how to upload compatible formats to that column. This is a bit more complex than previous examples because you need to know how to create a read-write connection to the back-end Microsoft Azure SQL Database (which is where the web App tables are stored). You will find this described in detail in Chapter 9, in the section "Creating an ODBC system DSN."

However, if you worked through the previous section—in particular, the end of the section where I demonstrate a clever technique for converting all the linked tables in a reporting database, to use Read-Write enabled connections, which is what you need in this section—you will find the process significantly simpler than it could be.

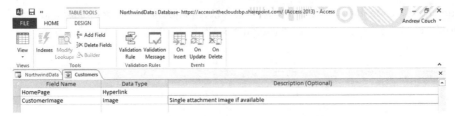

FIGURE 3-32 Adding an Image field to the Customers table.

In our sample database ConvertAttachments.accdb, delete the existing links Customers and Customers?Images, and then import your linked table for Customers and Customers?Images from the Read-Write database you created after reading the "Reporting" section in this chapter. This gives you a read-write connection to the Customers and Customers?Images tables in Microsoft Azure SQL Database , as shown in Figure 3-33.

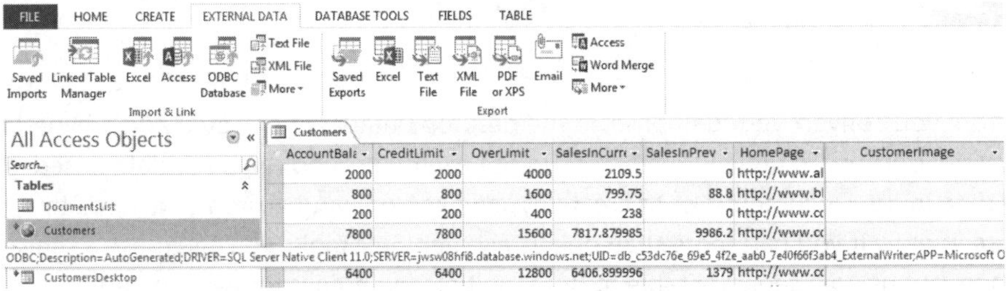

FIGURE 3-33 Importing the Linked Access table with Read-Write permissions.

The final step is to write a code routine that can transfer the extracted saved attachment image files to the new image data type.

The technique you use here uses a Stream object for uploading the image file. To use this technique if a reference to ADODB is not already present, you first need to enable a new reference to ADODB (Microsoft ActiveX Data Objects Library), as shown in Figure 3-34. (In a VBA module, click on Tools – References. You should find this has been already added in the sample database.)

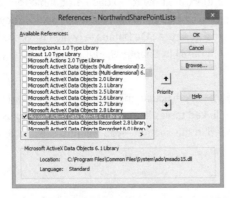

FIGURE 3-34 Adding a reference to the ADODB Library.

To upload the files, do not use the linked table Customers. (You will use that later in this section.) Instead, perform the operations in code using an ADO recordset. The following procedure can be used to perform the upload:

```
Sub modAttachments_Upload()
    strFilePath = CurrentProject.Path & "\Docs\"
    modAttachments_UploadAttachments "Customers", _
                                     "CustomerImage", _
                                     "CustomerID"
End Sub
```

In the main routine shown next, you need to edit your own values in the server, database, user, and password strings (*strServer*, *strDatabase*, *strUID*, and *strPWD*):

```
Sub modAttachments_UploadAttachments(strTablename As String, _
                             strImageFieldName As String, _
                             strKeyFieldName As String)
' Upload compatible image formats to our web app.
' This code assumes that we have only one image to upload for each record

Dim db As Database
Dim rstImageList As Recordset
Set db = CurrentDb
Dim rstWebApp As New ADODB.Recordset
Dim cnWebApp As New ADODB.Connection
Dim iStream As ADODB.Stream
Dim strImageListSQL As String
Dim strcnWebApp As String
Dim strWebAppSQL As String
Dim lastKeyValue As String
Dim strServer As String
Dim strDatabase As String
Dim strUID As String
Dim strPWD As String
Dim lngNewID As Long
Dim strSQL As String

' Get list of image files to upload
strImageListSQL = "SELECT * FROM DocumentsList " & _
                  " WHERE DocumentFileType " & _
                  " IN('jpg','png','gif','jpe','jfif')"
Set rstImageList = db.OpenRecordset(strImageListSQL, dbOpenDynaset)

'Open a connection to the SQL Server
strServer = "jwsw08hfi8.database.windows.net"
strDatabase = "db_ee7a8cd0_35d4_40b0_b28c_27b47d5284f6"
strUID = "db_ee7a8cd0_35d4_40b0_b28c_27b47d5284f6_ExternalWriter"
strPWD = "H1Keo3V:ZS4BhrP"

strcnWebApp = "ODBC;Description=TEST;DRIVER=SQL Server;SERVER=" & _
              strServer & ";Trusted_Connection=No;DATABASE=" & _
              strDatabase & "; UID=" & strUID & _
              ";PWD=" & strPWD
' open connection to Web App
cnWebApp.Open strcnWebApp
```

```
' open recordset on the ?Images table
strWebAppSQL = "SELECT * FROM Access.[" & strTablename & "?images] " & _
               "WHERE ID = -1"
rstWebApp.Open strWebAppSQL, cnWebApp, adOpenDynamic, adLockOptimistic
lastKeyValue = ""
Do While Not rstImageList.EOF
    ' prevent duplicates from being written
    ' we could have multiple source attachment images
    If rstImageList!KeyFieldValue <> lastKeyValue Then
        ' upload the file
        'Open an ADO Stream and load the image in it
        Set iStream = New ADODB.Stream
        iStream.Type = adTypeBinary
        iStream.Open
        iStream.LoadFromFile strFilePath & rstImageList!DocumentName

        ' Add the image to the ?Images table
        With rstWebApp
            .AddNew
            .Fields("Image").Value = iStream.Read
            .Fields("srcID").Value = rstImageList!KeyFieldValue
            .Update
        End With
        ' close the stream
        iStream.Close

        ' Get the new unique id for the image from ?Images
        lngNewID = cnWebApp.Execute("SELECT @@Identity")(0)

        'update the main table with the new key to image data
        ' This uses DAO, but could have used ADO
        ' Find record to update
        strSQL = "UPDATE [" & strTablename & "] SET [" & strImageFieldName & _
                 "] = " & lngNewID & " WHERE [" & strKeyFieldName & _
                 "] = " & rstImageList!KeyFieldValue
        CurrentDb.Execute strSQL, dbSeeChanges

        ' record key for record written
        Debug.Print rstImageList!KeyFieldValue & " " _
                 & rstImageList!DocumentName
        lastKeyValue = rstImageList!KeyFieldValue



    End If
    rstImageList.MoveNext
Loop
' close recordset
rstWebApp.Close
cnWebApp.Close
rstImageList.Close
MsgBox "Images Uploaded"
End Sub
```

> **Note** This code was adapted from code provided in the public domain by Kevin Bell, who works on the Access team at Microsoft.

After running the code, you should find that displaying records in a browser window displays the corresponding images, as shown in Figure 3-35.

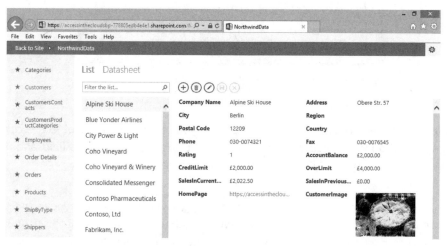

FIGURE 3-35 Image displayed in a browser window.

Returning to the desktop database used for the conversion, if you open the link to the Customers table you will see values in the CustomerImage field that act as foreign keys to the actual image data that is held in the table Customers?Images. In Figure 3-36, I show an example of the foreign-key values in the CustomerImage field.

FIGURE 3-36 Displaying the foreign-key values held in the main data table.

Figure 3-37 shows the Customer?Images table, which contains the image data. In this example, Access uses the SrcID column to record the primary key of the Customers table record to help us check the data that has been uploaded. In the example, the SrcID field is populated with the primary key of the matching record in the Customers table to indicate which images have been uploaded. The Image column could already contain data where *SrcID* would not contain any values. The *SrcID* field is an internal system field that was used when Microsoft rolled out the new Image data feature. If you insert a new image using the web app, this field would not contain any values. This means that it is a useful field to use when uploading images, but it should not be used for any other purpose.

If you try to double-click on an image to display the image in the Access design environment, you will receive a warning that the image cannot be displayed.

FIGURE 3-37 Attempting to display an image from the desktop database.

 Warning If you right-click and choose Insert Object, you can insert an OLE object, such as an image. Do not do this, because that stores a true OLE object in the Image field, and that will cause your web app to fail if it tries to display the object.

Notice that the Customer Image field is displayed showing the new image data type as an OLE object. This demonstrates that the new image data type, although shown as an OLE object, does not contain data in an OLE object format. It holds the data in a new Image data format. This means that the limitation on the new Image data types is that they cannot be displayed in a desktop reporting database using an OLE data control. However, with a single line of programming code, you can get around this limitation.

OLE objects, image data, and Microsoft Azure SQL Database

When you create an IMAGE data type in a web app table, in the background a VARBINARY(MAX) field is created in Microsoft Azure SQL Database . When a desktop database links to a VARBINARY(MAX) field in Microsoft Azure SQL Database, Access displays it as an OLE object, and Access will allow you to store OLE objects in the field. OLE objects use a special encoding format that cannot be understood by a web app in a browser window, because the new Image data type expects the data in a different format and an Access desktop database does not understand this new format. (It assumes the data is in an OLE format.) You cannot use a desktop database to manipulate this data using a linked table.

Earlier in this section, you used a special ADO technique to upload images in a format that will work in a web-app browser window, but this format is not compatible with the OLE-object format expected when displaying an object in a desktop database.

Because Access needs to maintain compatibility with existing applications linked to SQL Server, and because a desktop database bypasses Access Services and links directly to Microsoft Azure SQL Database, you cannot make this type of field behave in two different ways at the same time.

Warning At the time of this writing, there is an issue with the following approach working with linked tables generated by the reporting database created using the Report On My Data feature. To make this feature work, you need to replace the linked tables with the links created from within Access using a Machine Data Source. (See Chapter 9 for details about creating a Machine Data Source.)

If you create a desktop form that displays a single record from the image table (in our example, Customers?Images), the default choice of an OLE-object control cannot be used to display the image data and should be removed from the form—add an Image control to the form, and click Cancel when prompted to select an image. This image control cannot be bound to the image data. To display image data, rename the control ImageControl and then add the following code to the On Current event:

```
Private Sub Form_Current()
    Me.ImageControl.PictureData = Me.Image
End Sub
```

As shown in Figure 3-38, the form will render to display the image data in the control.

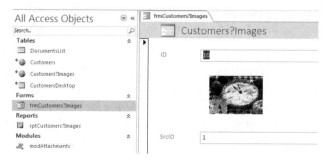

FIGURE 3-38 Rendering an image in a single record form with an image control.

Tip Although you can render this in a single form, you will not be able to produce the same result in a continuous form. But the good news is that you can tabulate the images in a report.

A similar technique is used when you want to display the image on a report. In this case, you want to add the bound control to the OLE data field but set the visibility to *False*. Then, in the detail section, add an image control and name the control *ImageData*.

Then add the following code to the On Format event for the detail section:

```
Private Sub Detail_Format(Cancel As Integer, FormatCount As Integer)
    Me.ImageData.PictureData = Me.Image
End Sub
```

The resulting report displayed in Print Preview is shown in Figure 3-39. (It will not render in Report View because it relies on the format event used in Print Preview.)

FIGURE 3-39 Rendering an image in a report with an image control.

Summary

In this chapter, you saw how a desktop database table structure, relationships, and data can be imported into a web app. You started by looking at how web-app tables are automatically assigned a numeric AutoNumber primary key if the table does not have a primary key, or if the primary key is not a long integer. You saw that this can have implications for existing foreign keys if a new primary key is added to a table. I demonstrated how you should restructure foreign and primary keys prior to importing the data to resolve any issues.

A great feature of web apps when importing data is that for table name or field names containing unsupported characters, the characters are removed and replaced with an underscore character. Also, when an unsupported data type is encountered in a field, the field is removed (or converted, for example, to a Long Text data type) but the data in other fields is preserved and imported into the new tables.

When working with a web app, you discovered how relationships and lookups are combined into a new single UI lookup, and you saw examples showing that, when possible, existing lookups or relationships are automatically converted into the new web-app lookups.

I provided examples of VBA code for assisting you in identifying field and table properties that are not converted but that can be later manually added to the imported design. I also provided code to assist you in extracting documents from existing attachment fields and, where an attachment contains supported image data formats, to directly transfer the data into a new Image data type in a web app.

An example creating a reporting database was used to demonstrate how desktop links to the SQL back-end could be easily changed from read-only to read/write using the External Writer user account.

In Chapter 4, "Creating a blank web app and using templates," I will build on your understanding of working in the web-app design interface, looking at how to create new tables and add lookups, indexes, and calculated fields.

Creating a blank web app and using templates

In this chapter, you'll see how you can create a new blank web app using design tools without needing to import existing data. You'll also look at basic design activities such as creating lookups and relationships, adding validation rules, indexing, and using calculated fields.

The web app you create in this chapter is not used in subsequent chapters.

Creating a blank web app

When using Access, you can create either a desktop database or a web app. The list of choices for each option also includes built-in templates for creating popular database structures, both for the desktop and for a web app. The templates for the desktop databases begin with the word "Desktop" in their name, as listed on the Office Start screen. In a web app the idea of a template database is of more limited importance, which you'll see when working with the new feature for table templates in the next section.

After you start Access, select Custom Web App, as shown in Figure 4-1.

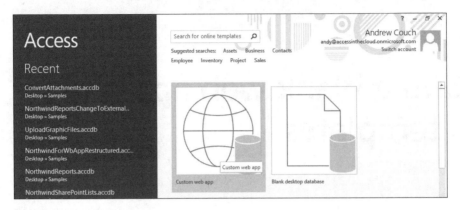

FIGURE 4-1 Creating a blank web app.

After you make this selection, you will be prompted to select a name and location for the application. As shown in Figure 4-2, name your web app **NewBlankDatabase**.

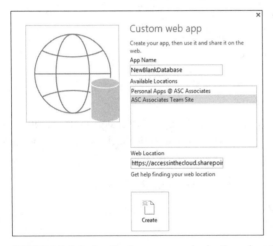

FIGURE 4-2 Entering the App name and selecting a location.

Adding template tables

After creating your blank web app, you will be presented with the screen shown in Figure 4-3. Notice that below the search box are hyperlinks for suggested searches on Person, Order, Service, and Sell.

FIGURE 4-3 The Add Tables page.

If you type **Orders** in the search box, Access will try to match your request with the set of options most appropriate to your needs. You will notice that the results can show either a box with a single outline, such as Customers (which means you get one table), or a box named Orders with a shadowed outline (which means you get more than one table). Select the Orders table option shown in Figure 4-4 to follow the example in this chapter.

FIGURE 4-4 Selecting a template table.

The result of making this selection is shown in Figure 4-5, where not only have new tables been added, but on the Table Selector on the left the Order Details view is hidden from the user.

FIGURE 4-5 Multiple tables displayed in the Table Selector.

 Tip Access 2013 tries to get you started with a productive business solution by helping to structure your data and then, with the data structures created, adding views to display the data. The underpinning concept to this scaffolding is the relationships between the tables. With one or two clicks, you have a set of tables and views for the data. This is the true power of this new design tool, and later you will see that this approach of automatically creating views also applies when you construct your own blank or imported tables.

Creating a new table

To create new tables, click the Table icon on the home ribbon or, at the bottom of the Table Selector, click the Add New Table button. Either method will display the Add Tables screen shown in Figure 4-6. On the right side of the screen at the end of the second paragraph of text, click the Add A New Blank Table hyperlink.

FIGURE 4-6 Add Tables page.

After you click the link, Access displays the design interface. Here you need to add two new fields to the table design (FirstName and Surname, which are both Short Text data types), as shown in Figure 4-7. In Chapter 3, "Converting a desktop database to a web app," in the section "Importing different data types." I listed the available data types for use in a web app.

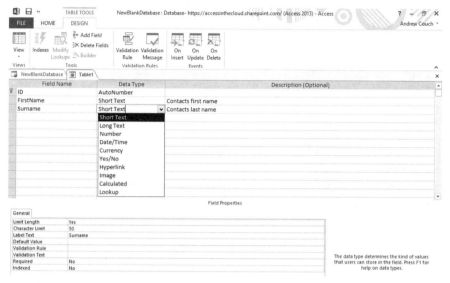

FIGURE 4-7 A new table viewed in the design interface.

Each table will automatically be assigned a primary key AutoNumber called *ID*. This field can be renamed but not deleted from the table design. You can change the name of the key to a more meaningful name—for example, ContactID, which is used for the new table design in this chapter.

Save the table with the name CustomerContacts. Before getting deeper into the design, you will change the names of all the primary and foreign-key fields to make them easier to understand, rather than accepting the default names for the fields.

Editing the design of a table

When viewing the Table Selector, you can choose from one of two methods to quickly switch a table into design view to change the table structure. You can double-click on the table caption in the Table Selector. Or you can click once on the table caption, either right-click on the table or directly click on the Settings/Actions charm, and then choose Edit Table, as shown in Figure 4-8. You could also display the navigation pane and double-click or right-click on a table.

FIGURE 4-8 Opening a table in Design view.

Warning Don't click on the large edit button in the center of the screen because that is for editing the view that is displayed in the design preview on the screen, and in this situation we want to change the design of the table and not alter a view layout.

Make the following name changes to the primary and foreign keys in the tables, and save your changes.

TABLE 4-1 Changes for the primary and foreign keys

Table Name	Old Field Name	New Field Name
Orders	ID	OrderID
	Customer (Lookup)	CustomerID
	Employee (Lookup)	EmployeeID
Customers	ID	CustomerID
Employees	ID	EmployeeID
Products	ID	ProductID
	Supplier (Lookup)	SupplierID
	Category (Lookup)	CategoryID
Suppliers	ID	SupplierID
Categories	ID	CategoryID
Order Details	ID	OrderDetailsID
	Product (Lookup)	ProductID
	Order (Lookup)	OrderID

As you are going through this, you can also change the captions on the foreign keys and primary keys—for example, change *ProductID* to *Product*. That has not been done for the example used in this chapter.

If you look at Figure 4-9, you will see how the web app has altered all views to reflect the changes you made to the field names—in this case, OrderID and ProductID in the Order Details table.

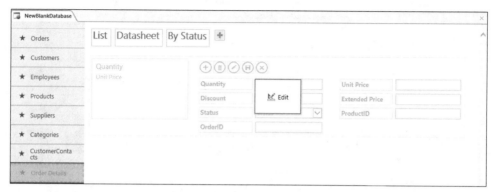

FIGURE 4-9 Automatic updates to the design of the quickly created views.

> **Tip** As long as you have not edited any of the quickly created views, any changes to elements in the table will be automatically reflected in the views (which have not been edited). This means that making any significant structural changes before starting to work on view design will save you design effort.

Creating lookups and relationships

In Chapter 3, I described the rules that are applied when importing lookups and relationships, and I described how lookups and relationships are combined into one feature in the user interface even though behind the scenes real relationships can be created in the back-end Microsoft Azure SQL Database.

Before looking at how to create a new lookup, you'll find it useful to see how to display existing lookups. View a table in design view, select a field that is a lookup, and then click the Modify Lookups button on the Design contextual ribbon tab. Access opens the Lookup Wizard, as shown in Figure 4-10.

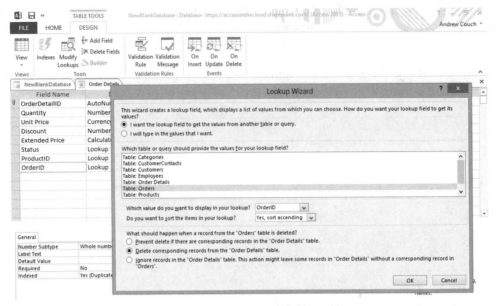

FIGURE 4-10 The Modify Lookups selection, displaying the Lookup Wizard.

You will notice that the Lookup Wizard supports both a lookup to data in a table and a list of values you typed in. In the Order Details table, if you choose to modify the lookup for the Status field, you will see an example of a value-based lookup.

Return to the new CustomerContacts table. Using the design view, type in the foreign-key name **CustomerID** on a new line and change the data type from Short Text to Lookup, as shown in Figure 4-11.

Field Name	Data Type	Description (Optional)
ContactID	AutoNumber	
FirstName	Short Text	Contacts first name
Surname	Short Text	Contacts last name
CustomerID	Short Text	
	Short Text	
	Long Text	
	Number	
	Date/Time	
	Currency	
	Yes/No	
	Hyperlink	
	Image	
	Calculated	
	Lookup	

Field Properties

FIGURE 4-11 Adding a new lookup field.

In the Lookup Wizard, select the first option, I Want The Lookup Field To Get The Values From Another Table Or Query. Select the Customers table from the list of tables, and then select Company from the drop-down list to be the field displayed. You can also change the sorting order if required, as shown in Figure 4-12.

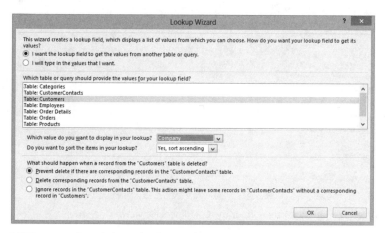

FIGURE 4-12 Completing selections in the Lookup Wizard.

In the lower part of Figure 4-12 are three choices that control how the relationship will operate:

- **Prevent Delete If There Is Are Corresponding Records In The "CustomerContacts" Table** This option creates a relationship with referential integrity between the two tables.

- **Delete Corresponding Records From The "CustomerContacts" Table** This option acts similar to the preceding one, but it adds a cascade delete to the relationship.

- **Ignore Records In The "CustomerContacts" Table** This action might leave some records in "CustomerContacts" without a corresponding record in "Customers." No relationship will be created.

The web app does not have any point at which you can view all the relationships to see a diagram of how the tables fit together. (There is no equivalent to a desktop database diagram.)

> **Tip** The information on lookups that enforce referential integrity is stored inside the Microsoft Azure SQL Database. How to extract this information is described in Chapter 9, "Looking under the hood at Microsoft Azure SQL Database."

After you create this new lookup between Customers and CustomerContacts choosing the first option to enforce referential integrity, if you display the Customers table caption and select the list view, at the bottom of the view you will see that the web app has automatically added a new tab to the related item control (RELIC). It now displays the related CustomerContacts tab (in addition to the existing Orders tab), as shown in Figure 4-13.

FIGURE 4-13 Automatic changes to related information for the Customers list view.

Adding indexing

If you create a new table, the primary key for the table will be indexed, and if you add a lookup, the foreign key for the lookup will also be indexed. The indexing on foreign keys is created to help improve performance when joining together two tables of data to return with queries.

Adding additional indexes is useful when you have a commonly searched field and you believe an index could help to retrieve the data. An index can also be created that is unique, and then you can use the index to enforce a business rule ensuring unique values.

Take a look at the design of the Employees template table. If you click the Indexes button on the Design contextual ribbon tab, Access opens the Indexes dialog box and displays all indexes defined in the table, as shown in Figure 4-14.

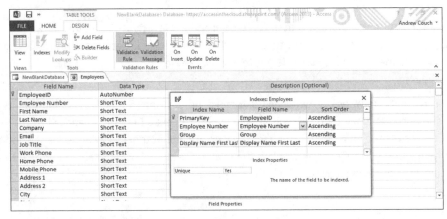

FIGURE 4-14 Displaying indexing on the Employees table.

In Figure 4-14, although the PrimaryKey index is unique, the Employee Number index is also unique. This means that the second index is enforcing a business rule stating that each employee has a unique employee number.

> **Tip** A value of NULL (no value) is treated as also being unique, so this index seems to allow one employee, and only one, to have no value for the employee number. But because the field is a required field (NOT NULL), there is no inconsistency. If you created a field that was not required (NULLABLE) and created a unique index, you could get some strange side effects.

If you have an activity that is slow to execute, adding an index on, for example, a field used for filtering the data can improve performance. The only way to test this is to add the index and then see if the performance has improved. Indexes can also be created using multiple fields. One key question to ask before adding an index is, "Will the field values have sufficiently varied values to make the index selective?" For example, indexing a field with only four or five distinct values is unlikely to be of great benefit, while indexing a field for a postal code is likely to be beneficial if you are constantly filtering or searching on this field.

You also incur a cost with having indexes: the database will need to update the indexes when data changes. This means that adding many indexes to a table can result in operations to change the data slowing down (because the indexes will need to be updated). It is a good idea not to create too many indexes. Exactly what is meant by too many is difficult to quantify. However, if you kept the number of indexes to 5 or 6, that would not be an unreasonable number of indexes.

> **Tip** Although the Microsoft Azure SQL Database has tools for displaying how indexing is being used (specifically, showing the execution plan for your SQL), unfortunately at the time of this writing, you will not have sufficient permissions in Microsoft Azure SQL Database to use these features.

Adding validation rules

A web app has validation features similar to a desktop database, but it uses a different set of functions to support validation. Each table is allowed a validation rule and message. The table-level validation rule is used to cross-validate data and compare the values in several fields. Depending on the data type, each field can have a separate validation rule, which normally refers only to the field but can make references to the values in other fields. (This is a feature that is not available in desktop database field validation rules.)

In the sample web app in this chapter, look at the template table Customers and click the Validation Rule button on the Design contextual ribbon tab. You will see the rule displayed in the Expression Builder dialog box, as shown in Figure 4-15.

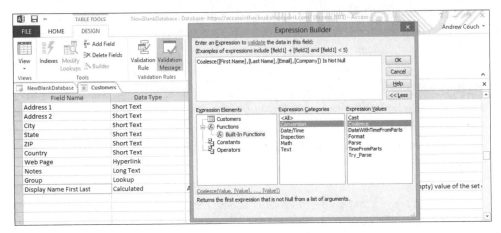

FIGURE 4-15 Expression Builder dialog displaying a validation rule.

> **Tip** In addition to the help information provided within Access, the validation rule functions (such as COALESCE, which returns the first NOT NULL value from a list of choices) are SQL Server functions.) You can find detailed examples and further information when looking in the SQL Server help; this information is most easily found either by searching online or by using the help features in the SQL Server Management Studio (SSMS), which is described in Chapter 9.

The preceding example of a table-level validation rule ensures that one of the four specified fields has to contain a value:

```
- Coalesce([First Name],[Last Name],[Email],[Company]) Is Not Null
```

Individual fields can also have a single validation rule. For example, in the Products table, if you want to ensure that each product code starts with the string "01-", you could add the validation rule shown in Figure 4-16.

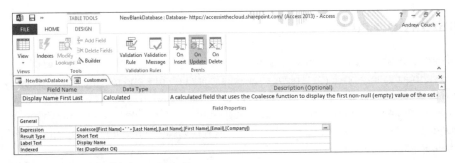

FIGURE 4-16 Field validation rule and text.

In this example, you find the rule `Left([Product Code],3) = "01-"`, which checks that each product code starts with "01-". When entering the rule, you can choose to use single quotes (such as '01-'), which would also be accepted.

> **Tip** To delete a field or table validation rule or message, display the text and remove the text or rule using the backspace key.

Adding calculated fields

Tables support the use of calculated fields, where the calculation can be based on a combination of other fields in the table. There are two advantages to using a calculated field rather than an expression in a query. The first advantage is that rather than possibly repeating the calculation in several places, the calculation is defined in one place in the design of the table.

The second benefit is that it might give you better performance, because the web app holds the results of the calculation with the data in the table. This means that it needs to recalculate the result only if any data in the dependent fields change, which it will do automatically. The storage type used for the calculated field will vary to suit the needs of the calculation, as defined in the Result Type field property for the calculation (which is a read-only property).

> **Tip** Because the calculation results are saved, you are not allowed to use expressions in a calculation that could vary over time. For example, you can calculate the number of days between two date fields in the table but not the number of days between a date field and today's date (because that calculation varies depending on the current date). In SQL Server terminology, you are allowed to use only *deterministic* expressions, not *nondeterministic* expressions.

Figure 4-17 shows an example of a calculated expression in the Customers table.

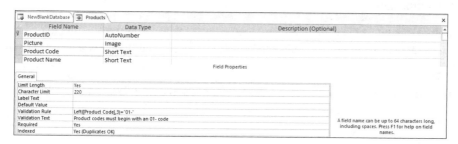

FIGURE 4-17 Calculated field expression.

In this example, the calculation used is the following:

```
Coalesce([First Name]+" "+[Last Name],[Last Name],[First Name],[Email],[Company])
```

The *Coalesce* function returns the first non-null value in the list of expressions. Notice that the plus sign (+) symbol is used for string concatenation; this is because that is what SQL Server uses for concatenating strings. An Access desktop database can use either + or & for string concatenation. The advantage of using & is that if one part of the expression is NULL, it will still give a result. Here is an example:

```
"Andrew" + NULL = NULL, but "Andrew" & NULL = "Andrew"
```

To obtain a similar expression to the Access desktop database expression `Trim$([First Name] & " " & [Last Name])`, you would need to protect the string concatenation against a NULL—because you cannot use the & symbol but must use the + symbol.

You could use the following expression:

```
LTRIM(RTRIM(COALESCE([First Name], "") + " " + COALESCE([Last Name], "")))
```

Here you need to use the combination of left and right trim operations because the TRIM function has no equivalent function in SQL Server.

> **Tip** If you examined this calculation in Microsoft Azure SQL Database, you would see the following expression:
>
> ```
> (ltrim(rtrim((coalesce([First Name],N'')+N' ')+coalesce([Last Name],N'')))),
> ```
>
> Here you can see that the double quotes have been switched to single quotes, and the use of the *N* symbol next to the string expressions indicates that they should be read as Unicode strings.

Summary

In Chapter 3, I focused on dealing with converting an existing desktop data. In this chapter, I described the alternative scenario, where you need to create new table structures or alter the design of imported table structures.

You started by creating a blank database and then adding tables using the built-in table templates. You used this great new feature to add individual tables or sets of tables to either a new or existing web app.

This chapter also demonstrated the essential skills you need to do the following:

- Create a blank new table.

- Edit the design of an existing table.

- Create lookups and relationships.

- Add indexing to improve performance.

- Add validation rules.

- Define calculated fields.

Now that you understand both how to manage the importing of data from existing databases and the creation of new database structures, you can move forward in Chapter 5, "Displaying data with views." In that chapter, you develop an understanding of how to customize the basic UI interface displayed when new tables are created or imported into a web app.

Displaying data in views

This chapter looks at how to develop the user interface for a web app using views. In Chapter 2, "Finding your way around Access 2013," you created a blank web app called NorthwindData and imported data from Access. If you do not have this web app but want to follow along with the different techniques, repeat the steps at the beginning of Chapter 2 to create the web app and import the sample data before continuing.

To demonstrate many of the great techniques you can use to control view presentation, this chapter introduces some simple user-interface macros. Chapter 7, "Programming a web app using macros," provides a more detailed examination of the macro design interface and examines the process of constructing more advanced macros.

Chapter 2 also introduced view controls; later in this section, you'll explore the more advanced controls in greater depth.

Customizing the table selector

By renaming a caption on the table selector, you can create more meaningful captions. Click the table caption of the table you want to rename to highlight it, click the Action/Settings charm, and then click the Rename option from the list of options, as shown in Figure 5-1.

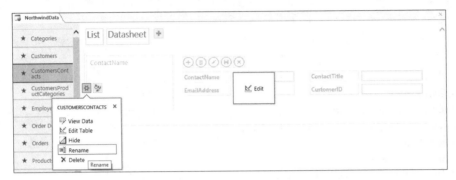

FIGURE 5-1 Selecting the Rename option for a table caption.

After you select the Rename option, the cursor will be positioned in the existing table caption, which is editable. Rename the table caption from CustomersContacts to **Contacts**.

You will also find it useful to hide table captions. Figure 5-2 contains several table captions that were hidden by selecting the Hide option, which you can see in Figure 5-1. After they are hidden, the captions move to the bottom of the table selector and appear grayed-out; these captions will not be visible when the web app is shown in a browser. In Figure 5-2, you can see that by displaying the Settings/Actions drop-down list for a hidden caption you can unhide the table caption.

FIGURE 5-2 Display the Unhide option for a hidden table caption.

You can re-order the table captions by clicking on a caption and then dragging the caption to a new position in the list. Figure 5-3 shows the captions re-ordered. Also, the icons on table captions can be changed, as shown in Figure 5-3, by using the formatting popup window.

FIGURE 5-3 Changing the table caption icons.

Warning Deleting a table caption also deletes the actual table. In contrast, when hiding the table caption you can remove the element from the user interface without removing the table.

Customizing the view selector

Before continuing through this section, check that your table caption names and the order of the table captions match that shown in Figure 5-4.

Each table caption can have a number of views that are displayed across the top of the screen. You can delete, rename, or duplicate views, and you can add new views using the plus sign (+) button to the right of the existing views. Figure 5-4 shows the settings and actions available when selecting a view caption in the view selector.

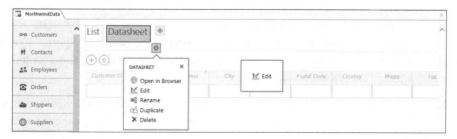

FIGURE 5-4 Settings and actions for a view.

Figure 5-5 shows an example where captions were renamed for the two views and the order of the views was changed using drag and drop.

FIGURE 5-5 Changing the title and display order of a view.

Creating a pop-up window interface

You normally create views from the view selector and associate them with a table caption. However, you also can create a standalone view that is not associated with a table selector. This example illustrates how you can create a blank standalone view with a set of buttons that provide an alternative interface to the normal table selector–driven application interface.

When you click the Advanced button in the ribbon, you'll see three view types available: Blank View, List View, and Datasheet View, as shown in Figure 5-6. If you click the Blank View option, and Access opens the design window for a blank view.

FIGURE 5-6 Creating a blank standalone view.

When the design tool opens, you are presented with a blank view; double-clicking on the button icon in the Controls area on the ribbon adds a control button to the view. (See Figure 5-7.) After adding a button, you can use the formatting charm to change the button caption, add a tooltip, and if desired, specify whether the button is visible or hidden.

In Figure 5-7, I added two buttons, named Customers and Contacts, to the blank view and clicked the Save icon on the Quick Access toolbar (at the top left, above the ribbon) to save the view with the name NavigationView.

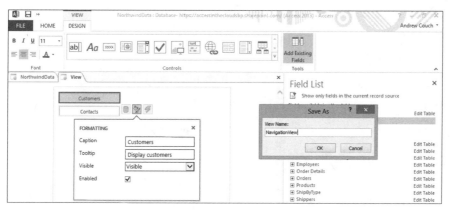

FIGURE 5-7 Adding buttons to the blank view.

 Tip The Quick Access toolbar provides commands to Save, Undo, Redo, and Launch App. In Figure 5-6, you can see all these options on the toolbar. To the right of the Save button are two arrows that expand the bar to show more controls. In Figure 5-6, on the right of the toolbar is a small downward pointing arrow that can be used to display options to customize the toolbar. In Figure 5-7, the toolbar is shortened.

Figure 5-8 shows the result of clicking to select a button and then clicking the Settings/Actions charm. This shows that a button has a single action called On Click. Clicking this button displays the macro design interface.

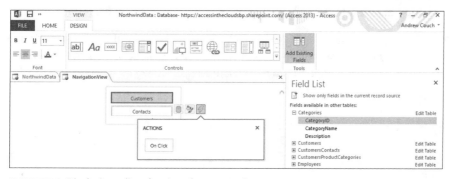

FIGURE 5-8 Displaying a list of actions for a control.

In the macro design window, type the command **OpenPopup** and then press Enter. From there, you can then set the various arguments used with the macro action. In this case, for the view argument, choose Customers List from the list of available views, as shown in Figure 5-9. In Chapter 7, you will look at macros in more detail.

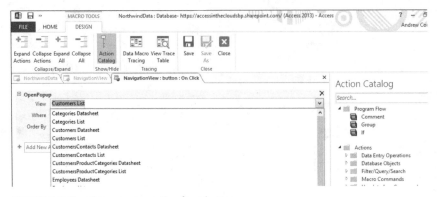

FIGURE 5-9 Creating a macro action for a button.

After saving and closing this window, you can repeat the steps to add a macro command to open the CustomersContacts List Details view when the Contacts button is clicked. After you close the macro design window and save your macro, you will see that the action is highlighted with a green color to indicate that there is macro code behind the action. You can now save and close the blank view.

> **Tip** After you write macro code behind an event for the view or for controls on the view and then save and close the macro editor, it is easy to forget that you also need to save the view to cause any of the new actions or changes to operate with the view. The view must be saved before any embedded saved macro changes will be saved.

The OpenPopup macro action is often used in a special macro named *On Start* to display a popup view when the application starts. We will use this feature to create our popup interface.

In Figure 5-10, on the left, you can see the navigation pane. It contains the new NavigationView view. (Remember that the views are shown as forms when displaying information in the navigation pane.) Select the On Start menu option from the Advanced drop-down list of operations.

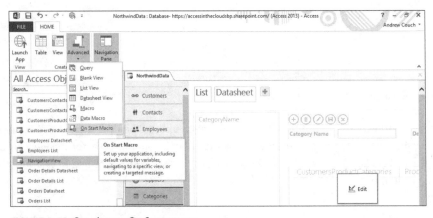

FIGURE 5-10 Creating an On Start macro.

Tip You can click the On Start Macro option only when you select the main application tab (NorthwindData, in our example), which shows the table selector. If you have focus on any other tab, such as when working on the design of a view, and click the Advanced drop-down list of actions, you will find the On Start Macro action is disabled (grayed out).

In the macro design tool, type **OpenPopup** and select the NavigationView, as shown in Figure 5-11, for the View argument in the macro action.

FIGURE 5-11 Setting the On Start macro to open a popup window.

After saving the macro, you need to hide all the table captions because the application would still display the standard interface. Note that hiding all the table captions is not something you would normally do in a web app, but you do it here because you want to create a popup-driven interface without using the table selector for navigation. In Figure 5-12, you can see the initial menu popup window, and the resulting view that is displayed when you click the Customers button has been moved to the right.

Tip You could add a dummy table to your application and change the table caption to give your application a title. Then delete any views from the view selector, and add a blank view, which could then contain text describing the application, or add an image to the blank view to create a more pleasing background screen for the application. Adding a button to display the navigation popup window is also a good idea; otherwise, if this is closed, the user would be left with a blank screen.

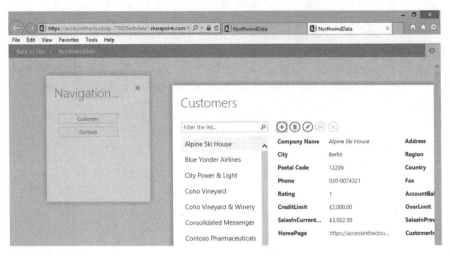

FIGURE 5-12 Using a popup window to navigate your application.

To return the web app to the standard interface and continue with the examples in this chapter, right-click and unhide any table captions you chose to hide in the preceding steps. Using the Advanced menu, click to open the On Start macro in the design view. Shown in Figure 5-13 on the right of the macro command is a Delete button (X). Click on that to delete the macro command and save the empty design window. This removes any commands from the On Start macro.

FIGURE 5-13 Deleting a macro command from the On Start macro.

Datasheet view

The humble datasheet achieves functionality that would require considerable programming if you were working with other developer products, such as Microsoft Visual Studio. This control provides a tabulation of data for which you can scroll, filter, and sort information, and you can simply type into any cell and move on to the next row to enter more data.

> **Tip** One restriction with this view is that you cannot easily undo changes you make to the data, because changes are saved when you move to another record. If, before moving to another record, you refresh the page or navigate to another view or table caption, you will be prompted to discard your changes. You will see later in this topic how you can improve on that behavior by adding an Undo button to the action bar.

Before delving further into customizing the behavior of the datasheet, take a look at the built-in filtering and sorting feature. Figure 5-14 shows the drop-down list on a column header for filtering and sorting data.

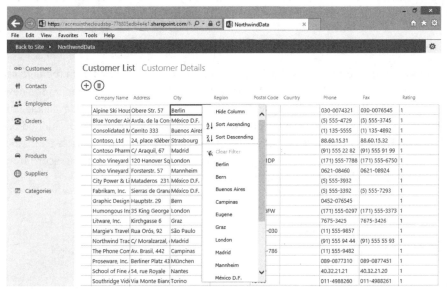

FIGURE 5-14 Filtering data displayed in a datasheet.

If you look at the action bar in Figure 5-15, you will see only two icons: one for adding new records and the other for deleting records. This is a reduced set of actions compared to a List Details view; the reason is that the datasheet opens in edit mode, which means fewer buttons are required to interact with the data. (You can add additional buttons to the action bar.)

In this example you have a datasheet view for the Customers table where the caption has been renamed to *Customer List* and selected in in the view selector. In Access, the layout of the view is shown in *view preview*. (This is the term used to refer to a view when it has been selected in the design interface and is shown as a preview of the layout of controls on the view.) Click on the Edit button in the center of the screen in Figure 5-15 to edit the view.

FIGURE 5-15 Selecting a datasheet view in view preview.

More Info You can prevent a blank row from being displayed at the bottom of a datasheet in your browser only for a read-only user of the web app or with the view Record source set to Read Only (applies to all users). You can allow users to save changes but prevent them from inserting or deleting a record using data macros, which are described in Chapter 7.

On the right side of the design tool is the Field List area. You can drag fields from the field list onto the design surface, and other fields will move to the right to make space for positioning the new field. Notice that the controls shown in the Ribbon in Figure 5-16 are a reduced set of all available controls. This reflects that not all controls are available on a datasheet, and controls can be positioned only in a horizontal row. There is no header or footer area. You will notice that the controls on the ribbon do not include a hyperlink. However, if you drag and drop a hyperlink field onto the record from the Field List area, it will be displayed with a hyperlink control.

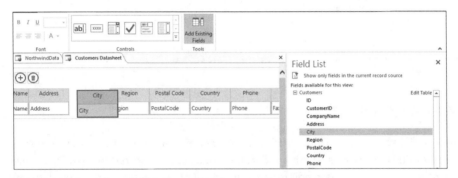

FIGURE 5-16 Dragging a field from the field list onto a datasheet view.

Tip In a datasheet, you cannot display images or adjust the height of each row to display multiline text. In both cases, you could add a button to display a view showing additional information. A tabulation of images is available in the list control, which is part of a List Details view.

If you click on the Data charm for the column, you will see the column data properties, as shown in Figure 5-17. The Control Name text box is automatically filled with a name that incorporates the control type and field name. The Control Source and Default Value text boxes have accompanying ellipses build buttons you can use to construct expressions.

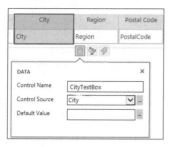

FIGURE 5-17 Using the Data charm to display data properties.

If you click on the Formatting charm for a column, as shown in Figure 5-18, you can define a tooltip, set visibility, enable or disable the control, and set a datasheet caption.

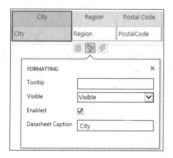

FIGURE 5-18 Formatting charm for a control.

You will notice that fonts and color are not displayed in the formatting properties. At the end of this chapter, you will see how to set a control's color presentation properties using a macro command. For other formatting, you should refer back to Chapter 1, "Finding your way around Office 365," to see how themes can provide additional formatting features.

In the datasheet view, after entering data but not moving out of a cell, you can press the ESC key to undo a change. However, once you move to another cell in the same row, you cannot undo changes in other cells (other than by refreshing the page before moving to another row).

To simplify correcting mistakes made in entering data, you can add your own Undo button to the action bar.

If you click on the plus sign (+) button next to the action bar, you can add a control, as shown in Figure 5-19. You can see the Data charm is used to name the control, add a tooltip, and change the icon (in this example a cross icon is selected).

FIGURE 5-19 Adding a button to the action bar.

Click on the Action charm. Then click on the On Click event button shown in Figure 5-19. This displays the macro editor. Type **UndoRecord** as the macro action as shown in Figure 5-20. Then save and close the macro, and save the datasheet view. You will now have an undo button on the action bar in your datasheet.

FIGURE 5-20 Adding the UndoRecord macro command.

> **Tip** You are allowed a maximum of 12 action buttons on a view. On a blank or list details view, you can also add more button controls in any position on the view, and on a datasheet, you can add more button controls in the row—for example, to display additional details on the record.

Navigation buttons—such as first, previous, next, and last—can also be added to the action bar. In Figure 5-21, four extra buttons have been added to the action bar for record navigation. The On Click button is green, indicating code behind the event has been written.

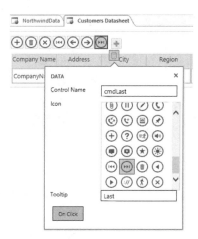

FIGURE 5-21 Adding record navigation buttons to the action bar.

 Tip Unfortunately, if you add new buttons to the action bar, you cannot use the clipboard to copy the buttons to another view. The process of adding the buttons needs to be repeated on all required views.

Using the On Click event for each button, you then add the GoToRecord macro action with the Record choices of Previous, Next, First, and Last, as shown in Figure 5-22.

FIGURE 5-22 Adding the GoToRecord macro command.

You can also add your own buttons in a row, which can be used to either display another view that shows more information, using the OpenPopup macro. Or you can navigate to display a different view on the table selector using the ChangeView macro action. Both these actions have *where* clause arguments you can use to filter the displayed information to match the current record you are working on. In Figure 5-23, I placed a button control onto the datasheet. Note that you cannot drag and drop the control onto the design surface. Click the control once in the Ribbon, and it will be placed at the end of the row. Then drag the control across the screen to the desired position.

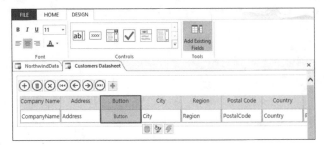

FIGURE 5-23 Adding a button to the datasheet.

You can use the Formatting charm to change the button caption and datasheet caption, as shown in Figure 5-24.

FIGURE 5-24 Changing the datasheet caption and button caption.

If you then display the Actions charm, as shown in Figure 5-25, and click the On Click event, you can write appropriate macro code behind the button.

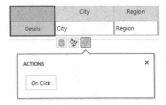

FIGURE 5-25 Displaying the On Click event for a button.

Figure 5-26 shows the OpenPopup macro action, which was entered in the On Click event for the button.

FIGURE 5-26 The OpenPopup macro action.

The syntax for the *where* clause argument has the following general form:

```
[TableName].[FieldName1] = [FieldName2]
```

In this case, *[FieldName1]* is the name of the field on the target view and *[FieldName2]* is the name of the field on the source view.

> **Tip** When you refer to the target view, you must prefix the field with the table name (or query name) used in the target view. The field on the source view does not need to be shown on the view because Access can still retrieve the value at runtime. You can also choose to use unbound controls on the source view.
>
> If the target view was based on a query—for example, qryCustomersDatasheet—rather than the table Customers, the syntax would be *[qryCustomersDatasheet].[ID]*. Note that this technique does not work if the target view uses an *embedded query* (discussed in the next section) as its record source because you, as the app designer, do not know the internal name Access uses for embedded queries. You should consider changing the embedded query to a saved query object visible in the Navigation Pane if you want to use this technique.

The resulting button and popup window are shown in Figure 5-27.

FIGURE 5-27 An example datasheet using a popup window to display further information.

Tip If you create a datasheet based on more than one table using a query, you will be able to edit the data only on the *many* side of the relationship. I will discuss queries in Chapter 6, "Creating data sources using queries."

Views and record sources

The Access environment will try and help you when you are creating views by offering you a restricted choice of options for the source of data (Record Source) when you start to create a view. The available list of record sources will include the table associated with the table caption on which you are creating the view and any queries that include the table (excluding parameterized queries, which we will discuss in Chapter 6). But this is not a real restriction; it is only an aid to get you started. After the view has been created (with the exception of a summary view), you can change the record source.

Figure 5-28 shows the screen you get after you locate the table caption and click the + icon on the view selector to add a new view. After entering a name for the view, you select datasheet from the View Type drop-down list. (The options are List Details, Datasheet, Summary, and Blank.) The only option you have in the Record Source drop-down list is the table name, Categories—because you have no queries containing the Categories table and you are creating this view on the Categories table caption.

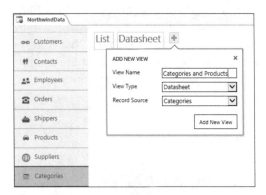

FIGURE 5-28 Creating a new view.

When editing this view, you have several techniques to choose from if you want to change the record source. In Figure 5-29, the data properties for the view are displayed. (Note the check box you can select to make the view read only.) When you click the build button next to the Record Source drop-down list, you get a popup window that prompts you to invoke the Query Builder. If you click Yes, you can create and save a named query or create what is called an *embedded query*. Queries are discussed in Chapter 6.

Tip An embedded query is where the SQL is not held as a named query but is internally tied to the view that the Record Source will display [Embedded Query]. The SQL for the *embedded query* is held as a Windows SQL Azure View and is given an internal alphanumeric code. Using an embedded query for a view can result in reduced features. For example, when I described filtering in the last section, I indicated that the filtering technique cannot be used with an OpenPopup macro action when the view is based on an *embedded query*.

FIGURE 5-29 Invoking the Query Builder to change the record source for a view.

A second option for changing the Record Source setting is shown on the right side of Figure 5-30. You can see the related Products table in the Field List area. When you expand this table, its fields can be dragged and dropped onto the view, creating a view displaying information from both the Products and Categories tables. This combined view is shown in Figure 5-31.

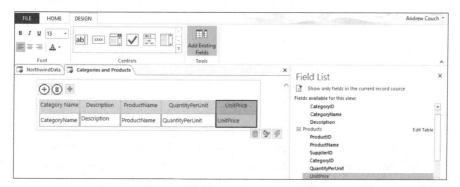

FIGURE 5-30 Adding fields from a related table using the field list.

Note that using this technique of adding fields from related tables in the Field List will automatically create an *embedded query* for the view. After the *embedded query* is created, you could use the Record Source build button shown in Figure 5-31 to edit and then save the *embedded query* as a named query.

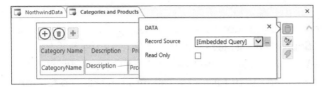

FIGURE 5-31 Displaying the record source as an embedded query.

If you use SQL Server Management Studio (SSMS) to look into your database, you will find that these queries are actually saved as views in SQL Azure. Figure 5-32 provides an example. Unlike queries you will see later that get saved with the name you provide, an embedded query is saved with a unique code. (You will not see these queries listed when looking in the navigation pane.)

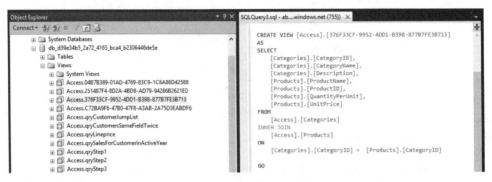

FIGURE 5-32 Displaying the embedded query by viewing it in SQL Azure using SSMS.

> **Tip** An advantage of having a named query is that it can be re-used on several views. But the disadvantage is that you have more objects to manage in your web app. Using an embedded query means you will have fewer objects to manage in the web app. In both cases, the queries are saved as views in SQL Azure, so there will be no performance differences between the techniques.

In this section, you saw that after a view is created, it can be adapted to use data from either multiple tables or from sources other than the table associated with the table caption. This means the initial restrictions on choosing a source of data are present to make it easier to get started developing a view, not to place a restriction on which data source is used for a view. It is your responsibility when changing the data source to ensure that control sources are present in any new data sources.

Duplicating views

In the previous section, I described how the record source for a view need not be tied to a table caption. In this section, I demonstrate how, by duplicating views, copies of a view can be transferred from one table caption to another. You can think of the table caption more clearly as a menu item for organizing your views rather than as a restrictive way to interact with only data from the underlying associated table.

Maintenance tables, or *lookups*, are an excellent example of where you want to gather up several datasheets for different tables and place them on a single table caption. In Figure 5-33, the Products table caption was changed to *Maintenance*, the Products list-view was deleted and the Products datasheet-view was retitled with the caption *Products*. This allows other datasheets for different tables to be gathered together under the single maintenance table caption.

FIGURE 5-33 Changing a table caption for gathering lookups.

If you then locate another datasheet view as shown in Figure 5-34, clicking on the Settings charm for a selected view displays the option to duplicate the view.

FIGURE 5-34 Displaying the Duplicate menu item for a view.

The Duplicate View popup is shown in Figure 5-35. After entering a name for the new view, select the table caption onto which you want to copy the view. Notice that the underlying table name is shown, not the table caption. In this example, I chose *Products*, for which we previously renamed the table caption to *Maintenance*.

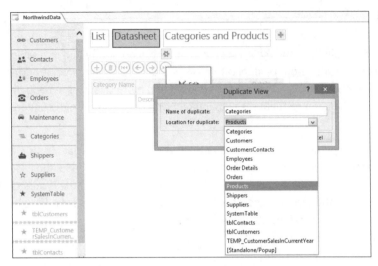

FIGURE 5-35 Duplicating a view to a different table caption.

This results in a table caption for Maintenance containing the views shown in Figure 5-36.

FIGURE 5-36 The resulting Maintenance table caption with the duplicated view.

In Figure 5-35, at the bottom of the list of destination tables, is the option to duplicate a view to [Standalone/Popup]. Choosing this option creates a view that is independent of a table caption. After they are created, these views can be displayed only with the OpenPopup macro command as a popup window in your browser.

Tip To see a list of all your views, including standalone views, look in the navigation pane under the Forms grouping.

Figure 5-37 provides a roadmap to help you understand how views can be duplicated between both table captions and the navigation pane. A view on one table caption can be duplicated to another table caption or standalone view, and a standalone view can be duplicated to a table caption.

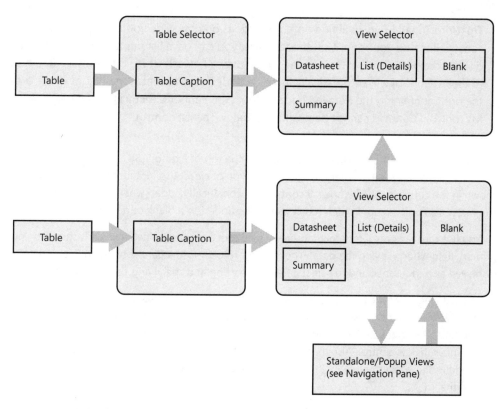

FIGURE 5-37 Roadmap for duplicating views between table captions and the navigation pane.

List Details view

A view that is more flexible than the datasheet is the List Details view. A sample List Details view is shown in the design view in Figure 5-38. A key characteristic of this view is the list control shown on the left of the view.

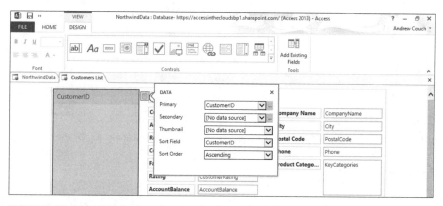

FIGURE 5-38 A List Details view showing the list on the left and details on the right.

Tip Unfortunately, you will find tight restrictions on how wide you can make the list control. Because you cannot set the font size, you can have list information that will not be displayed entirely until you hover the cursor over a line of text in your browser. The height of the list control will automatically increase or decrease to match the height of the area on the right containing the detailed information. (You cannot directly alter the height of the list control.) Controls cannot be positioned below the list control.

Looking at the controls shown in the ribbon at the top of Figure 5-38, you will see that the full set of controls are available when designing this type of view. Also, note that the list control is not shown in the controls set. This special control is automatically added when you create either a list or summary view and cannot be deleted. It cannot be added to a blank or datasheet view.

You use the list control to select a primary field and a secondary field (which is shown below the primary field when viewing the data). You also use it to choose a field containing image data to be displayed as a thumbnail and to select a field for sorting and specifying the sort direction.

The List Details view can also be added as a subview (which is discussed later in this chapter) onto another view, which can create very interesting graphical presentations when combined with thumbnail graphics. In Figure 5-39, you can see a List Details view containing a second List Details view shown in a subview control. Also, notice the restriction where, in the subview, the list cannot be made wide enough to show the full text; the full text will be displayed when you hover the cursor over an item in the list.

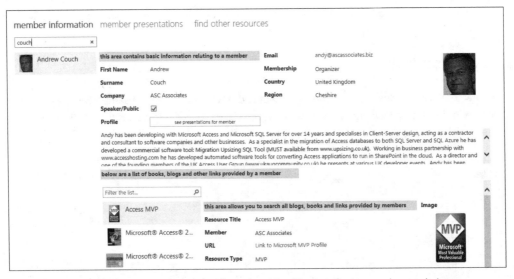

FIGURE 5-39 A List Details view with thumbnails, and another List Details view used as a subview.

Tip When you open a List Details view using the drill-through from a related items control, the list control portion of the list view will be hidden and the view opens in a popup window. However, if you add a List Details view as a subview within a parent view, the list control will be displayed, allowing users to further search related items. You can also use the OpenPopup macro action, which will display both the list control and details. The OpenPopup action also supports the use of a *where* clause to further filter the data. This means that depending on the context within which a List Details view is displayed, the list control part of the view can be automatically hidden. This is an example of the framework making available a suitable popup presentation using an existing List Details view without needing to create an additional view that would need to hide the list control part of the List Details view.

Both the List Details view and the blank view have the same default action bar options, which allow you to add, delete, edit, cancel, and save changes when working with a record. The icons are shown in Figure 5-40.

FIGURE 5-40 Action bar for a List Details view or blank view.

As you work with the data in the view and, for example, start to edit data, the Cancel and Save buttons become enabled. Also, the action bar buttons will become enabled or disabled as appropriate for your operation.

 Tip If you add your own action bar buttons, you will not get the same automatic features where controls are enabled or disabled according to the context of actions with the built-in buttons. If you need this level of functionality—for example, only making a button available when editing a record—you will need to take full control and replace all the built-in buttons in the action bar. This also applies to enabling and disabling other buttons you place on your view.

If you want to prevent a user from undertaking a certain operation, or make that operation conditional on other logic, you can add macro commands to either hide or display the built-in action bar buttons. If you delete one of the built-in action bar buttons Access created with the view, you can never add it back onto the view. As you develop an application, you can find yourself needing to duplicate a view to use for another purpose, so hiding rather than deleting a built-in action bar button is often a good idea.

To hide a built-in action bar button, you need to add a macro command to the On Load (or On Current) event for the view. When you click on the background of the view, away from any other controls, on the right you will see charms for the view. The Action charm will display the button for adding macro code to the On Load event, as shown in Figure 5-41.

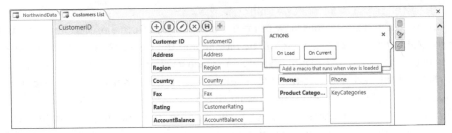

FIGURE 5-41 The On Load and On Current event buttons available for List Details views are displayed on the Actions property callout menu.

In Figure 5-42, you use the SetProperty macro action to hide the action bar delete button.

FIGURE 5-42 A SetProperty macro action attached to the On Load event of a List Details view.

The names for the built-in buttons on the action bar are as follows:

- deleteActionBarButton

- editActionBarButton

- saveActionBarButton

- cancelActionBarButton

- addActionBarButton

One further use of the SetProperty macro action is to change the caption shown in the browser title bar. Do not select a control, and leave the Control Name argument blank. Then set the Property argument to Caption, and fill in text or an expression for the Value argument, as shown in Figure 5-43. This configuration changes the text displayed in the browser title bar.

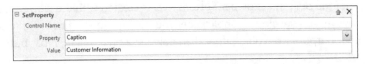

FIGURE 5-43 Macro logic to change the title shown on a tab in the browser window.

The SetProperty macro action can set six control properties. Note that not all properties can be changed for a selected control type using the SetProperty macro action. For example, you cannot change the colors of the built-in action bar buttons. These are the six control properties you can set:

- Enabled

- Visible

- ForeColor

- BackColor

- Caption

- Value

More Info In Chapter 7, you will see a technique where you can replace the built-in action bar buttons with custom buttons to gain finer control of view behavior.

Caution As you start typing in the control name in Figure 5-43, you will see IntelliSense display options. There are a number of built-in control names—such as Section, Form, and Report—which might make you think you have discovered previously unknown programming features. This is not the case. Parts of the UI for a web app are shared with components used in desktop databases.

Summary view

Summary views are used to summarize information by grouping and counting records, but they also provide a way to drill down into the summarized information. These views are read only and do not display an action bar.

In Chapter 6, you will read more detail about queries, but in this section I want to quickly create a simple query which will summarize data. I will do this to demonstrate how a summary view can be constructed. Click the Advanced icon in the ribbon and then choose Query from the drop-down list, as shown in Figure 5-44.

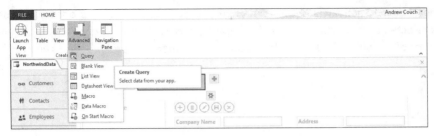

FIGURE 5-44 Creating a query using the Advanced menu options.

Figure 5-45 shows the Products table selected. After closing the Show Table dialog, double-click on the * to select all fields in the table to displayed on the query grid.

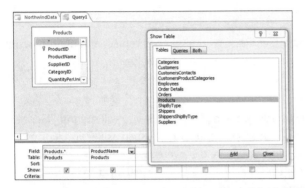

FIGURE 5-45 Creating a simple query that selects all fields from a table.

You then need to add a calculated field with the expression `Product:Left([ProductName],1)`, as shown in Figure 5-46. You can do this by first double-clicking on the ProductName field, dragging the field to the left of the existing field, and then replacing the field name with the expression. The Shift+F2 Zoom box is useful in displaying the detail of the expression. This expression uses the `Left` string function to extract the first initial in the ProductName. I saved this query with the name *qryProductsJumpList*.

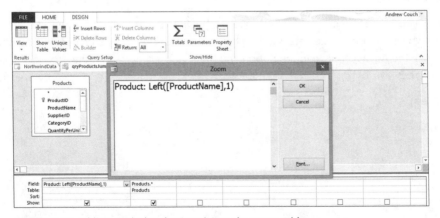

FIGURE 5-46 Adding a calculated expression to the query grid.

At this point, you can also use the view icon on the left of the ribbon to display a datasheet preview of your data, as shown in Figure 5-47.

FIGURE 5-47 Displaying the query results in a datasheet preview.

> **Tip** Once you finish working with an object, such as the query created in this example, it is a good idea to close the object. If you try to work with other objects depending on an open object, you might not be allowed to perform certain operations.

The next step is to create a summary view based on the query we created called *qryProductsJumpList*. Because we are working on Products, we will use the appropriate table caption, which we have retitled as Maintenance, to add a summary view as shown in Figure 5-48.

FIGURE 5-48 Creating a summary view based on a query.

When editing a summary view, you will observe that the view shows two boxes: on the left is the list area, and on the right is the summary information. Both areas appear blank, and it is only when you display the data properties of each area that you will see the summary information. In Figure 5-49, you can see data properties for items in the list area, including a calculation header, field, and type. The options for the Calculation Type property are SUM and AVG. In this example, I set the Calculation Header property to display the text *Stock* and selected UnitsInStock for the Calculation Field.

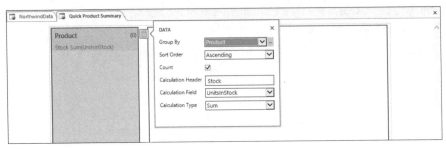

FIGURE 5-49 Setting the list area properties for a summary view.

Tip Once you have created a summary view and selected the Record Source for the view, you cannot change the Record Source to use a different query or table of data.

Figure 5-50 shows the Data-charm properties for the detailes area of the summary view. You use the details area to include up to four display fields, each with an appropriate caption. I selected the fields *ProductName* (caption *Product*), *SupplierId* (caption *Supplier*), *CategoryID* (caption *Category*), and *QuantityPerUnit* (caption *Quantity Per Unit*). Sorting is also supported. I selected an ascending sort for the *ProductName* field.

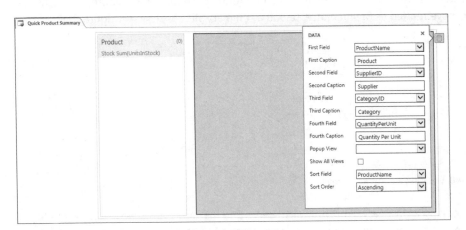

FIGURE 5-50 Setting the summary area properties for a summary view.

Figure 5-51 shows the resulting summary view in a browser window after all the properties are set. This view is often called a *jump list*, because the list groups all products with the same first letter in the product name and users can type that letter to more quickly access the product listing.

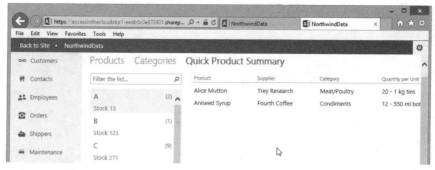

FIGURE 5-51 The summary view displayed in a browser window.

Return to Figure 5-50. Notice that the summary area also supports a Popup View property. When this property is defined, it provides the ability to drill down in the summary area, popping up a detailed view for each product. The popup selection contains only the name of the view we created, as shown in Figure 5-52. If you select this and try to drill down on the data, you will get an error (so don't make this selection).

FIGURE 5-52 The Popup View box, showing the same named view as the only popup option.

> **Tip** In Figure 5-52, the drop-down list for popup views does not allow you to choose from all the views in your web app. However, in Figure 5-50 you see a check box named Show All Views. By clicking to select this option, you can select from a full list of views in your web app.

To create a new view based on the query, you will create a standalone view. This example is continued in the next section, where you create a blank standalone view that can be used for the Popup view shown in Figure 5-52.

Standalone view

Views that have been automatically created for you are associated with a table caption in the table selector. On the Advanced menu, shown in Figure 5-53, you will see options to create either a Blank View, List View, or Datasheet View; these are standalone views.

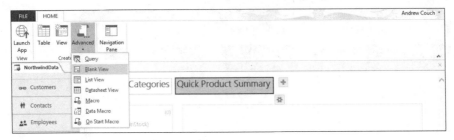

FIGURE 5-53 Creating a standalone view with the Advanced menu.

When you create a standalone view, it will not have a record source initially, and you can choose from any of the available existing queries or tables defined in the web app. The view will be displayed only in the navigation pane and is not associated with a table caption.

> **Tip** Earlier in this chapter, I described how to create standalone views by duplicating an existing view; the only view type that cannot be created as a standalone view is the summary view. (This is not shown on the Advanced drop-down list of objects.) However, a standalone view can be created by choosing the duplicate option from a summary view associated with a table caption and choosing the Location for the duplicate as [Standalone/Popup].

Assume you chose to create a blank view. After you select a record source, the action bar will be displayed, and the field list will reflect your chosen record source, as shown in Figure 5-54.

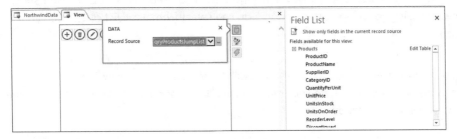

FIGURE 5-54 Selecting the record source for a blank view.

You can drag and drop items from the field list, but a quicker method is to double-click the field names in the Field List to add each field to the blank view. The view in Figure 5-55 has been saved with the name Product Jump List Details.

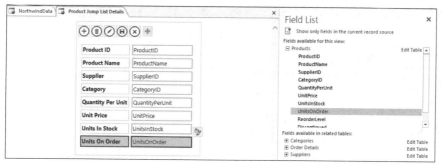

FIGURE 5-55 Adding fields to a blank view.

> **Tip** Within the Field List area, you can use the Shift key to select multiple fields, but the fields can be added only one at a time to the view. The Shift key selection is not supported as a method of adding multiple fields to the view within web apps, but this technique does work in desktop databases.

Standalone views can be displayed only as either a popup view or on an existing view as a subview, unless you duplicate the view to an existing table caption. Returning now to the design of our summary view described in the last section, you can use this view as the popup for the summary view, as shown in Figure 5-56.

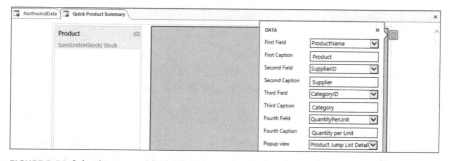

FIGURE 5-56 Selecting a new blank standalone view as the popup for a summary view.

In Figure 5-57, the summary view is shown in a web browser displaying the popup information for a selected product.

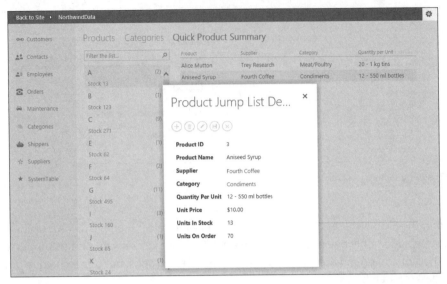

FIGURE 5-57 A summary view using a blank standalone view as a popup.

> **Tip** Notice in the popup view shown in Figure 5-57 that the action bar buttons are not enabled. This means that the popup associated with the summary view is read-only.

Related items control

The related items control (RELIC) is the key control that the framework uses, based on lookups, to display related information. The RELIC is a multitabbed control, which means it is a good choice for displaying a brief list of related records you can drill down into for further details.

The RELIC is restricted to displaying only four fields in a list of the related records.

In Figure 5-58, you can see in our sample database that the relationship between orders and order details has been automatically constructed to reflect the relationship between the parent and child records.

FIGURE 5-58 The RELIC relating data between two tables.

In the design view, you can look at the data properties on the RELIC, as shown in Figure 5-59.

FIGURE 5-59 Data, Formatting, and Calculation charms for the RELIC.

The Data charm for the control is shown in Figure 5-60. The RELIC has a data source for the related table, and it has options to select four related fields and captions to be displayed. The final options provide for sorting and an associated popup view. Two recent additions to the properties are the Show All Views selection which allows more flexibility in choosing a view for the popup selection and Hide Add Link preventing users adding new records from the related items control tab.

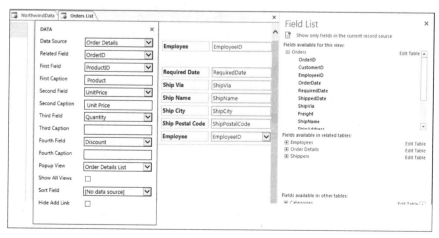

FIGURE 5-60 The RELIC data properties.

Tip If you retitle the caption in the view selector for a view, such as the Order Details List in our example, there are a few things you need to be aware of. Because the retitle operation is in the view selector, if you display the view as a popup, the name of the view is displayed as a caption, not the retitled caption on the view selector.

You can change the view caption by editing the formatting property of a view. Or, for more flexibility in changing the caption for a List Details view, use the macro action SetProperty in the On Load event for the view, leave the Control Name argument blank, select the Caption property, and enter the following value:

```
="your caption text"
```

Because of the natural way in which the mechanism for drilling down through data operates, you should either edit the caption or add this code to every list details view in your web app. If you do this, all the popups will display a meaningful caption. The only downside to the macro action approach is a noticeable delay when the popup opens before the caption is changed.

Subview control

Although the RELIC provides a quick method of displaying related records, you might want either more sophisticated filtering or additional fields included in the related information area. This can be achieved using the subview control, which allows you to add a control that displays information in a related view.

In Figure 5-61, you can see a subview control added to a List Details view. After selecting a view name for the Source Object property, specify the Link Master Field and Link Child Field values to link the records in the parent view with those displayed in the subview. In our example, I made a copy of the Customers Details view, named Custom Details Subview, and then deleted the RELIC and added a subview control.

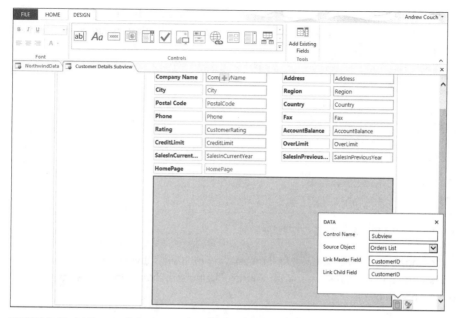

FIGURE 5-61 Adding a subview control to display a view within a view.

In Figure 5-62, you can see the subview, which is a List Details view. The subview displays both the detailed records and the list control for searching and filtering.

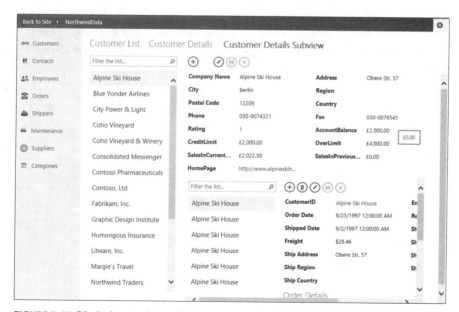

FIGURE 5-62 Displaying a subview that is a List Details view.

In Figure 5-63, the subview was changed to display a tabulation of data using the Orders datasheet. Alternatively, you could choose to use a summary view. (This view has been saved with the name Customer Details Subview List.)

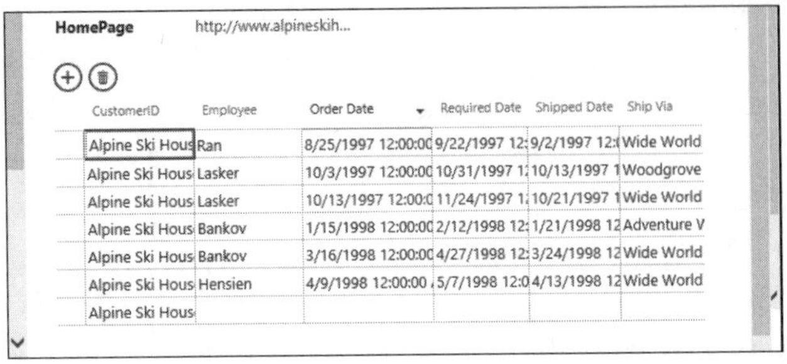

FIGURE 5-63 Displaying a subview that is a datasheet view.

Although doing so is allowed, you will find that having multiple subviews often makes it difficult to sensibly arrange them in the screen area without introducing scrollbars. (Remember, the subview does not support multiple tabs.)

A great technique for getting around this problem is to make use of the view selector. In the previous steps, I wanted to show the subview as a list and also as a datasheet. Adding both subviews to a single view could make the layout overcomplicated. To work around this problem of complexity in a single view, you can create two views.

Start with a view using the subview to display the data as a datasheet, and then duplicate the newly created view. In the duplicated view, change the subview from displaying a datasheet to displaying the List Details view of the data. In Figure 5-64, you can see the two views. On each view, I added a button and wrote macro code to navigate to the alternative view.

FIGURE 5-64 Creating two views you can navigate between using a button.

Next you need to write a single macro action attached to the button that will navigate to the alternative view and display the matched record with a different subview, as shown in Figure 5-65.

FIGURE 5-65 Macro action ChangeView for navigating to the alternative view.

> **Caution** The Macro Editor does not always provide as much assistance as you might expect. In this example, make sure you do not put square brackets around the view name, and make sure in the *where* clause that you prefix the key field (CustomerID, in our example) in the target view with the table name. (Square brackets will be automatically added.) If you based your view on a query, precede the field name with the name of the query supporting the view.

In Figure 5-66, you can see the two views on the view selector. When you navigate from one view to the other using the control button titled Subview (Details), the automatic filtering in the *where* clause is applied. You cannot see the value displayed in the filter box, but the filter has been applied. When displaying the filtered result, you can also enter alternative filter searching criteria. The ability to use this technique means you achieved an effect similar to having a multitab control action but using the view selector to navigate between two views. This avoids having to handle tricky layout issues involving multiple subviews on a single view.

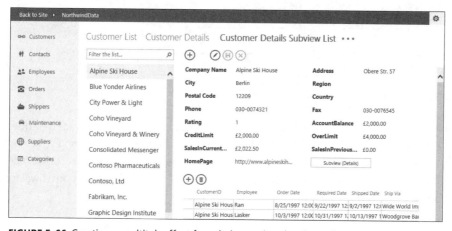

FIGURE 5-66 Creating a multitab effect for subviews using the view selector.

Tip In this chapter, you have seen the two most important user-interface macro actions for navigation. They are OpenPopup, which opens a new popup window, and ChangeView, which navigates to a new position on the existing table selector without opening a popup view.

View controls

In this section, I want to take a look at the controls you can add to your views. I already described restrictions on the controls that can be added to a datasheet or summary view. Figure 5-67 shows the full list of controls available in a view that are subject to those previously described restrictions.

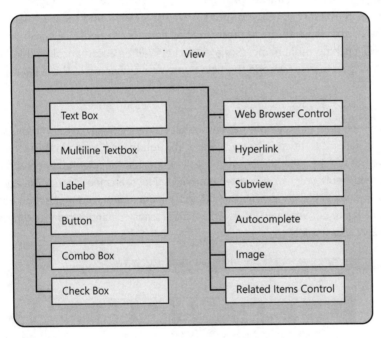

FIGURE 5-67 Roadmap of available controls for adding to views.

Image, label, text box, check box, and hyperlink are standard controls that I will not describe in more detail. The multiline text box control is a text box in which, rather than pressing Ctrl+Enter keys to generate a new line, you press the Enter key. I already described the related items control and subview controls and showed examples of the button control. In the upcoming sections, I will focus on the combo box, web browser, and autocomplete controls.

> **Tip** There are restrictions on setting the control source when adding an unbound control to a view when you bind the control to a source of data. For example, you cannot bind a text box to a lookup data type; these require the use of the combo box or autocomplete controls. As another example, a check box can be bound only to a Yes/No data type field.

Combo box control

The combo box is one of the most-used controls in a desktop access database. As you type, it identifies a match based on the letters you type. The problem is that the control needs to have all the possible data values available in a list, and lists could contain thousands of values. Such a large amount of data would slow down a view while the data was loaded to create the web page for display.

The web app combo box drops down a list of values, but it does not offer the freedom to type in text and match the results. This control is also restricted to displaying a maximum of 500 values.

> **Tip** In the next section, I will describe the new autocomplete control, which delivers similar functionality but with optimized performance. You might have noticed that no combo boxes are automatically added to your views when you create your tables. Instead, the autocomplete control is used to display lookup data.

Figure 5-68 shows the Products Datasheet tab displaying the Data properties for a combo box. The combo box Control source is CategoryID. On the right, the CategoryID field is highlighted under the Products heading in the Field List pane. The combo box has a Row Source set to lookup values from the Categories table displaying the CategoryName from the Categories table and the bound field links the CategoryID between the two tables.

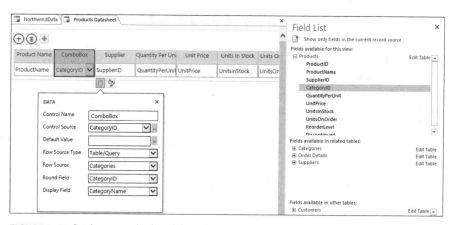

FIGURE 5-68 Setting a combo box for use in a datasheet.

As shown in Figure 5-69, as you start to type and press the first letter, the combo box will locate the first matching record.

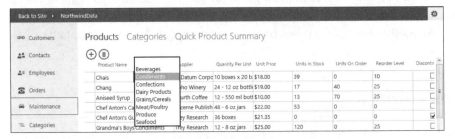

FIGURE 5-69 Interacting with a combo box control in a datasheet view.

> **Tip** A presentation you might want to achieve is to have a pair of controls, such as a text box and a combo box, in which one control restricts the choices based on the first control that is chosen. This is often called *synchronization of controls*. Although these techniques are not fully supported with all controls, it is possible to synchronize combo boxes.

When you display a combo box while editing data, it will provide a drop-down list of choices. When data is not being edited, it will display the current value. Also, if you define a popup view, it will be displayed as a hyperlink that, when clicked, displays a detailed view of the data in a popup window. (This additional property is not shown in Figure 5-67 because it is not available on a datasheet view. However, it is available on a blank or List Details view.)

In summary, the combo box control is an excellent choice when you need to choose from a small list of values that are provided by a table or entered directly into the control as a Value list. However, when you have larger lists of choices, you will find that the autocomplete control is a better and more flexible choice.

Combo box synchronization

In the book's Introduction I mentioned how new capabilities could be added on a more regular basis. The feature described here was added in July 2013. If you have an on-premises implementation of Microsoft SharePoint 2013, you might have to check with your administrator regarding the availability of updates for this feature.

Figure 5-70 shows a blank view called Combo Box Synch, which has the *Categories* table caption. The view contains two combo boxes. The first one provides for a selection of category, and the Control name is *cboCategory*. The second one allows a corresponding product to be selected, and the Control name is *cboProduct*. The two new properties, Parent Control and Related Field, allow the combo boxes to be synchronized with the data choices in the second box as governed by the choice made in the first combo box.

FIGURE 5-70 Synchronizing two combo boxes using the Parent Control and Related Field properties.

Figure 5-71 shows the combo box selections being made in the browser window.

FIGURE 5-71 Combo box synchronization in the browser window.

 Tip When you use the synchronization (cascading controls) feature, the Parent Control property can be shown in either a combo box or autocomplete control, but the child control can only be a combo box.

Autocomplete control

The autocomplete control is shown in the design view in Figure 5-72. The control properties are similar to those associated with a combo box, but an additional Secondary Display Field property is available. When a value is specified for this property, it is displayed below the Primary Display Field in a list of matched values.

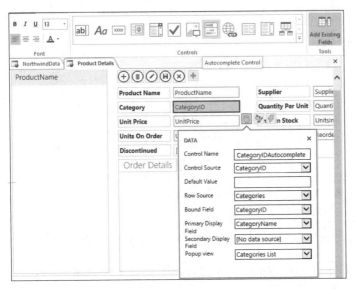

FIGURE 5-72 Defining the data properties for an autocomplete control.

When you are editing data, as shown in Figure 5-73, as you type the autocomplete control will provide up to eight matches in a list that match the pattern of letters you have entered. The drop-down list also provides an Add New Item option if you defined an associated popup view for the control.

FIGURE 5-73 Editing data using the autocomplete control.

Tip When using a combo box or autocomplete control that is not tied to a field in a table, the control is unbound. You are not restricted with regard to the choice of table or query that provides the data choices. However, if the control is bound to a field in the table, you are restricted to using only the lookup table as a data source; you cannot look up values from a query. You could work around this problem by using an unbound combo box, and then using the SetProperty macro action to save the value to the field in the table.

Web browser control

The web browser control is intended to display the results of a URL as content within the control. If you have an on-premises implementation of the SharePoint 2013 web app, you can display unsecured content in the URL for the control. However, for Office 365, you are prevented from displaying unsecured content, which means you can show content only when using the *https* protocol.

Tip Finding examples that can be used in the web browser control can be difficult. For example, if you try to link to a spreadsheet or Microsoft Word document you have stored in Office 365 (referenced using an *https* link), you will get an error when attempting to display the data.

As an example of a valid link for Office 365, you could use the following URL to display the map information shown in Figure 5-74:

```
https://maps.google.com/maps?q=Washington, DC, USA
```

FIGURE 5-74 Displaying map information using the web browser control.

The preceding example demonstrates that you can display map information in your views.

Adding color to controls

At first sight on examining the formatting properties for a control such as a text box, you will notice that there is no color palette for setting the background text color. (The ribbon does support commands to alter text alignment, Font Color, Font Size, Bold, Italic and Underline.) However, using a simple SetProperty macro action in the On Load or On Current event for the view will enable you to add color to a control.

In Figure 5-75, I added a label at the top of our view to help distinguish the purpose of different areas in the view.

FIGURE 5-75 A label with formatting properties, which do not include color information.

In Figure 5-76, a SetProperty macro action is added to the On Load event for the view. The color is entered as an HTML color code and represents the color yellow.

FIGURE 5-76 A SetProperty macro action in the On Load event, used to color a control.

Figure 5-77 shows the resulting title with background color in a browser window.

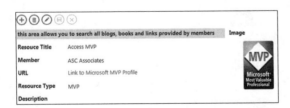

FIGURE 5-77 The completed label displayed with a yellow background color.

Tip If you need to have a title that wraps over several lines, use a text box or multiline text box control, because the label control cannot be used for this style of presentation.

Summary

In this chapter, you started by looking at customizing the table and view selectors. I described the role of popup windows, and you then looked at how to create the different types of views: datasheet, list (or list details), and summary. I demonstrated how views can be duplicated and how to create standalone views that are displayed in popup windows.

After giving you a tour of the different types of views, I described some key controls in detail. This included the related items control (RELIC), which is used to display related data. I contrasted that with the alternative choice of the subview control, which also displays related data. You also had a look at the web browser control, autocomplete control, and combo box control; you saw an example of a recent enhancement to web apps when I described how to use control synchronization when working with two combo box controls or an autocomplete control and combo box.

Throughout the chapter, I included several examples of macro actions that can be used to alter the presentation of views. In Chapter 6, you will see techniques that can be used to construct more sophisticated data sources to display data using a view.

Creating data sources by using queries

In this chapter:

In this chapter, we will look at how to create queries in a web app. These queries can then be used either with views to display information or with data macros to process information. If you are familiar with this subject, you will notice that in the contents there are no topics on creating queries to modify data. Queries that modify data are not supported in a web app; instead, you use data macros to perform equivalent operations.

In Chapter 5, "Displaying data in views," I demonstrated creating a simple query for creating a jump list to summarize product data in our application. In this chapter, I provide a more detailed explanation of how queries are created and how they can then be used in your application. As you did in Chapter 5, you'll use some simple user-interface macros to link your queries to views. In Chapter 7, "Programming a web app by using macros," I will provide a more detailed discussion of macro design.

If you want to follow along with the design steps in this chapter, continue to use the NorthwindData web app used in Chapter 5.

Creating basic queries

Queries are created using the Query option on the Advanced menu, as shown in Figure 6-1.

FIGURE 6-1 Creating a query.

When the query designer opens, the Show Table popup is displayed. It has three tabs you can click on to display tables, queries, or both. If you double-click a table or query in the Show Table popup (or click the Add button when the table or query is highlighted), it will be added to the query, as shown in Figure 6-2. If you close the Show Table popup, you can return later to add other tables or queries by clicking the Show Table icon on the ribbon. If tables are related, lines will be added between the linking fields as the tables are added to the query.

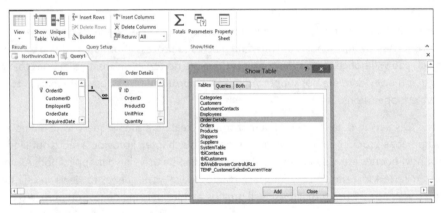

FIGURE 6-2 Adding tables or other queries to a query.

> **Tip** Joining-relationship lines can be removed by clicking on the line and pressing delete. New lines can be added by clicking to select a field in one table and dragging the mouse over the related table. If tables are not joined, this produces a display multiplying all rows in one table by all the rows in another table. This is called a *Cartesian product*. Normally, you will not want to see this, but in certain situations it can be useful. In those situations, you are likely to either have only one record in one of the tables or need to add additional filtering criteria to the query grid to reduce the number of returned records. (You will see an example of this in Chapter 7.)

After you select the tables and queries to be used in creating a new query, the next step is to select the fields to work with. Fields can be added using several different techniques:

- Double-click or drag and drop the * at the top of the list of fields to add all fields to the query grid. This would be shown, for example, as Orders.*

- Double-click or drag and drop a single field onto the query grid.

- Press the Shift key to select multiple fields, and then drag and drop the multiple selections onto the query grid.

- From the query grid, in a blank column, use the Field drop-down list to select a field.

Select all the fields from the Orders table by dragging and dropping the * at the top of the field list for the Orders table onto the query grid, as shown in Figure 6-3. Then select multiple fields—such as ProductID, UnitPrice, Quantity, and Discount—holding down the shift key to select the fields from the Order Details table, which are then dragged onto the query grid.

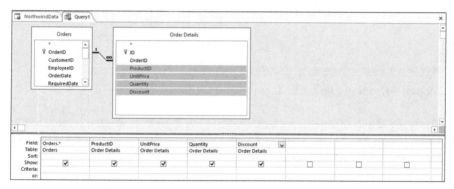

FIGURE 6-3 Adding fields to the query grid.

 Tip The advantages of using the * to select all fields are that it's easy and does not clutter up the query grid. The disadvantages are that you need to again select again a field in the set if you want to sort or filter by the field. Also, if you ask for more fields than needed, displaying all the data will take more time than if you select only the fields you need.

Fields on the query grid can be selected by clicking just above the field name, as shown in Figure 6-4. After a field is selected, the column will appear darkened to indicate it is selected. After the fields are selected, they can be re-ordered using drag and drop, or deleted by pressing the Delete key; the Shift key can be used to select multiple fields.

FIGURE 6-4 Hovering the cursor to select a field.

Tip Avoid selecting to show the same field name more than once. If you use the * and then need to add a field for filtering or sorting, clear the Show box below the added field. This means the field can be used for filtering or sorting but is not displayed. Having a field selected more than once is allowed, but that can lead to confusion when you are linking views to the query or working with data macros.

A field name can be changed by prefixing the field using an alternative name ending with a colon, as shown in Figure 6-5. I displayed the Zoom box by pressing Shift+F2 and adjusted the display font to display the expression.

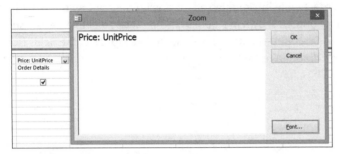

FIGURE 6-5 Changing the name of a field.

You can display the results of your query by clicking on the View icon, which is located at the top left on the Design ribbon. You will be prompted to save the query before viewing the results. Save the query with the name *qryOrdersWithCriteria*.

Adding criteria to queries

Figure 6-6 shows an example of criteria being added below some of the fields. I started with the previously created query, qryOrdersWithCriteria, and used the Show Table icon on the design ribbon to add the Products table to the query. Note that I cleared the Show box below [Order Date] because I already included this field using Orders.*. Also, note that the date range is displayed using the standard # symbols around the date, but the *like* criteria uses the % symbol as a wildcard and not the * (which is not supported). You can surround the text string by either single or double quotation marks. I chose double quotes in this example.

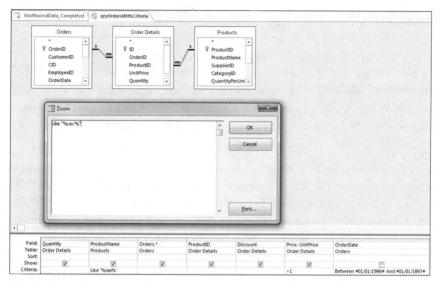

FIGURE 6-6 Sample query with criteria against numeric, date, and text fields.

If you looked at this saved query (which is saved as a view) in Azure SQL Database, you would notice that the criteria looks like this:

```
WHERE
    [Order Details].[UnitPrice] > 1.0 AND [Orders].[OrderDate]
    BETWEEN DATEFROMPARTS(1996, 1, 1) AND DATEFROMPARTS(1997, 1, 1)
    AND [Products].[ProductName] LIKE N'%rav%'
```

From this code, you can see how the web app displays the information in a format that is more familiar to people working with Access for the date criteria, but it actually saves the query in a true Azure SQL Database format.

> **Tip** For a wildcard search against text criteria, to save typing you can enter ***rav***. This will then be displayed as *Like "*rav*"*. You can then change the * to %. Although the resulting view will use single quotes, the information you enter is preserved for display in either double or single quotes, depending on what you typed in. Getting used to using single quotes will help when switching between the web app and the Azure SQL Database. When searching on a Yes/No field, you cannot use True/False; you can use Yes/No or 1/0 or <>0/0. (In the Azure SQL Database, 0 is false and 1 is true.)

The query grid has multiple lines, each starting with the keyword OR. This allows you to construct several alternative sets of criteria for filtering the data. When you have multiple criteria against multiple columns on a single line of criteria, they act together to filter the data, such as criteria1 AND criteria2 AND criteria3. Each line of criteria acts as a set of alternatives. If we had criteria1 on the first line and criteria2 on the second line this would be criteria1 OR criteria2.

Adding calculations to queries

If you are familiar with creating calculations using a desktop database, you will find that the calculations in a web app are significantly different. The reason for this is that the queries are stored in Azure SQL Database as views and must conform to the SQL language syntax used in the Azure SQL Database, the built-in Azure SQL Database functions, and additional Access support functions in the Azure SQL Database—not the syntax and functions used in a desktop database.

> **Tip** The query calculation syntax does not allow the use of the & symbol when concatenating strings. In a desktop database, developers often use the & when concatenating strings because it protects against a NULL value causing the resulting string to be NULL. In the web app, you must use the plus sign (+) when concatenating strings and use a built-in function to avoid problems with NULL values, such as COALESCE([FieldName], ''). The COALESCE function takes multiple arguments and returns the first non-null value.

There are 52 built-in functions you can use in web app queries, together with 25 constants. Rather than simply listing all of these (which you can see when using the builder in the query design tool), I will provide a few guidelines about using popular functions to get you started constructing expressions.

The Azure SQL Database has more strict rules than the desktop Access environment when it comes to adding together different data types and performing arithmetic operations—for example, on dates.

For example, if you try to construct the following expression, you will get an error:

```
NameAndID: [Products].[ProductID]+' '+[ProductName]
```

In this case, you need to convert *ProductID* to a string, and you do this by using the CAST function to change one data type to another data type. (Note that the data types used here—for example, ShortText—are not true Azure SQL Database data types; they are the data type names used when creating fields in a web app.)

```
NameAndID: Cast([Products].[ProductID],ShortText)+' '+[ProductName]
```

If you want to remove spaces from the beginning and end of a string, you need to use the following syntax because the *Trim* function is not supported:

```
NoSpaceField: LTRIM(RTRIM([FieldName]))
```

To replace a substring inside a larger string, use the REPLACE function. To extract part of the text in a string, use the SUBSTR function. There are also STUFF and REPLICATE string functions.

Another useful feature in a query is if you divide, for example, an integer by 10, you will find that in the view this is replaced by division by 10.0. This is because in the Azure SQL Database *3/10 = 0* and *3/10.0 = 0.3*. However, you need to be a bit careful with this. Figure 6-7 shows the result of dividing two whole-number columns and an alternative calculation that forces the divisor to be a floating point number. Note that this happens only because we are using whole-number columns for the FirstNumber and SecondNumber fields.

FirstDividedBySecond	FirstNumber	SecondNumber	FirstDividedBySecondFloat
0	3	10	0.3

FIGURE 6-7 Dividing 3/10 is zero when using integer arithmetic.

The two expressions are as follows:

```
FirstDividedBySecond: [FirstNumber]/[SecondNumber]
```

```
FirstDividedBySecondFloat: [FirstNumber]/Cast([SecondNumber],Float)
```

Calculations can also be constructed using the Builder icon (shown in Figure 6-8) on the design ribbon, or by right-clicking in a column header or criteria and selecting Build.

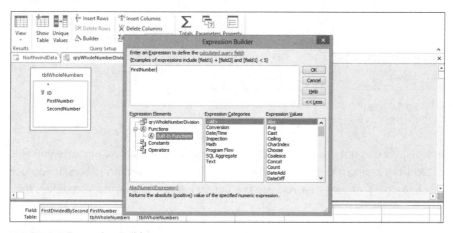

FIGURE 6-8 Expression Builder.

 Tip You might think that the integer division issue is a bug or problem in the web app, but this is not the case. This is simply a contrast between how an Access desktop database performs a calculation and how the Azure SQL Database performs calculations. You will also find that when you add a Number field to a table, the default Number Subtype is Fixed-Point Number (6 decimal places), and because this is not an integer, the division issue does not arise.

Adding parameters to queries

Parameters enable you to create a query that has a placeholder that can be populated at runtime to filter the data. Unlike a desktop database, where a user can directly open a query (or an object using the query) and enter a value for the parameter, in a web app you need to provide the values for any parameters before opening a view that has been constructed to use the parameterized query.

You start by creating a query from the advanced menu. For this example, select all fields from the Customers table, select the City field, and clear the Show check box for this field. Then click on the Parameters icon on the design ribbon, select a name for your parameter (CityFilter), and specify an appropriate data type (Short Text), as shown in Figure 6-9. Click OK to dismiss the Query Parameters dialog when you finish defining the new parameter.

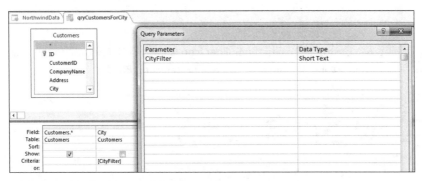

FIGURE 6-9 Creating a query and adding a parameter.

Tip Ensure that you do not enter any spaces in your parameter names, because you will be prevented from saving a query when the parameter names contain spaces. If you use parameters in a query, ensure that you use the Query Parameters window to define the parameters.

As you start to type the parameter name in the criteria below the City field, IntelliSense will assist in selecting the parameter. Once you are done, the parameter name is shown in square brackets, as you can see in Figure 6-10.

Field:	Customers.*	City
Table:	Customers	Customers
Sort:		
Show:	☑	☐
Criteria:		[CityFilter]
or:		

FIGURE 6-10 Adding the parameter as a filter against an existing field.

If you look at this using SQL Server Management Studio (SSMS) in the Azure SQL Database, you would find that your query is saved using a special type of function called a *table-valued function*. This is shown in Figure 6-11. (I deleted some fields in the select statement to make this clearer.)

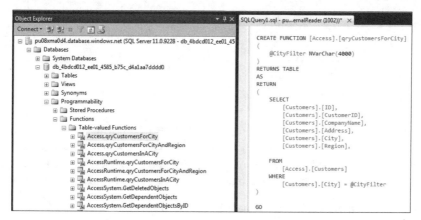

FIGURE 6-11 Displaying the resulting table-valued function in SSMS.

Tip The advantage of Access using a table-valued function in the Azure SQL Database rather than a stored procedure is that the table-valued function can return results that might be updateable, whereas the results from a stored procedure are always read-only.

After creating the parameterized query, you then construct a View that uses the parameterized query as a record source, as shown in Figure 6-12. However, you will not be able to directly open the view from the table selector, because we must use the OpenPopup macro command to supply a value for the parameter. This means you should create this as a standalone view using the Advanced Menu. Choose to create a datasheet view.

FIGURE 6-12 Selecting the parameterized query as a datasource for a datasheet view.

Figure 6-13 shows the Field List on the right being used to select the fields ID, CustomerID, CompanyName, Region, and PostalCode to display on the datasheet. The view has been saved with the name CustomersDatasheetForCity.

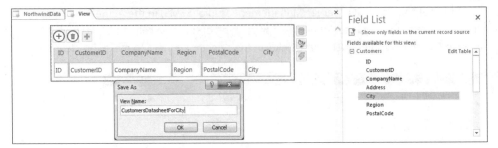

FIGURE 6-13 Adding fields to the datasheet view, and saving the view.

You have now created a parameterized query and associated view. Next, you need to provide a point from which to display the data. Normally, a blank form with selection controls is a good choice of starting point, but here you will add a button to the Customers datasheet. Clicking the button displays your view, which shows customers in the same city for the currently displayed customer.

Figure 6-14 shows a button on the Customers datasheet that will be used to open the new parameterized view.

FIGURE 6-14 Adding a button to open a parameterized view.

By clicking the On Click event for the button, you can then add the OnPopup macro action and select your CustomersDatasheetForCity view. As shown in Figure 6-15, a great feature of a parameterized view when combined with the OpenPopup action is that it automatically identifies the parameters and displays a list of the parameters on the macro design surface, which can then be set to reference a control or field on the view. In our example, I refer to the control called [CityTextBox].

FIGURE 6-15 Adding the OpenPopup macro action and providing the Parameters.

Tip In Figure 6-15, the City field value is referred to by using the control name [CityTextBox], because that is the option offered with the IntelliSense. However, you could have entered the equivalent field name [City].

In Figure 6-16, you can see the related records displayed in the browser window.

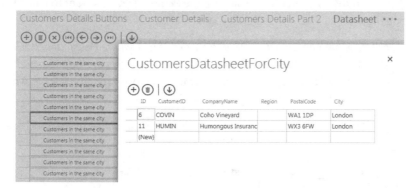

FIGURE 6-16 The view will display another popup window based on a parameterized query.

Tip If you edit data in the popup, when you close the popup, the underlying data will not reflect any changes. It is not possible to automatically refresh the data, but you could add an action button that uses the RequeryRecords macro action to refresh the data.

Looking back at Figure 6-15, you'll notice that the OpenPopup macro action also supports a Where argument for filtering. This can be used either as an alternative to using a parameterized query or to provide additional filtering. Figure 6-17 shows the equivalent macro argument expression used to filter by city without using a parameterized query.

FIGURE 6-17 OpenPopup macro action with an expression entered in the Where argument.

It is up to you whether you want to use parameterized queries or *where* clauses. By choosing the *where* clause approach, you can use the target view in several parts of an application, by using different *where* clauses. The parameterized query is fixed in terms of the parameters. But the parameterized query can seem simpler to work with, because it automatically detects the parameters and provides separate options for each parameter.

> **Tip** In a parameterized query, you can create columns that use the parameter values for calculations and other expressions. You cannot do this using the *where*-clause technique.

In the Customers table, you assume that all customers have a city, but sometimes a customer also has a region. The question is how you can make your parameters conditional so that there is additional filtering by region when the customer has a value for the Region field. You want to construct optional parameter filtering.

The choice of whether to use a parameterized query to solve this or a *where* clause depends on how confident you are at writing *where* clauses, and how much you prefer to have popup boxes and graphical assistance. You should also consider, if you start to add more conditional logic, which method would be simpler for you to remember and understand.

The *where* clause approach with the OpenPopup macro action is shown in Figure 6-18 and uses the *where* clause:

```
[Customers].[City]=[CityTextBox] And Coalesce([Customers].[Region],'')=
Coalesce([RegionTextBox],[Customers].[Region],'')
```

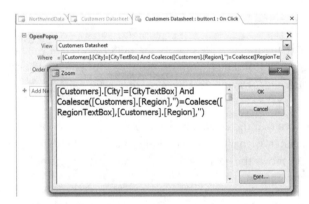

FIGURE 6-18 Conditional logic in a *where* clause for optional filtering.

Remember that the COALESCE function returns the first non-null value. So if a for a customer record you have a value in `[RegionTextBox]`, this is compared against `Coalesce([Customers].[Region],'')`, which will either match the region value or return an empty string that will not match the region value.

If the current record has no value or NULL in `[RegionTextBox]`, the expression `Coalesce([RegionTextBox],[Customers].[Region],'')` returns either the region value `[Customers].[Region]` or an empty string. This is equivalent to comparing `[Customers].[Region]= [Customers].[Region]` or " ".

You might be wondering why you create the comparison `'' ='' `. The reason is that you cannot allow the comparison NULL = NULL, because this expression is never true in a database or web app and would not match any records.

Tip You could, as an alternative to our logic, use IIF conditional logic in these expressions. You will see an example of that in the following description of using a parameterized query.

Before I show how to create a parameterized query approach to this problem, you need to understand that you are not allowed to have a parameter that can have a value of NULL, because Variant type parameters are not supported. This means that in a later step you will force the values provided to your parameterized query to have a safe value, such as an empty string, when the value is NULL.

Figure 6-19 shows a parameter query with two parameters, `[CityFilter]` and `[RegionFilter]`, which are both Short Text data types. The `[CityFilter]` has already been explained earlier in this section. For the region filter, you create a column expression `Coalesce([Region],'')`. (Remember you can't compare NULL values, and you stated that NULL values will be converted to empty strings.) Then you compare this in the where clause against the expression `IIf([RegionFilter]='',Coalesce([Region],''),[RegionFilter])`. The explanation of this logic is the same as previously described for the *where* clause example.

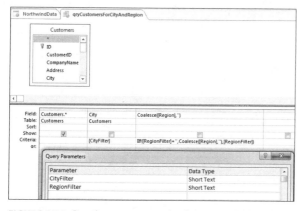

FIGURE 6-19 Creating a parameterized query with optional parameters.

If you look in the Azure SQL Database, you would see the following table-valued function. (I removed the list of fields to focus on the important part of the SQL—the parameter data types and the *where* clause.)

```
CREATE FUNCTION [Access].[qryCustomersForCityAndRegion]
(
    @CityFilter NVarChar(4000),
    @RegionFilter NVarChar(4000)
)
RETURNS TABLE
AS
RETURN
(
```

```
SELECT
    ...
FROM
    [Access].[Customers]
WHERE
    [Customers].[City] = @CityFilter
    AND COALESCE([Region], N'') =
    IIF(@RegionFilter = N'', COALESCE([Region], N''), @RegionFilter)
```

Next construct a new view based on our parameterized query called *CustomersDatasheetForCityRegion*; this method for constructing a standalone datasheet was described earlier in this section. Then add a button on your customers datasheet view to open the parameterized view as shown in Figure 6-20. Note that the RegionFilter parameter uses the expression `IIf([RegionTextBox] Is Null,'',[RegionTextBox])`; remember you indicated earlier that you cannot pass NULL as a parameter, so you convert that value to an empty string.

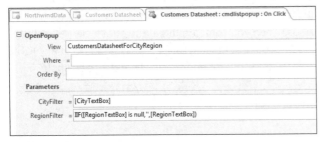

FIGURE 6-20 Protecting a parameter from passing a NULL value.

 Tip Another benefit of using parameterized queries rather than a *where* clause is improved performance. Because the parameterized query is saved as an object in the Azure SQL Database, it can offer slightly better performance.

Totals and queries

In this section, we look at how to use the Totals feature to produce summarized data; these queries are read only.

Figure 6-21 shows the new query with the Totals icon clicked on the design ribbon. This results in a new Total row on the query grid. The default choice below each field is GroupBy in the Total row, where the query groups records with similar values. Other options include the aggregate functions SUM, Avg, Min, Max, Count, the statistical function StDev, Var, Expression for calculations, and Where for filtering data.

Tip When working with a calculation and entering an aggregate such as SUM in the Total row, after saving and re-opening the query, you will see Expression in the Total row and the SUM operation moved into the column title. This is because the web app standardizes the way it saves the SQL. So the look of your layout can change, although the resulting data that is displayed will be unchanged.

In our example we have the expression OrderValue:SUM([UnitPrice]*[Quantity]).

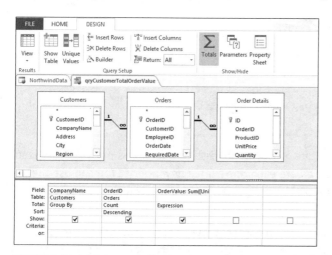

FIGURE 6-21 A totals query allowing data to display summarized calculations.

The datasheet preview for this Totals query is shown in Figure 6-22. In the results of this query, you can see that grouping for each company name displays the count of orders (CountOfOrderID) and sum of order values (OrderValue) as totals.

FIGURE 6-22 Summarized results of a Totals query in the datasheet preview.

Top value queries

Another feature of queries is to limit the number of records displayed, either specifying this as a number of records or as a percentage of the total records that could be displayed.

Figure 6-23 shows a summary query that counts the number of orders for each customer.

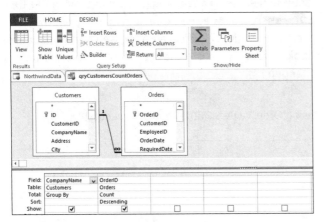

FIGURE 6-23 Customers sorted by the greatest number of orders.

Tip In a web app, you cannot create a copy of an existing query. This means if you need several similar queries, you must create each one from a new query. (You can use the clipboard to copy and paste complex query expressions from one query to the next.)

Figure 6-24 shows the query results in the datasheet preview. Note that in the 13 records displayed, the last three records in the screen shot show the same count of 7. This is an important point to note for the following discussion of how the Top feature works in a web app.

FIGURE 6-24 Resulting datasheet preview showing customers sorted by the greatest number of orders.

Returning to the design view, you can use the Returns icon on the design ribbon to select to display only the top 10 records, as shown in Figure 6-25. (In our example, we typed in the value 10, which is not shown in the drop-down list of choices.)

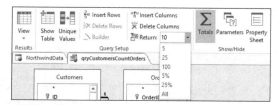

FIGURE 6-25 In the design view, a screen that shows the use of the Returns drop-down list to return the top 10 records.

 Tip If you look at the query properties, you will see that although the ribbon displays the word *Returns*, the property is called *Top Values*.

Figure 6-26 shows the resulting top records.

FIGURE 6-26 The Top Values property returns the top matched records.

If you are familiar with using TOP in an Access desktop database, you might know that it would have returned more than 10 rows in the previous example. This is because if the last row ties with other rows, all matched rows that tie in value are displayed. This is called TOP WITH TIES. Because the web app relies on the Azure SQL Database, which by default does not show tied values, you see only the first of the records that tie for last place.

 Tip The Azure SQL Database does offer a special TOP WITH TIES feature, but this is not available for you to use in a web app.

Unique values in queries

When you create a query, one row will be displayed for each underlying record, regardless of which fields you choose and whether the output shows several records with the same value. The Unique values property enables you to eliminate any duplicate values and makes the output of each record unique across the combination of selected fields. These queries are useful when summarizing data, making lists of unique choices, and when re-organizing data to identify new lists of unique combinations with which to construct new tables. These queries are read only.

> **Tip** Although you cannot create a "make table" query or "append" query in a web app, you can create an empty table and then use SSMS to execute an "append" query to populate the data.

As an example of this, Figure 6-27 shows a query to select the City field from the Customers table and display a list of unique values when clicking on the Unique Values icon on the design ribbon. We also add a criteria to exclude any null values and sort the results.

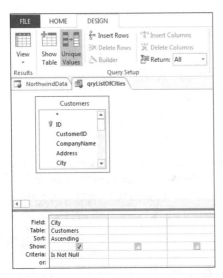

FIGURE 6-27 Specifying the Unique Values setting for a query.

> **Tip** When you specify unique values in the Azure SQL Database, the SELECT DISTINCT syntax will be added to the query. An equivalent technique to using the unique values property is to use a Totals query and the Group By operation.

You can then edit your customers view and replace the text box for the City field with an Autocomplete control, which uses the query qryListOfCities as the row source for the control, as shown in Figure 6-28.

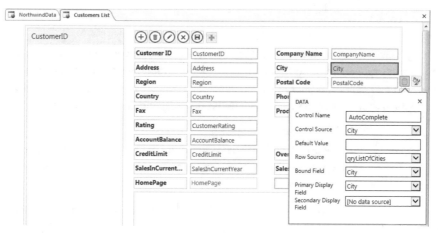

FIGURE 6-28 Using a Unique Values query in an autocomplete control.

In Figure 6-29, you can see the result of using the autocomplete control to display a list of values for the City selection based on the unique values used in the existing customer records.

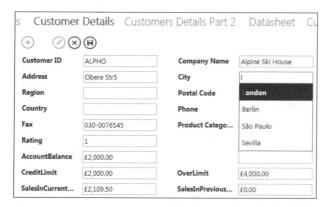

FIGURE 6-29 Completed view with autocomplete control.

In Figure 6-29, the autocomplete control sorts the results based on matching characters. The word *London* is displayed before *Berlin*, because the letter *l* is first matched as the first letter in the word *London*. This means that the autocomplete control will override any sorting you specified earlier when constructing the underlying query qryListOfCountries (where you had an ascending sort on the City name).

> **Tip** This method, although it makes queries very quick to construct and avoids the need to create a new table, does not allow you to enter a new value for City, which is not already in the list of values. In this case, you need an alternative view, such as a datasheet view, to enter a new value.

Summary

In this chapter, you saw how to create queries that can then be used to construct views that display your data. You can use queries to bring together data from several tables or other queries and construct calculated expressions. A query can contain criteria to filter the data, provide totals to summarize the data, use unique values to remove duplicate data, and limit the results using the Top property.

The most complex feature of working with queries is in using parameters to supply values to a query at runtime. This technique requires both the construction of a parameterized query and the use of a macro to supply the runtime parameters.

In Chapter 7, we will look at further examples of working with macros and queries to enhance your applications.

Programming a web app by using macros

In this chapter, we will take an in-depth look at macro programming. At several earlier points in this book, you added a sprinkling of macro code behind view and control events to fit the user interface together. In this chapter, you will dive into a much more detailed description of the subject.

Two other topics introduced earlier in the book were how objects are stored in Microsoft Azure SQL Database and how to use Microsoft SQL Server Management Studio (SSMS) to look behind the scenes at the detailed construction of the objects. In Chapter 9, "Looking under the hood at Microsoft Azure SQL Database," I provide information on using SSMS. If you want to follow along and look at what is produced in the data macro sections of this chapter, you might want to read through Chapter 9 to ensure you can connect to the back end in Azure SQL Database. Although this is not essential, when I write data macros, I nearly always have a copy of SSMS connected to the back end to help me design and debug my macro code.

So far in this book, you have been building a sample web app called NorthwindData, but in this chapter you are going to stop building that web app and create a new web app.

In this new sample database, I introduce a design flaw, and I will demonstrate how to resolve the problem it causes. This exercise will also provide an opportunity to demonstrate some of the exciting ways you can both work within the Microsoft Access environment and extend your skills into Microsoft SQL Server.

To get started, create a new custom web app called **NorthwindRestructuredMacros**, and then import all the tables from the desktop database NorthwindRestructuredMacros.accdb. If you can't remember how to do that, look back at Chapter 2, "Finding your way around Access 2013," where you created the custom web app.

The difference in this new sample database is that in the Customers table, rather than providing a numeric AutoNumber primary key called *CustomerID* (as in the NorthwindData web app), you have a primary key that is a Short Text data type. Because that is not a supported data type for a primary key, the web app will add a new primary key ID when importing the data. So existing foreign-key references from the Orders table to the Customers table will be invalid with respect to any new data added to the two tables. Also, there will be no lookup relationship between the two tables.

Macro-programming capabilities

Access desktop databases offer both macro programming and Microsoft Visual Basic for Applications (VBA) programming to write code supporting your database application. In a web app, you have only macro programming. The reason for this is that whatever you write in Access has to then be translated into another form of programming language, because neither the browser window nor the Azure SQL Database directly support the VBA Access programming language. Microsoft decided that the more appropriate environment for translation and support when working with web apps is the macro environment, not VBA.

Before you start programming macros, you'll find it useful to have a good overview of what I mean by *macro programming* and to see how the different types of macro programming fit together in supporting your web app development.

In the Introduction, I mentioned that macros were translated into something else, but I did not say what that was. Program code can be executed in one of two places. It either executes on the client-side in your browser or inside Azure SQL Database. The Azure SQL Database has a full programming language called *Transaction Structured Query Language (TSQL)*. SQL is the international standard for working with relational databases, and all the large database vendors provide extensions to the standard. Microsoft's standard is called TSQL. Because in a web app you have two places where code can execute (in the browser or in the Azure SQL Database), you have two different types of macros:

- **User-interface macros**   These execute in your browser and manage the user interface.

- **Data macros**   These execute in Azure SQL Database and manipulate data.

Because each type of macro executes in a different technology, the action set and programming techniques will be different for each.

It is also common in software programming to both write code behind an object and write common code that can be referenced by other parts of your application in common objects that are not tied to other objects, which are called *standalone macros*. Both user-interface (UI) macros and data macros can be written as standalone macros:

- **Standalone user-interface macros**   These are called *macros* in the design tool on the Advanced menu.

- **Standalone data macros**   These are also known as *named data macros*. They are referred to as *data macros* in the design tool on the Advanced menu.

> **Tip** Both types of standalone macro code can be displayed only in the Navigation Pane in the Macro grouping. Note that the same graphical icon is shown for both types of macro, so I suggest that you prefix all data macros with *dm_* or an equivalent notation. By doing that, you can easily spot the different types of macros in your application.

The second place to write macro code is attached to an object. UI macros are written inside views, on either the view or control events. Sometimes macro code written inside a view is called *embedded macro code*, because it is embedded inside another object. Embedded data macros are held inside the design of a table. They are written on one of three table events: On Insert, On Update, or On Delete. Here's a short description of the two types of embedded macros:

- **Embedded UI macro**   Written inside a view on view and control events

- **Embedded data macro**   Written inside a table on table events

With both types of UI macros, standalone and embedded, your macro programming is translated to use a combination of the *JavaScript Object Notation (JSON)* and *Asynchronous JavaScript and XML (AJAX)*. This translation mechanism is like a black box, and you cannot easily dig into what is going on. (You would not want to do this unless you were very well acquainted with those technologies.)

Standalone data macros are translated into TSQL, which is held inside parameterized stored procedures in SQL Server. Embedded macros are translated into SQL Server *After Triggers* held against the appropriate table.

Figure 7-1 is a roadmap I prepared to guide you through where the macro code can be written. It illustrates quite a flexible path for making different types of macros call other macros. For example, the small loops on the standalone macros indicate that a standalone macro can call another standalone macro. The line from an embedded data macro to a standalone named data macro indicates that the embedded macro can call the named data macro.

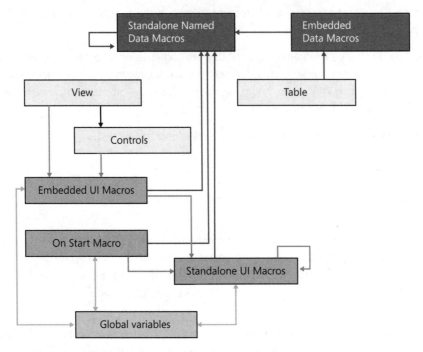

FIGURE 7-1 Roadmap for where macro code can be placed and how it can interact with other macros.

Tip Although a named data macro cannot call an embedded data macro, if a named data macro alters data in a table that has an associated embedded data macro, that code will be executed. It thereby indirectly executes the embedded data macro code.

Figure 7-1 also shows the On Start macro, which executes when the application starts. This macro will be described later in the chapter in the "On Start macro" section.

Another important idea to grasp is how variables operate. In a UI macro, all variables are global variables. When you define a variable, it exists until the browser session is closed or the user refreshes the browser window. In a data macro, you can define *local variables*. These variables are declared and exist only inside the stored procedures and triggers that get generated for the duration of their execution.

Global variables are important because they exist for the duration of the user's session when interacting with your application. They become important as you seek to preserve a record of choices and settings appropriate for a user as the user works with different parts of your application.

One further significant feature is the ability of named data macros to accept input parameters and provide return values. This functionality is the only link you have between code executing in the browser and code executing in the Azure SQL Database.

Tip You cannot directly reference a global UI variable inside a data macro, because the UI defines the global variable in the browser context, which the Azure SQL Database cannot see. But you can pass a global variable to a named data macro (but not an embedded data macro, which is an event on a table). Global variables are created as JS (JavaScript) variables on the server behind the scenes.

Macro editor and standalone user-interface macros

In this section, you will start by creating a simple standalone macro. However, because a macro needs a point from which it can be activated, you also need to create some embedded macro code to execute the operations.

The main purpose of this section is to describe both how to create a standalone macro and how to familiarize yourself with the macro editor.

To create a standalone macro, from the Advanced menu select the Macro option as shown in Figure 7-2. In this example, you will create a standalone user-interface macro.

FIGURE 7-2 Creating a new user-interface macro.

The macro editor needs some explanation before you can productively work with the interface. The blank macro interface is shown in Figure 7-3.

FIGURE 7-3 The macro editor.

On the left is a drop-down list of macro actions. You can either select from the list or type in text to locate a match. On the right is the Action Catalog, which provides a structured grouping of actions. (This area can be closed and re-opened using the Action Catalog button on the design ribbon.)

> **Tip** You can run into a problem when you have a long section of macro logic with many actions. In such a scenario, adding a new action with the drop-down list and moving the action can be difficult. However, you can more easily drag and drop an action from the Action Catalog to a specific position in the list of macro actions.

To get started, you will create a simple macro involving two actions. The first action is a comment, and the second action is a message box. These are shown in Figure 7-4, save this macro with the name **MacroSimpleMessage**.

FIGURE 7-4 Simple macro actions.

To test the macro, you need to either activate the macro from the On Start macro or create a view with a button to activate the macro. Because you will have to do this for several macros, create a blank view called **ViewToAddMacros** based on the Customers table caption as shown in Figure 7-5.

FIGURE 7-5 Creating a blank view for testing macros.

After the view is created, edit the view and set the Record Source value for the view to No Data Source, as shown in Figure 7-6. (You could leave the view bound to the Customers table. Because this view will not directly manipulate data in a record source, it is a good practice to remove the reference to the record source when it will not be used.)

FIGURE 7-6 Setting the view data source to No Data Source.

Next, add a button control to the view, change the button caption to Simple Macro Action, and click the On Click event for the button to add embedded macro code, as shown in Figure 7-7.

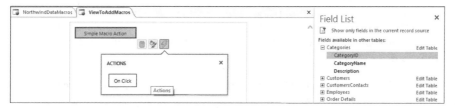

FIGURE 7-7 Adding a button to execute a standalone macro.

Figure 7-8 shows the RunMacro action. This macro action will execute our standalone macro.

FIGURE 7-8 Creating an embedded macro that calls a standalone macro.

To test the form, you need to save and close the macro and then also save the view. Then display the view in your browser and click the button, as shown in Figure 7-9.

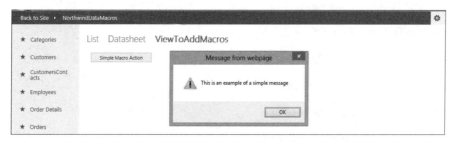

FIGURE 7-9 Executing the embedded macro from a blank view.

This example demonstrated the basic operations involved in creating both a standalone macro and then an embedded data macro.

User-interface events for views and controls

At first sight, you might feel that there is a limited set of events on a view from which you can program, and this is true. But this set of events can be extended, as I will describe in this section. Even after you extend the set of events, it might still feel limited. However, you need to appreciate that developing a solution that has a runtime browser experience will be limited by the features offered in web browsers, so you cannot get the same set of events in a web app as you do with a desktop database experience.

Views have only two events to which you can attach macros:

- **On Load** Executes when the view loads

- **On Current** Executes when a user moves to a new record or a different record from the current record

But when you look at the action bar, you will see icons to save a record, add a record, edit a record, delete a record, and cancel editing a record.

The *action bar* is a special object. It does not give you the opportunity to add to the built-in button code, but you can replace the built-in buttons and then mimic their operations. This is where you can exploit the interface to get additional events.

 Warning If you decide to take control of how the interface handles basic operations like Save, you will face a lot of programming effort to fulfill your requirements.

Once you take control of the built-in actions, you will have to execute the action, such as when saving a record. However, because you have control of when the action is executed, each button effectively represents two events. (One event consists of instructions before you execute the main action, and the other event consists of instructions following the execution of the main action.) This gives you a total of 10 additional events:

- Edit, Before Edit, and After Edit

- Save, Before Update, and After Update

- Delete, Before Delete, and After Delete

- Insert, Before Insert, and After Insert

- Cancel, Before Cancel, and After Cancel

To get a better understanding of why you would want to take control of the built-in actions, think about adding a button to a view where you want the button to be available only when you are editing in the view. If you leave the Action buttons available, you can never figure out whether to make your button available. You can't replace the Action Bar control itself with something else. You can replace the built-in Action Bar buttons, though.

There are five macro actions: EditRecord, NewRecord, SaveRecord, DeleteRecord, and UndoRecord. These correspond to the actions on the action bar buttons.

You start by creating five standalone user-interface macros as shown in Figure 7-10; each macro will enable or disable the other action buttons on the view depending on the required action.

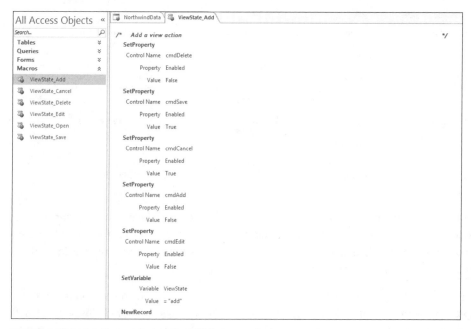

FIGURE 7-10 Macro for producing the Add Button action.

Each of the macros will control the button's Enabled property as described in Table 7-1. (The final actions are added after manipulating the enabled properties of the buttons.)

The macro logic makes use of the following macro actions:

- **SetProperty** This macro action is used to control whether other action buttons are enabled.

- **UndoRecord** This macro action is used to undo changes to a record.

- **RequeryRecords** This macro action is used to refresh the data.

- **SetVariable** This macro action is used to set a UI macro programming variable.

TABLE 7-1 Macro command actions for new action bar buttons

Macro Name	Enable	Disable	Final Actions
ViewState_Add	cmdSave, cmdCancel	cmdAdd, cmdDelete, cmdEdit	ViewState="add" NewRecord
ViewState_Cancel	cmdAdd, cmdDelete, cmdEdit	cmdCancel cmdSave	If the ViewState is "add", RequeryRecords; otherwise, UndoRecord. ViewState = "cancel". (See Figure 7-11.)
ViewState_Delete	cmdAdd, cmdDelete, cmdEdit	cmdSave, cmdCancel	ViewState="delete" DeleteRecord
ViewState_Edit	cmdSave, cmdCancel	cmdAdd, cmdDelete, cmdEdit	ViewState="edit" EditRecord
ViewState_Open	cmdAdd, cmdDelete, cmdEdit	cmdSave, cmdCancel	ViewState="open"
ViewState_Save	cmdAdd, cmdDelete, cmdEdit	cmdSave, cmdCancel	ViewState="open" SaveRecord

The macro action for Cancel has more steps than the other macros, and the additional steps are shown in Figure 7-11. If adding a record, you need to requery the view to correctly update the view. Note that you also created a global variable called *ViewState* to help refine the logic in displaying buttons and taking appropriate actions.

To enter an IF code block, type **IF** in the new macro action and then enter the condition **ViewState = "add"**. (Access will add square brackets after the macro is saved.) Inside the IF action, you can enter the RequeryRecords macro action. If the conditional test is true, any macro actions will be executed.

On the left of the IF block (when the IF action is highlighted), you will see hyperlinks titled Add Else and Add Else IF. Click on these commands to add additional conditions to the IF action. In this example, I clicked on Add Else and then entered the *UndoRecord* macro action. Macro actions entered in the *Else* code block are executed if the condition on the IF action is *false*. In Figure 7-11, you can see the Add Else If link on the right. The Add Else link is not shown because I already used that selection to alter the IF macro action logic. You can use the Add Else If logic to extend an IF macro action with further conditional logic.

> **Tip** Because these macro actions are similar, once you write one macro you can use Ctrl+A to select all the macro actions and then Ctrl+C to copy to the clipboard. Then create another macro, click on the background (and not in the macro action box), press Ctrl+V to paste in all the macro steps, and then adjust the macro actions to correspond with the correct button context.

```
⊟ If  [ViewState]="add"  Then
    ⊟ RequeryRecords                                                    ⬆ ⬇ ✕
              Where  =
            Order By

    ✛  Add New Action          ▾                                   Add Else If

  ⊟ Else
        UndoRecord
    End If
⊟ SetVariable
          Variable  ViewState
            Value  = "cancel"
  ✛  Add New Action          ▾
```

FIGURE 7-11 Final steps in the Cancel action macro.

The next steps on your view are to delete all the built-in action buttons on the Customers List View, add your own set of custom action bar buttons with similar icons to those used with the built-in action buttons as shown in Figure 7-12, and name the custom action bar buttons **cmdAdd**, **cmdDelete**, **cmdEdit**, **cmdSave**, and **cmdCancel**. Then write the macro actions behind each new button to execute the appropriate macro, either *ViewState_Add*, *ViewState_Delete*, *ViewState_Edit*, *ViewState_Save*, and *ViewState_Cancel*.

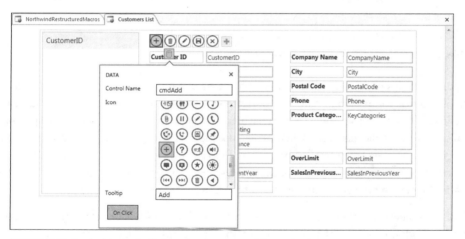

FIGURE 7-12 Replacing the built-in action buttons on the action bar.

Behind each custom action bar button on the On Click event, you add a single RunMacro action as shown in Figure 7-13 to execute the appropriate macro.

FIGURE 7-13 Calling the standalone UI macro from the new action buttons.

> **Tip** This technique also solves another important issue if you add a button to a view. How can you enable or disable the button based on whether you are viewing or editing a record? The code to do this can now be added behind the button and view events.

The last points to consider are that you need some code on both the On Load event, to set the default display of buttons (and initialize the ViewState variable), and the On Current event, to handle the situation where a user clicks away to select another record. For the On Load event, simply run the macro *ViewState_Open*, but for the On Current event, you need to remember that it will fire when you click on the add action button. The code to handle this is shown in Figure 7-14.

FIGURE 7-14 On Current and On Load event handling the add action.

The result of all this hard work is that you will have a view that displays a set of custom action bar buttons identical to the standard action bar buttons. But in addition to having the standard On Current and On Load events for the view, you have now created the opportunity to write specialized code in response to the five new user activities. Each of these activities allows you to add additional macro operations before completing the action and then perform additional operations after the action is completed. This is equivalent to having Before Edit, After Edit, Before Save, After Save, Before Delete, After Delete, Before Insert, After Insert, Before Cancel, and After Cancel events.

Controls on a view can potentially have two events: On Click and After Update. The availability of the events depends on the type of control, and it also can depend on the type of view. (For example, a datasheet view will not support an After Update event on controls.) Here are the events available in each case:

- **On Click**   Text Box, Label, Button, Image, Autocomplete, Hyperlink, Multiline Textbox
- **After Update**   Text Box, Hyperlink, Multiline Text Box, Check Box, Autocomplete, Combo Box.

The Web Browser, RELIC, and Subview controls have no events.

User-interface macros

In the last section, you used *NewRecord*, *SaveRecord*, *UndoRecord*, *DeleteRecord*, and *EditRecord* macro actions. These are the data-entry macro operations, and the *RequeryRecords* operation is the only action in the Filter/Query/Search category.

In Figure 7-15, you can see how the UI macros are organized into categories.

FIGURE 7-15 UI macro action sets.

In terms of the program flow, you saw an example of the If and Comment action sets. The *Group* action offers no functionality other than to gather a set of macro actions in a collapsible element.

In the Database Objects category, you have the following actions:

- **GoToControl**   This macro action moves the focus to a control.

- **GoToRecord**   You used this macro action in earlier chapters to add navigation buttons.

- **SetProperty**   You saw that this macro action can change the properties of controls.

> **Tip** You need to be careful with the *SetProperty* macro, because you need to make sure that the control supports the property you are setting. For example, trying to set the background color on an action button will fail, but the macro action is not sensitive to the control type.

In the final category of macro actions, you already used the *SetVariable* and *RunMacro* actions. The *RunDataMacro* action will be described in the next section when we discuss data macros.

Named data macros and stored procedures

In the sample web app that I hope you have been using to follow along with this chapter, I intentionally created a problem. If you look at the Customers table, you will see that the primary key is *ID*, but it also has the old text key called *CustomerID*. Then if you look at the Orders table, you will see that it has the old foreign key called *CustomerID*, but that links to the old field, not the new primary key field *ID*.

I could have fixed this before importing the data, but I wanted to demonstrate the steps to rectify this problem. You will need to remap the data to link the two tables on a new foreign key. Because web apps don't support update queries, you will need to look at an alternative technique.

To start resolving this problem, you need to add a new foreign key lookup field to the Orders table called *CID*, which is shown in Figure 7-16. This will look up the ID field in the Customers table, not the old text CustomerID, and display the CompanyName field.

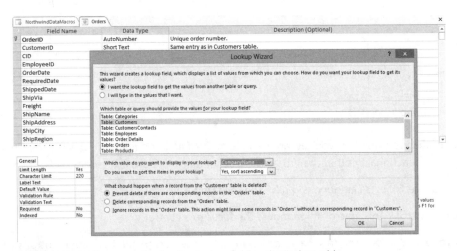

FIGURE 7-16 Adding a new foreign key lookup field to the Orders table.

After saving your work, select the Advanced menu and then select the Data Macro option, as shown in Figure 7-17.

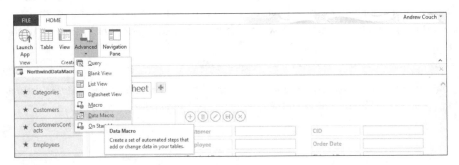

FIGURE 7-17 Creating a data macro.

You start the data macro, which is named *dm_RemapOrdersForeignKey_CID*, by declaring two local variables, as shown in Figure 7-18.

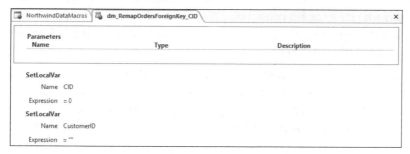

FIGURE 7-18 Declaring and initializing two local variables.

The main part of the data macro code is shown in Figure 7-19. This consists of an outer loop that iterates through all the customer records and then executes an inner loop for each customer's orders based on matching the old foreign key, CustomerID, to update the new foreign key, CID.

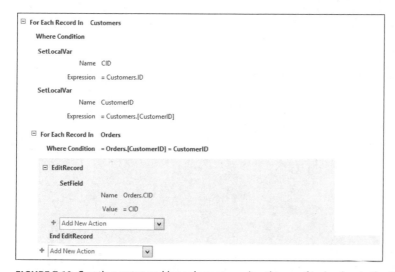

FIGURE 7-19 Creating outer and inner loops to assign the new foreign key in the Orders table.

In the following code, I examined the resulting stored procedure that is created in the Azure SQL Database and removed a significant amount of code, without removing the essence of the processing that takes place. Highlights to notice in the code are the variables being declared and assigned and a cursor (the TSQL equivalent to a VBA recordset) that is opened with a *while* loop, which checks the status to see if processing is complete. Inside the loop, a second cursor is opened and another *while* loop runs through all the orders for the customer record. Then inside the inner loop, UPDATE actions are executed to update the records.

> **Tip** You will find that examining the resulting stored procedure code in the Azure SQL Database when writing data macros provides an excellent method for checking that your variable definitions are in the correct place. Using this approach, you can ensure the variables have the correct scope, they are available when needed, and the nesting of any processing loops is correctly organized.
>
> If you are not that familiar with TSQL but feel more at home with macro programming, you will also find that looking into the generated code is a great learning tool for coming to grips with TSQL. Just remember that the code is generically written by code generators, so it is often more verbose and general purpose than code you would write for yourself.

```
CREATE PROCEDURE [Access].[dm_RemapOrdersForeignKey_CID]
WITH EXECUTE AS 'AccessWriter'
AS
BEGIN
    BEGIN TRY
        DECLARE @CID Decimal(28,6)
        DECLARE @CustomerID NVarChar(Max)


        SET @CID = 0.0
        SET @CustomerID = N''
        DECLARE _dm_cur1 CURSOR LOCAL STATIC FOR
            SELECT
                [ID],
                [CustomerID]
            FROM
                [Customers]

            ORDER BY [Customers].[ID] ASC
        OPEN _dm_cur1
        FETCH NEXT FROM
            _dm_cur1
        INTO
            @_dm_temp1,
            @_dm_temp2
        WHILE @@FETCH_STATUS = 0
        BEGIN
            SET @CID = @_dm_temp1
            SET @CustomerID = @_dm_temp2
            DECLARE _dm_cur2 CURSOR LOCAL STATIC FOR
                SELECT
                    [OrderID],
                    [CID]
                FROM
                    [Orders]
                WHERE
                    [CustomerID] = @CustomerID
                ORDER BY [Orders].[OrderID] ASC
            OPEN _dm_cur2
```

```
        FETCH NEXT FROM
            _dm_cur2
        INTO
            @_dm_temp3,
            @_dm_temp4
        WHILE @@FETCH_STATUS = 0
        BEGIN
            SET @_dm_temp4 = @CID
            IF @_dm_cancelRecordChange = 0
                UPDATE
                    [Orders]
                SET
                    [CID] = @_dm_temp4
                WHERE
                    [OrderID] = @_dm_temp3
            FETCH NEXT FROM
                _dm_cur2
            INTO
                @_dm_temp3,
                @_dm_temp4
        END
        CLOSE _dm_cur2
        DEALLOCATE _dm_cur2
        FETCH NEXT FROM
            _dm_cur1
        INTO
            @_dm_temp1,
            @_dm_temp2
    END
    CLOSE _dm_cur1
    DEALLOCATE _dm_cur1

END TRY
```

A large amount of the code I have not shown here is connected with being able to activate a trace table to help debug data macros, as well as code for transaction processing and error handling.

> **Tip** Because the Azure SQL Database allows you to run update queries, if this was a one-off operation, you could have executed a SQL update command using SSMS to perform this operation. (This would require the use of a connection with read/write permissions to the database.) Here's the code you would use to perform the SQL update:

```
UPDATE Orders
    SET CID = ID
FROM Orders
    INNER JOIN Customers
        ON Orders.CustomerID = Customers.CustomerID
```

After creating your data macro, you need to add a button on a view and create an embedded macro action in the On Click event to run the data macro. Figure 7-20 shows the button being added to the view.

Start by editing the Orders List view for the Orders table caption. From the list of controls on the ribbon, add a button to the view with a caption **Re-map CID**. Then, from the button actions, click on the On Click action.

FIGURE 7-20 Creating a button to run the new data macro.

Figure 7-21 shows the UI macro action you add to the On Click event of the button on the Orders List view. In the On Click event, add the *RunDataMacro* macro action, selecting to run the *dm_RemapOrdersForeignKey_CID* macro you created previously. Save the macro and then save the view.

FIGURE 7-21 Creating a UI macro to execute the data macro.

Display the Orders List view in the browser window and then click the *Re-map CID* button. Figure 7-22 shows the new CID field on the Orders list view displayed in the browser window, which has now been correctly populated with data after running your data macro. (Remember that although CID is a number, when you defined the lookup, you specified it to display the CompanyName from the Customers table.)

FIGURE 7-22 Orders view showing the new Remap CID field and action button.

Now that you have remapped your data, we will look at constructing a second data macro example that depends on the previous data macro work being completed and the data being remapped.

You start by creating a table called SystemTable, which in addition to the unique identifier has a single whole number field called ActiveSalesYear, as shown in Figure 7-23.

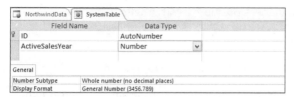

FIGURE 7-23 SystemTable containing the field ActiveSalesYear.

Figure 7-24 shows the table in the datasheet preview. Enter the year **1997** in the ActiveSalesYear column. (This will match your existing data.) Note that this table must contain only one row. Later you will see how triggers on the table can help enforce this rule.

FIGURE 7-24 SystemTable in the datasheet preview.

In your Customers table, you have a Currency field called SalesInCurrentYear, as shown in Figure 7-25.

Field Name	Data Type	Description (Optional)
SalesInCurrentYear	Currency	Sales made in the current financial year
SalesInPreviousYear	Currency	Sales made in the previous financial year

FIGURE 7-25 The SalesInCurrentYear field in the Customers table.

You are going to modify your web app so that as data is changed, the SalesInCurrentYear field for a customer is updated to reflect those changes. This approach then can be generalized to maintain account balances and previous years' sales if required.

You will start by creating a query that will calculate the sales in *ActiveSalesYear*, using the Orders, Order Details, and SystemTable tables. Figure 7-26 shows a totals query, which calculates the total sales value for all customers in the ActiveSalesYear. Note that the SystemTable table is not joined, but you use the value of the single record in this table to filter the data. This query demonstrates a technique called *creating a Cartesian product*. Here are the steps:

1. Start by creating a new query.

2. Add the tables Orders, Order Details, and SystemTable to the query grid.

3. Click on Totals.

4. Scroll down the Orders table, and double-click on CID to add this to the query grid as a Group By option.

5. In the Field row, type the following in the expression SumOfLinePrice:

Sum([UnitPrice]*[Quantity]*(1-[Discount]))

6. Below the expression in the Totals row, change Group By to Expression.

7. In the Field row, enter the expression **Year([OrderDate])**. You can ignore the text Expr1: Year([OrderDate]) that Access adds. After saving the query, Access removes the text *Expr1:*. In the Total row for this column, change the selection to Where.

8. In the Criteria, below Where, type in **[ActiveSalesYear]**.

9. Save the query as **qrySalesForCustomersinActiveYear**.

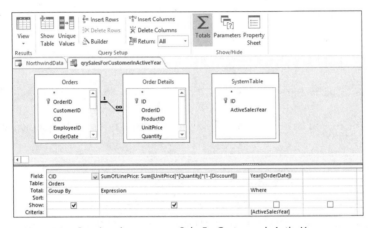

FIGURE 7-26 Creating the query *qrySalesForCustomersinActiveYear*.

Your next steps are to create a data macro that can update the data for a single customer and then generalize that to produce a data macro that uses the first data macro to update for all customers. This is because you will also be re-using the first data macro.

1. Start by creating a new data macro.

2. Click the Create Parameter link, enter a parameter called **SelectedID**, and select the data type Number No Decimal.

3. Add a For Each Record In macro action for the Customers table.

4. Add the following *where* clause: [Customers.ID] = [SelectedID].

5. Use the macro action *SetLocalVar* to set the variable *OrdersThisYear* to *0*.

6. Add a Lookup A Record In macro command for the query *qrySalesForCustomersinActiveYear*.

7. Add the following *where* condition:

[qrySalesForCustomersinActiveYear].[CID] = [SelectedID]

8. Add a *SetLocalVar* action to set the following variable:

```
OrdersThisYear = [qrySalesForCustomersinActiveYear].[SumOfLinePrice]
```

9. Save the macro with the name **dm_CustomerSalesInAYear**.

Figure 7-27 shows the top part of a new macro called *dm_CustomerSalesInAYear*. This named data macro has a parameter called *SelectedID*. The outer For Each Record loop filters to locate one record with the required ID; you need to do this because you are going to edit the record. To find the value for the sales, you can use the Lookup A Record In action to return a single value, rather than another For Each Record In loop. Notice that the *SetLocalVar* action must be indented correctly so that it lies inside the Look Up A Record In code block.

> **Tip** If you need to check the indentation level on your code, you can easily collapse and expand the indentation on each section of code. This is the technique I used when writing the code in this chapter.

FIGURE 7-27 A data macro that uses named parameters.

Below the final *SetLocalVar* in Figure 7-27, add an *EditRecord* to update *SalesInCurrentYear* for the customer, as shown in Figure 7-28.

FIGURE 7-28 Final macro actions to edit and save the sales value in the customer record.

Caution When you add the macro command shown in Figure 7-28, it will be associated with the Look Up A Record In action, and you want it to be associated with the outer loop. You need to click the Move Down button (the downward-pointing arrow) shown on the right in Figure 7-29 to ensure that the action moves to the correct level of indentation.

FIGURE 7-29 Preparing to move down a macro action.

Figure 7-30 shows the macro action block for the Look Up A Record In action collapsed to show the correct position for the final macro action after you click the Move Down button.

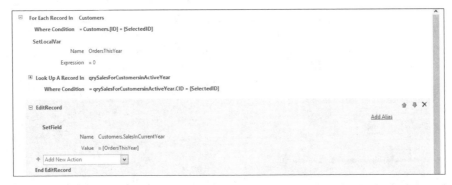

FIGURE 7-30 Final completed data macro showing the correct position for the final *EditRecord* macro action.

After you have saved and closed the *dm_CustomerSalesInAYear* data macro, you need to create a second data macro that will call the first data macro to process records for all your customer records.

Figure 7-31 shows a new data macro called *dm_AllCustomersSalesInAYear*. This macro loops through each customer record, calling your previously defined data macro *dm_CustomerSalesInAYear*. Notice the *RunDataMacro* action automatically displays the *SelectedID* parameter and that you also include a *SetReturnVar* action to pass back to the calling program a count of the number of processed records. Here are the steps you need to complete:

1. Start by creating a new data macro.

2. Use the *SetLocalVar* macro action to initialize the local variable *intCustomerCount* to *0*.

3. Then add a For Each Record In macro action for the Customers table.

4. In the For Each Record loop, add a *SetLocalVar* macro action to increment the *intCustomerCount* by 1.

5. Add a second macro action within the loop to run the data macro *dm_CustomerSalesInAYear*, setting the data macro parameter to *Customers.ID*.

6. Outside of the For Each loop, add a *SetReturnVar* macro action with the name *CountOfCustomers* and the variable *intCustomerCount*.

7. Save the data macro with the name *dm_AllCustomersSalesInAYear*.

When you enter these macro actions, check to see that the indentation on actions are correct. The *SetLocalVar* and *RunDataMacro* actions are both contained within the For Each Record In macro code block. After you add these two actions to the bottom of the data macro, you need to use the Move Up button to reposition the actions within the correct code block. (Looking at Figure 7-31, you will see that the two macro actions are indented within the For Each Record In code block.) The Move Up button is next to the Move Down button, which was shown previously in Figure 7-29.

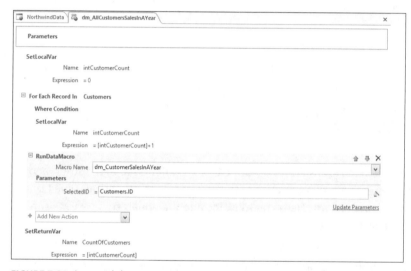

FIGURE 7-31 A named data macro that passes a parameter to another named data macro.

Tip If you rename your macros, you need to manually edit other references to the macro names. In Figure 7-31, at the bottom right of the RunDataMacro area is a link titled UpdateParameters. If you change the parameters in a data macro, you need to manually update the parameters using this link.

You can now add a button to your SystemTable datasheet view so that after saving changes for a year you can update all the customer records. The completed embedded macro action is shown in Figure 7-32. Follow these steps:

1. Open the SystemTable datasheet view in design view, and then add a command button.

2. Set the Control Name for the button to *cmdupdate*, clear the Datasheet Caption property for the button, and set the button Caption property to **Update sales in current year**.

3. Use the OnClick action for the button to enter macro code.

4. Enter the macro action **SetVariable** to create a variable called **intCustomerCount** with an initial value of *0*.

5. Use the RunDataMacro macro action to run the *dm_AllCustomersSalesInAYear* data macro, and enter **intCustomerCount** for the return value parameter.

6. Add a MessageBox action, and set the expression to the following:

   ```
   =Concat('Number of customers updated was ',[intCustomerCount])
   ```

7. Save and close the macro. Then save and close the view.

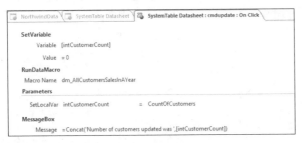

FIGURE 7-32 Embedded UI macro that updates all customer records for a change in the year.

Tip In the macro shown in Figure 7-32, I used the *Concat* function to join a string and numerical value. Alternatively, you can choose to just display the numerical value using the expression = intCustomerCount. Here you must include the equals sign (=) to ensure the value of the variable is displayed.

Refresh the datasheet view in the browser, and then click the button next to the year 1997, as shown in Figure 7-33.

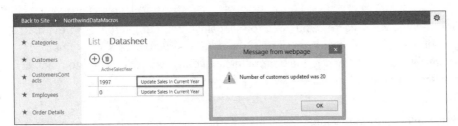

FIGURE 7-33 Running the macro actions from a button on a datasheet view.

> **Tip** You could run into problems when getting return values back from a data macro and receive error messages suggesting that you update parameters. If this happens, return to the RunDataMacro macro action. You will find that, after clicking on the macro action, a link is provided named Update Parameters. If updating a parameter still does not resolve a problem, sometimes it is worth deleting the SetReturnVar macro action in the data macro, saving and closing the data macro, and then re-opening the data macro and adding back the SetReturnVar macro action. Then, after saving the data macro, return to the place where you call the data macro and again update the parameters.

The method of updating the sales figures for all customers indicates you can set the values for each customer in a particular sales year (which would normally be the current sales year). If a new order is entered in the system, you need to recalculate the sales total for all customers by again clicking this button. You will see in the next section that you can improve on having a button on the view to manually perform this update. You do this by using triggers to keep values for a customer updated when dependent information is updated.

You might also wonder why we used two data macros in this instance: the first, *dm_CustomerSalesInAYear*, to update the information for a single customer, and the second, *dm_AllCustomersSalesInAYear*, to update the information for all customers. The reason is that you will make use of the data macro *dm_CustomerSalesInAYear*, which updates data for a single customer in the next section, when you are working with triggers.

Data macros and triggers

Each table in a web app has three events where you can embed data macro code in response to users inserting, updating, or deleting data in the table. Looking at the design of a table, as shown in Figure 7-34, you can see how the three events shown for the table have shaded icons. This indicates that embedded data macro code was written behind each of the following three events: On Insert, On Update, and On Delete. In this section, we will be looking at adding embedded data code on these events.

FIGURE 7-34 A table design in which embedded data macro code has been added to the table.

Each table can have code written behind the following three events:

- **On Insert** This macro action executes after the record has been inserted, but you can also use it to cancel the insert. It corresponds to On Insert After Trigger in the Azure SQL Database.

- **On Update** This macro executes after the record has been updated, but you can also use it to cancel the update. It corresponds to On Update After Trigger in the Azure SQL Database.

- **On Delete** This macro executes after the record has been deleted, but you can also use it to cancel the delete. It corresponds to On Delete After Trigger in the Azure SQL Database.

> **Tip** Azure SQL supports different kinds of triggers, and the triggers we are interested in are called *After Triggers*, because they execute after any referential integrity checks and other checks have been performed but before accepting changes. In the Azure SQL Database, the trigger code can see two virtual views of the data: INSERTED and DELETED.
>
> You use the INSERTED view to look at the "after" image of data, and DELETED shows the "before" image of the data. This means that trigger code can compare data values before and after the operation.
>
> These triggers execute in an implicit transaction and support the ROLLBACK command to undo the changes. You will see how this ROLLBACK and other trigger features correspond to commands and field references in the data macro code shown later in this chapter.

In the SystemTable table, you only want to have a single record, which can be edited but not deleted. To prevent a user from adding any new records to this table, you write data macro actions behind the On Insert event, as shown in Figure 7-35.

FIGURE 7-35 The *RaiseError* data macro action used to prevent records being added to a table

This data macro uses the *RaiseError* macro action. This action will cause any changes to the record to be undone, and the defined message text will be displayed as a popup in the user interface. You can write similar code for the On Delete action with appropriate message text.

1. Open the table SystemTable in design view.

2. Click the On Insert button on the ribbon.

3. Add the RaiseError macro action to the macro design surface, and then type the error description **Records cannot be added to this table**.

4. Save and close the data macro code in the event.

5. Save the table design.

Tip When you are working in the macro designer, you might notice in the title bar that it displays After Update for the On Update action. For On Delete, it displays After Delete; for On Insert, it displays After Insert. You can view each pair of terms as equivalent. Earlier I also pointed out that these actions map to After Triggers in SQL Server, which is what the *After* terminology is indicating.

Figure 7-36 shows the On Update data macro, which replaces the need for the button you added to the view earlier. That button is not needed after data is updated, because the data macro will be executed automatically when the data in the ActiveSalesYear field is changed. Notice that you do not need to use the return variable from the data macro. In fact, you cannot display that to the user because the On Update data macro executes in the Azure SQL Database and cannot pass back messages to the user interface, except when raising an error.

To add this macro code proceed as follows:

1. Open the table SystemTable in design view if it is not already open.

2. Click the On Update button on the ribbon.

3. Add the macro action RunDataMacro to the macro design surface, and then use **dm_AllCustomersSalesInAYear** for the Macro Name argument.

4. Save and close the data macro code in the event.

5. Save the table design changes.

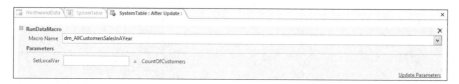

FIGURE 7-36 On Update event (After Update) executing a data macro.

To see how this works, proceed as follows:

1. Look at a customer List record—for example, ALPHO—where the SalesInCurrentYear is 2022.50 (for 1997).

2. Change the value of the ActiveSalesYear from *1997* to *1998* in the SystemTable datasheet, and click on the next row to save the record.

3. Return to the customer list record—for example, ALPHO—where SalesInCurrentYear is now shown as 2250.50.

4. Repeat and change back from 1998 to 1997. Then return to ALPHO. You will see the value 2022.50 has been restored.

The data macro will have been executed to update the sales information for all customers when the ActiveSalesYear is changed.

In the Azure SQL Database, if you expand the Tables folder and look at the Triggers folder inside the table SystemTable, you will see the data macros that were converted into Azure SQL Database triggers, as shown in Figure 7-37. To examine the contents of the trigger, right-click on the trigger and choose Script Trigger As, Create To, and then New Query Editor Window.

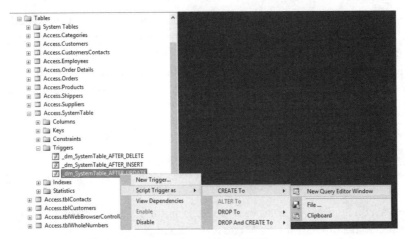

FIGURE 7-37 Displaying the triggers for a table in SSMS.

The following code sample is a fragment from the trigger code, which I simplified by removing a number of commands:

```
BEGIN TRY
    DECLARE _dm_cur1 CURSOR LOCAL STATIC FOR
        SELECT
            *
        FROM
            [DELETED]
    OPEN _dm_cur1
    DECLARE @_dm_temp1 Int
    DECLARE _dm_cur2 CURSOR LOCAL STATIC FOR
        SELECT
            [ActiveSalesYear]
        FROM
            [INSERTED]
    OPEN _dm_cur2
    FETCH NEXT FROM
        _dm_cur1
    FETCH NEXT FROM
        _dm_cur2
    INTO
        @_dm_temp1
    WHILE @@FETCH_STATUS = 0
```

```
BEGIN
    SET @_dm_actionRunning = N'If'
    IF @_dm_temp1 IS NULL
    BEGIN
        THROW 50000, N'You need to enter a year for the ActiveSalesYear', 1;
    END
    EXEC [Access].[dm_AllCustomersSalesInAYear]
        @_dm_temp2 OUTPUT
```

> **Tip** Notice that the trigger code starts by opening two cursors: one for INSERTED (the after image of the data) and the other for DELETED (the before image of the data). Then it enters a processing loop that tests the FETCH_STATUS to apply the processing for each record.
>
> Earlier in this section, I mentioned that INSERTED and DELETED are virtual tables that enable you to examine and accept or reject the data changes. If this was a DELETE trigger, you would again see the two cursors. However, for an INSERT trigger, you only need the INSERTED virtual table. Even when a simple trigger executes only a *RaiseError*, you will find that the general structure of the trigger code remains the same. This means that you ignore a great deal of the trigger code and focus on actions that relate to steps in your data macro.

When you write data macro code in a trigger and you refer to a field in the table, you will be referring to the INSERTED virtual table. To examine an old value in either an On Delete or On Update trigger, prefix the field name as follows: [OLD].[FieldName]. There is also a special Updated([FieldName]) command that can be used to test, in an On Update trigger, whether the value in a field has changed.

In this example, you have not taken into account how any changes made to the data in the Order Details table need to also potentially change the SalesInCurrentYear total for a customer. In the following example, you will also see some additional syntax available in data macros.

Here are the steps you need to follow:

1. Open the Order Details table in design view.

2. Click the On Delete button on the ribbon.

3. Add the For Each Record In macro action to the macro design surface, select the Orders table, and enter the where clause [Orders].[OrderID] = [Old].[OrderID].

4. Add a SetLocalVar macro action for the variable *OrderDetailsCID*, setting the value to *[Orders].[CID]*.

5. Add a RunDataMacro macro action that runs the *dm_CustomerSalesInAYear* data macro, and use the local variable *OrderDetailsCID* as the parameter value for the *SelectedID*.

6. Ensure that the macro actions just entered are within the For Each Record macro block, indented as shown in Figure 7-38.

7. Save and close the data macro code in the event.

8. Save the table design.

In Figure 7-38, you see that because the [Order Details] record was deleted before the data macro executed. You can find the details of the record only by looking in the [OLD] virtual image of the data. You then locate the customer from the Orders table and call your data macro to update the total sales for the customer.

FIGURE 7-38 An On Delete (After Delete) macro action demonstrating the use of [OLD].

 Caution After you have been working on the design tab editing a macro and you close the macro, it places the focus on the home tab and does not retain focus on the design tab.

In the previous example, you used a For Each loop. In the following example, for the On Insert data macro for the Order Details table, you need to type in a Lookup A Record In macro action, as shown in Figure 7-39. The question is does it make any difference whether you use a For Each Record In or a Lookup A Record In?

It turns out that if you examine the trigger code produced by both techniques, in both cases, inside the normal processing loop constructed on the virtual tables, an additional cursor is defined. However, with the Lookup A Record In macro action, the SQL is modified to include the TOP function in SELECT TOP(1) to ensure the loop processes only a single record. So, in the example, it makes very little difference which approach you take.

1. Open the Order Details table in design view.

2. Click the On Insert button on the ribbon.

3. Add a Look Up A Record In macro action to the macro design surface, select the Orders table, and enter the where clause [Orders].[OrderID] = [Order Details].[OrderID].

4. Add a SetLocalVar macro action for the variable *OrderDetailsCID*, setting the value to *[Orders].[CID]*.

5. Add a RunDataMacro macro action that runs the *dm_CustomerSalesInAYear* data macro, and use the local variable *OrderDetailsCID* as the parameter value for the *SelectedID*.

6. Ensure that the macro actions just entered are within the For Each Record macro block, indented as shown in Figure 7-39.

7. Save and close the data macro code in the event.

8. Save the table design.

FIGURE 7-39 An On Insert (After Insert) macro action using a Look Up A Record In macro action.

To complete the programming behind the events on this table, copy the code in the On Insert event and paste the code into the macro design editor for the On Update event on the Order Details table. (Use Ctrl+A to select all the macro code, use Ctrl+C to copy the code, and then in the On Update macro use Ctrl+V to paste the code.)

To test the three new data macros, proceed as follows:

1. Set the ActiveSalesYear field to 1997 in the SystemTable datasheet, and save the record.

2. Look in the Customers List view for the ALPHO record. The SalesInCurrentYear field will be 2022.50.

3. Navigate to the Orders table caption, and display the Orders List view. Search for the ALPHO record. The first order should be dated 1997. Add a new order details record. For the product Chai, set the unit price to 10, quantity to 10, and discount to 0. (You need to set the discount.) Save your record changes.

4. Return to the Customers List view, and find the ALPHO record again. You should now see the SalesInCurrentYear field showing 2122.50.

5. Return to the Orders List view again, and change the quantity field to 20 for the new record you previously created.

6. Return to the Customers list, and search for the ALPHO record. You should now see the SalesInCurrentYear field showing 2222.50.

7. Return to the Orders List view again, and this time delete the new order details for Chai that you entered.

8. Return to the Customers List view one last time, and search for the ALPHO record. You should now see the original SalesInCurrentYear field showing 2022.50.

When you look at the datasheet for the Orders Details table, you will notice that if you try to display the actual foreign-key value for OrderID, you cannot show the value. This is because if you add the default Autocomplete control, it will show the related value from the Orders table. Also, if you add a text box control, you cannot choose the underlying [OrderID] field because that is a lookup and is not available to display in a text box.

The workaround to this problem of displaying the true foreign-key value is to add the standard autocomplete control but then add an additional text box to the design grid that uses the autocomplete control as the data source; you need to use the expression builder to set this value. This is shown in Figure 7-40.

1. Open the Order Details datasheet in design view.

2. Add a text box to the view from the ribbon, an set the caption to read TrueOrderID.

3. Display the data properties for the control as shown in Figure 7-40.

4. Click on the build button (the ellipses next to control source).

5. Type in **OrderIDAutocomplete**, and click OK.

FIGURE 7-40 Adding a text box with the control source set to the autocomplete control.

Tip With regard to Figure 7-40, keep in mind that when setting the Control Source value, you need to use the build button. This is because the drop-down list of choices displays only the underlying field names, and you want to refer to a control. (It can also help if you first select the OrderID control and copy the control name to the clipboard to then later paste into the Expression Builder window.)

Figure 7-41 shows the result in the browser of adding the new text box titled TrueOrderID, which exposes the underlying value in the OrderID from the Autocomplete control.

ID	OrderID	TrueOrderID	Product	Unit Price	Quantity	Discount
1	GRDES	10254	Guaraná Fantást	$3.60	22	15%
2	GRDES	10254	Pâté chinois	$19.20	21	15%
3	GRDES	10254	Longlife Tofu	$8.00	21	0%
4	LITWA	10258	Chang	$15.20	50	20%

FIGURE 7-41 The true value behind the Autocomplete control exposed in a datasheet.

> **Tip** When you write event code on a table, after you save any changes to the macro code and close the macro design window, you do not need to then save the table. This is because the trigger code is saved when you save the macro code. Also, you do not need to refresh in the browser window to test the code changes, because the code is executing in the Azure SQL Database, not in the browser. This is different than when writing user-interface macros on a view, where after saving the macro code changes, you must save the view to see your changes. And if the view is already open in a browser window, you must refresh it to see your changes.

Data macro tracing

You saw in earlier sections how investigating the stored procedures or triggers in the Azure SQL Database to establish the detailed execution of your data macro and relating the TSQL back to the data macro is an invaluable tool in understanding how the data macro is executed. But there is also a built-in feature to trace data macro execution.

The data macro tracing feature is a switch that can be turned on or off for the database. This switch can be set on or off only when working inside the macro editor.

Inside the TSQL in the Azure SQL Database, you will notice code such as the following, which monitors the status of the trace flag. When set, this code will write the results to a system table in the web app called Trace:

```
SET @_dm_actionRunning = N'LookupRecord'
IF @_dm_traceOn > 0
    EXEC [AccessSystem].[LogActionTrace] @_dm_macroRunning,
    N'LookupRecord', N'Orders;WHERE [Orders].[OrderID]=
    [Order Details].[OrderID]', N'', N'', N''
```

To activate this feature, open any table in your web app in design view and go into an On Insert, On Delete, or On Update event (or alternatively edit another UI or named data macro). Then click the Data Macro Tracing button, as shown in Figure 7-42.

FIGURE 7-42 Activating data macro tracing.

Then switch to the runtime browser environment (you don't need to save anything before doing this), and execute anything that would fire a standalone data macro or trigger. In our example, you used the button on the SystemTable table datasheet to force the update of all customers for the ActiveSalesYear field for all customers. Now return to the design view of a table and click the View Trace Table button in the ribbon as shown in Figure 7-43.

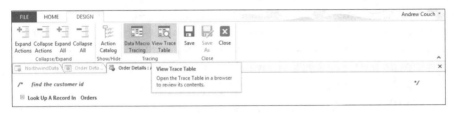

FIGURE 7-43 Viewing the data macro View Trace Table.

This displays the trace results, and an example of trace results as they appear in a datasheet view in Access is shown in Figure 7-44. (Your results might not exactly match the results shown in the figure.) The results include error messages, which will assist you in debugging the data macro.

ID	MacroName	ActionName	Operand	Output	TargetRow	Timestamp	RuntimeErrorMessage
1	dm_SetCustomerTab	ForEachRecord	Customers;WHE			5/29/2013 6:58:	
2	dm_SetCustomerTab	ForEachRecord			[ID] = 1 : [UpdatedBy] = NULL : [UpdatedC	5/29/2013 6:58:	
3	dm_SetCustomerTab	EditRecord				5/29/2013 6:58:	
4	dm_SetCustomerTab	SetField	UpdatedBy	Andrew Couch2		5/29/2013 6:58:	
5	dm_SetCustomerTab	SetField	UpdatedOn	2013-05-29		5/29/2013 6:58:	
6	dm_SetCustomerTab	ForEachRecord	Customers;WHE			5/29/2013 7:06:	

FIGURE 7-44 Data Macro Trace Table results in a datasheet view in Access.

> **Tip** There is no built-in feature to empty the trace table. This can be achieved by executing the SQL command DELETE FROM TRACE in the Azure SQL Database, or through an Access desktop application linked with Read/Write connections to the Azure SQL Database. Or you could write a simple standalone data macro to loop through and delete the records in the Trace table. (If you are using a data macro, ensure that you first turn off the Trace Table feature before attempting to empty the Trace table. Otherwise, you will contribute additional content to the Trace table.)

On Start macro

The On Start macro is a special macro that will be executed when your web app is first viewed or when a user refreshes any page in the web app. So you need to take the refresh action into account.

I described how all variables in UI macros are global, but you cannot refer to variables that have not been previously declared. So the On Start macro is a great opportunity to define your variables to ensure that they will not cause you subsequent problems when referring to them.

In Chapter 8, "Managing security and a public web app," you will see how to use the On Start macro in a real application, but for the moment we want to demonstrate how to create the On Start macro and emphasize when it will be activated. In Chapter 5, "Displaying data in views," we used the On Start macro to open a popup window when the application started.

The On Start macro is created or changed by using the On Start Macro option on the Advanced menu, shown in Figure 7-45.

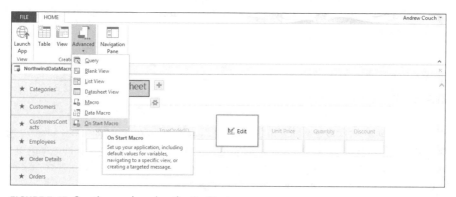

FIGURE 7-45 Creating or changing the On Start macro.

 Warning When working with the On Start macro, saving your changes is not enough to then be able to see the effect of the changes when you refresh the runtime browser window. You need to close the On Start macro editing window before any changes will become available. This causes Access to save the App Home View page as well. The On Start macro is attached to that view.

Figure 7-46 shows an On Start macro that saves the users display name and email address in global variables and, for the purpose of testing, displays these values in a message box.

FIGURE 7-46 Displaying the user's email address and display name.

You can then use this information to display a welcome message or actions that a user could undertake in the application.

Tip Because the On Start macro is executed if a user undertakes a browser refresh operation, you probably would not want to display a message box in your application. If a user refreshes a browser page, you need to assume that this is equivalent to their first visit to the site, because you cannot test to see if a global variable has a value without first assigning the variable a value.

Transactions and recursion

Recursion is the name for a process in which the code calls itself again repeatedly while executing the same code but with different parameters. It is a clever programming technique that allows people to write compact, powerful code. We are not going to be concerned with how this kind of code can be written, but instead focus on a how recursion can occur in a web app.

Indirect recursion

If you write a trigger on a table A and a trigger on table B makes a change to data in table A, the trigger on table A will be executed. This type of recursion is called *indirect*, and I will now discuss an example of how to demonstrate this effect.

Consider two tables, A and B. Table A has an On Insert event that writes to table B, and table B has an On Insert trigger event that writes to table A. If you insert a record in table A, you will create a game of Ping-Pong where you have an infinite loop. The Azure SQL Database can detect and stop this kind of problem; it has a limit on recursion to 32-levels, after which it will return with an error, which will be displayed as shown in Figure 7-47.

FIGURE 7-47 Access services warning when stopping a data macro.

Tip If you try to create your own recursive test that exceeds the permitted 32 levels, because all the changes are wrapped in transactions and all the changes get rolled back when the recursion limit is reached, you will not see any evidence of what has happened in the tables.

If you examine your event code in the Azure SQL Database, you will see that the data macro code results in transaction-processing statements. You will see commands such as BEGIN TRAN, which begins a transaction, and @@TRANCOUNT, which is a system variable that contains the depth of nested transactions; @@TRANCOUNT indicates how many transactions are open. You will also see SAVE TRAN, which is used to create a transaction save point, and ROLLBACK TRAN, which is used to roll back either the changes to a transaction save point or the changes for the entire transaction.

Direct recursion

This topic is crucial to understand, because the default behavior of SQL Server with which you might already be familiar is changed in web apps. You must take this setting into account when writing data macro code, especially if you consider yourself to be an experienced developer with SQL Server.

In SQL Server, if a trigger on table A attempts to make a change to the data in table A, the trigger normally will not execute again to take into account the change made when the trigger first executes. This is nonrecursive behavior and is the default behavior in SQL Server.

However, to support certain data-macro scenarios, a web app has the default SQL Server setting changed to allow for recursive triggers. This means that if your trigger code on table A changes the data in table A, the trigger in table A will again be executed. This means that without a little care you will generate infinite loops that will exceed the 32 levels of recursion described in the last section, where we looked at indirect recursion.

Tip The idea of triggers that can execute other triggers is also called *nesting triggers*. You can find out more on this subject by searching online for *SQL Server Using Nested Triggers*.

If you write a trigger that updates a field without making any test to see whether the field needs to be updated, this will cause an infinite recursion. Because each update causes the trigger to fire again, the next level fires the trigger again, and so the process repeats. (See Figure 7-48 for an example of how the EditRecord macro action would cause this recursion problem.)

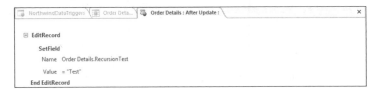

FIGURE 7-48 EditRecord macro action.

Attempting to edit a record in the datasheet will result in the same error message shown earlier in Figure 7-47, indicating that an endless loop will be generated.

You could test whether individual fields have been updated, but it is much simpler to add a new system field to the table that can then be used to detect whether the trigger has been called recursively. Figure 7-49 shows a field added to the table called RecursionFlag.

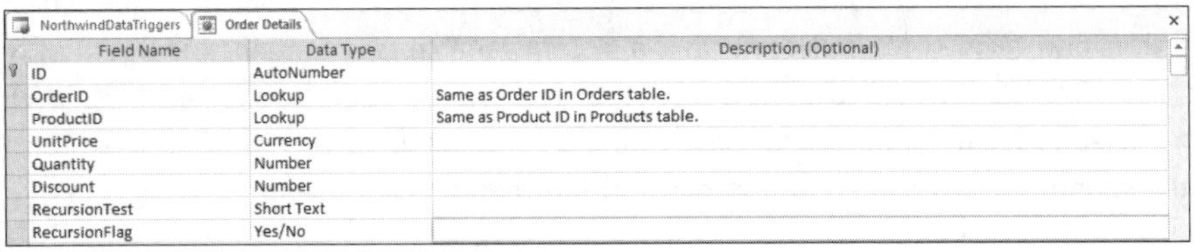

Field Name	Data Type	Description (Optional)
ID	AutoNumber	
OrderID	Lookup	Same as Order ID in Orders table.
ProductID	Lookup	Same as Product ID in Products table.
UnitPrice	Currency	
Quantity	Number	
Discount	Number	
RecursionTest	Short Text	
RecursionFlag	Yes/No	

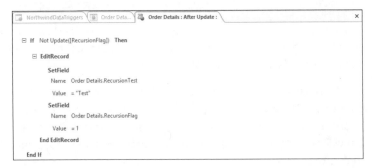

FIGURE 7-49 Adding a field to detect recursion.

In Figure 7-50, the macro code is modified so that it performs only the required operation if the RecursionFlag has not been updated. This is sufficient to prevent the endless loop.

FIGURE 7-50 Preventing recursion in a data macro.

An example of where you need a recursion flag is your needing to always update a field regardless of which other fields were changed by the user. In this situation, you could not use the update function because you cannot predict which field has changed. In general, you will find when writing complex macro code on events that having a flag to prevent recursion will simplify the design of your macro actions.

Presenting a view for printing

The normal page layout in the browser window is not suitable for printing. The layout includes the title bar at the top of the page and the table selector on the left side. The technique I describe in this section will enable you to construct a layout that can be used to construct a single-page layout suitable for printing.

In Figure 7-51, you can see the standard layout for a view.

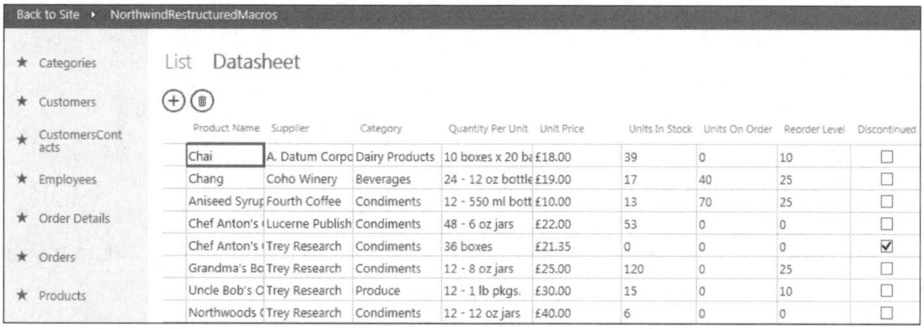

FIGURE 7-51 Example datasheet view showing titles and table selector.

If you look at a typical URL used when displaying a view, it has the following structure:

```
https://...default.aspx#Tile...
```

If you copy the link into a new browser window, change *default.aspx* to *viewer.aspx*, and then refresh the page, the top title bar will no longer be displayed on the page. The general form for the link is then

```
https://...viewer.aspx#Tile...
```

In Figure 7-52, you can see the resulting presentation when using viewer.aspx to display the view.

FIGURE 7-52 Example datasheet view hiding the top titles.

You next construct a blank standalone view called *ProductsDatasheetInSubView*, add the subview control to the view, and set the source object to display the view you want to use for the print layout, as shown in Figure 7-53.

FIGURE 7-53 Blank view containing a subview control configured to display a reporting view.

You can test this standalone presentation in the browser window by editing the URL to have the following form:

```
https://.. NorthwindRestructuredMacros/Viewer.aspx?page=ProductsDatasheetInSubView
```

This results in the presentation shown in Figure 7-54, where you can see that the layout is in a more suitable form for printing.

Product Name	Supplier	Category	Quantity Per Unit	Unit Price	Units In Stock	Units On Order	Reorder Level	Discontinued
Chai	A. Datum Corpc	Dairy Products	10 boxes x 20 ba	£18.00	39	0	10	☐
Chang	Coho Winery	Beverages	24 - 12 oz bottle	£19.00	17	40	25	☐
Aniseed Syrup	Fourth Coffee	Condiments	12 - 550 ml bott	£10.00	13	70	25	☐
Chef Anton's	Lucerne Publish	Condiments	48 - 6 oz jars	£22.00	53	0	0	☐
Chef Anton's	Trey Research	Condiments	36 boxes	£21.35	0	0	0	☑
Grandma's Bo	Trey Research	Condiments	12 - 8 oz jars	£25.00	120	0	25	☐
Uncle Bob's O	Trey Research	Produce	12 - 1 lb pkgs.	£30.00	15	0	10	☐
Northwoods C	Trey Research	Condiments	12 - 12 oz jars	£40.00	6	0	0	☐
Mishi Kobe N	Trey Research	Meat/Poultry	18 - 500 g pkgs.	£97.00	29	0	0	☑
Ikura	Trey Research	Seafood	12 - 200 ml jars	£31.00	31	0	0	☐
Queso Cabral	Trey Research	Dairy Products	1 kg pkg.	£21.00	22	30	30	☐
Queso Manch	Trey Research	Dairy Products	10 - 500 g pkgs.	£38.00	86	0	0	☐
Konbu	Trey Research	Seafood	2 kg box	£6.00	24	0	5	☐
Tofu	Trey Research	Produce	40 - 100 g pkgs.	£23.25	35	0	0	☐
Genen Shouy	Trey Research	Condiments	24 - 250 ml bott	£15.50	39	0	5	☐

FIGURE 7-54 Configuring the browser address to test the view ProductsDatasheetInSubView.

In this example, I show tabulation data that illustrates a limitation of this technique in terms of displaying a large tabulation of data, as can be seen by the right-side scroll bar.

Tip The layout can be improved by deleting the action bar icons and setting the view to read only. There is a restriction on the presentation to one page of information. If the view displays either too many records to fit on a page or is too wide, then regardless of how you size the subview control, the view will finally display horizontal and/or vertical scroll bars and restrict the information being displayed. This means that the technique is restricted to displaying a limited amount of data.

The technique described in this section is available from the SharePoint Store in a demonstration app called "Projects with Printable Sales Orders," which is shown in Figure 7-55. To follow along, download the app and complete the following steps:

1. In your site contents page, click to add an app.

2. Then select the SharePoint Store link.

3. Search or click on the Find An App box, and type **print**.

4. Then locate the application shown in Figure 7-55, and choose to Add It to select the application.

FIGURE 7-55 Locating "Project with Printable Sales Orders" in the SharePoint Store.

The app I just described is designed for use by a single user. In the remainder of this section, I will demonstrate how to create a modified version of the application that will support multi-user printing. The app has a Yes/No field on the Sales Orders table called Print Item. When printing a report, the Yes/No field for the record to display is set and the report uses this field to then filter the results to display a single record report.

Earlier in the chapter, I introduced the user-interface function *UserDisplayName()* as a means of identifying a user. You can make use of this function and construct a table that identifies each user and that user's print requests. Then when a user needs to print a record, you insert the primary key together with the user name in the print request table. The report is then based on a query that used the print request table to filter rows specific to the user. Figure 7-56 shows the design layout for the table used to hold print requests. Start by creating a table called tblPrintRequest in the application. The IDToReportOn field is a Number with subtype Whole number.

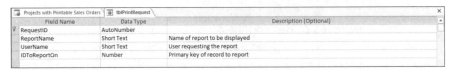

FIGURE 7-56 Table structure for tblPrintRequest.

Figure 7-57 shows an example of a print request. Later you will see how to create records in this table.

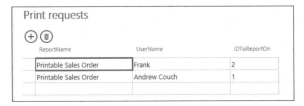

FIGURE 7-57 Sample data in tblPrintRequest.

The web app contains a view called Final Printable View that contains a subview where the source object is Printable Sales Order. This has been constructed using a similar technique to our earlier example shown previously in Figure 7-53.

Figure 7-58, shows the embedded SQL used in the Printable Sales Order view that filters the records to be displayed on the report. We saved the embedded SQL in a query called qrySalesOrderForUser.

1. Open the view Printable Sales Order in design.

2. Click on the Data Record Source, which is displayed as an [Embedded Query].

3. Change the embedded SQL to match that shown in Figure 7-58.

4. Add the table tblPrintRequest to the query grid, linking the IDToReportOn field to the ID field in the Sales Order table.

5. The existing query contains a Print Item field on the grid. This should be removed.

6. Select the UserName field from tblPrintRequest.

7. Select the ReportName field from tblPrintRequest, and add the criteria "printable sales order."

8. Save the query (by clicking the Save As icon on the design ribbon) with the name qrySalesOrderForUser. This makes it easier to check how the query is working.

9. Close the query, and answer yes when prompted to save the change in the record source property.

10. Save the view.

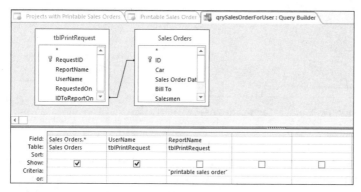

FIGURE 7-58 qrySalesOrderForUser used as the data source for the view Printable Sales Order.

Tip You cannot use the *UserDisplayName()* function in the query, because that function is available only in the user interface for UI macro code, and the query is saved and executed in the back-end Azure SQL Database.

The query qrySalesOrderForUser will be used to filter the Sales Orders table displaying a single selected report for the user. Next you need to add macro actions to create a record in tblPrintRequest when the user wants to print a sales order.

To present the report, the method will use a hyperlink to open the view called Final Printable View, which will use the viewer.aspx syntax. This raises another important point: when using the viewer. aspx syntax, any macro code on the view will not execute. However, macro code on the subview will execute. This means you can apply filtering on the Printable Sales Order view to restrict the records to match the current user, as shown in Figure 7-59.

1. Open the Printable Sales Order View in design view if it is not already open.

2. Click the On Load action for the view.

3. Below any existing macro actions, add a SetVariable macro action to set the variable *strUserName* to the value *UserDisplayName()*.

4. Add a RequeryRecords macro action with the where parameter set to *[qrySalesOrderForUser]. [UserName] = [strUserName]*.

5. Save and close the OnLoad action.

6. Save and close the view.

These additional macro actions will record the user name and requery the record source to filter the records for a particular user.

FIGURE 7-59 The On Load macro for the Printable Sales Order view.

The next step is to create a parameterized data macro that can delete any print requests for a user requesting a particular report and generate a new request for the record to be displayed. There is an existing data macro called *SetPrintableSalesOrder* that we will modify for our needs. Open this data macro, and edit the parameters and macro actions, as shown in Figure 7-60.

The data macro uses three input parameters, passing *paramID* as a number to identify the ID of a record to print, *paramUserName* as short text identifying the user, and *paramReportName* as short text indicating the requested report name. The data macro then uses a For Each macro loop with a *Where* condition to identify any records for the user and the requested report, and then it deletes the records. A final step in the macro uses the Create A Record In action to add a record to the tblPrintRequest table, setting the ReportName, Username, and IDToReportOn using the input parameters.

1. Delete the existing *SalesOrderID* parameter, and create the three new parameters.

2. Add a For Each Record In macro action for the table tblPrintRequest with a where parameter `[tblPrintRequest].[ReportName] = [paramReportName] And [tblPrintRequest].[UserName] = [paramUserName]`.

3. Add a DeleteRecord action inside the For Each Record action.

4. After the For Each Record In action, add a Create Record In macro action for the table tblPrintRequest.

5. Add three SetField macro actions inside the Create Record action to set the fields ReportName, UserName, and IDToReportOn to the appropriate parameters.

6. Save and close the data macro.

Parameters			
Name	Type	Description	Create Parameter
paramID	Number (No Decimal) ▼	ID of item to print	✕
paramUserName	Short Text ▼	Username requesting printing	✕
paramReportName	Short Text ▼	Name of report	✕

```
/*   Purge any records for this user and this report                                    */
⊟ For Each Record In   tblPrintRequest
      Where Condition   = [tblPrintRequest].[ReportName] = [paramReportName] and [tblPrintRequest].[UserName] = [paramUserName]
      DeleteRecord
            Record Alias
/*   Create a request for printing a record                                             */
⊟ Create a Record In   tblPrintRequest
      SetField
            Name   tblPrintRequest.ReportName
            Value   = [paramReportName]
      SetField
            Name   tblPrintRequest.UserName
            Value   = [paramUserName]
      SetField
            Name   tblPrintRequest.IDToReportOn
            Value   = [paramID]
```

FIGURE 7-60 Data macro *SetPrintableSalesOrder*.

The final step is to add a hyperlink for displaying the reporting view. You will edit an existing hyperlink in the web app. Because you cannot easily prevent the hyperlink from being activated before a new sales order is saved, and you cannot cancel the hyperlink action once the link is clicked, I altered the hyperlink control (which will be invisible by default) and added a button that will check for any illegal conditions and also save the user's record choice before making the hyperlink available. These controls are shown in Figure 7-61, where the hyperlink is selected. Below the link is a button with the caption Enable Hyperlink.

1. Open the view Sales Orders in design view.

2. Add a button below the hyperlink field, and give it the caption **Enable Hyperlink** and control name **cmdOpenHyperlink**.

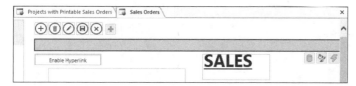

FIGURE 7-61 Design mode of the Sales Orders view, showing the hyperlink and command button controls.

Our view then has two sections of code. (I display only the code appropriate to the operation here and exclude any code associated with other activities, such as displaying totals.) Figure 7-62 shows the macro code for the On Current event in the view. This sets the hyperlink *Visible* property to *No* and the hyperlink *Value* to `Print this sales order#viewer.aspx?page=Final Printable View`.

1. Open the On Current event for the view.

2. Scroll to the bottom of the existing macro actions.

3. Add a new SetProperty macro action to set the visible property for the Hyperlink control to No.

4. Save and close the event.

5. Save the view changes.

FIGURE 7-62 On Current macro code for the Sales Orders view.

For the command button you added to the view earlier, add the macro code shown in Figure 7-63 to its On Click event. This code first checks to see if a new record is being entered. If that is the case, it displays a message box and stops the macro code from executing. If that is not the case, a new record then calls the *SetPrintableSalesOrder* data macro, passing in the ID of the record, user name, and report name. It then makes the hyperlink control visible, allowing the user to click on the hyperlink and display the report.

FIGURE 7-63 On Click macro code for the command button to enable the hyperlink.

6. Save the On Click event macro code.

7. Select the existing hyperlink control on the view and then go to the On Click macro action. The existing macro code contains an old reference to the RunDataMacro *SetPrintableSalesOrder*, which now has incorrect parameters. Delete this macro action because you already replaced it with the same macro action using different parameters in the code shown previously in Figure 7-63.

8. Save and close the view.

9. Refresh the web app in the browser window, and navigate on the Sales Order caption.

10. Display a sales order, and click on the Enable Hyperlink button. Then click on the Print This Sales Order hyperlink to display the sales order in a separate browser window.

Figure 7-64 shows the report in Print Preview in a browser window. In this layout, you need to adjust the report and the size of the subview to ensure that the data fits on a single page.

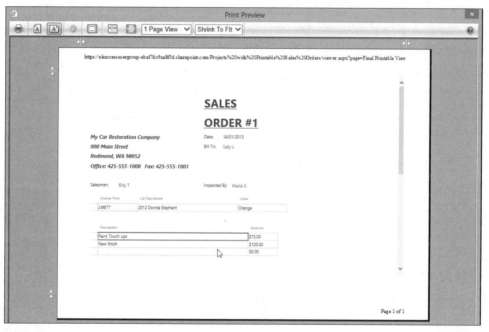

FIGURE 7-64 Print Preview view of the sales order.

> **Tip** You can also push this technique a little further to display more data from the view by zooming out on the data in the browser window before selecting Print Preview.

After running this sample code, you can also look on the tblPrintRequest table caption Datasheet View and you will see the values that the data macro writes into tblPrintRequest to enable the query qrySalesOrderForUser to filter and display the selected order record.

Creating a cross-tabulation of data

Access web apps do not support crosstab queries, which is a technique used in a desktop database to summarize data by creating new column headings which depend on the data. However, you can use data macro code to create a cross-tabulation presentation of data.

In this section, we return to using our web app created earlier in this chapter, NorthwindRestructuredMacros.

Figure 7-65 shows a totals query. (See Chapter 6, "Creating data sources by using queries," for more details on creating a totals query.) This query summarizes the order detail data grouped by OrderYear and OrderMonth.

1. Click the Query option from the Advanced menu on the ribbon.

2. Add the Orders and Order Details tables to the query grid.

3. Click the Totals icon on the ribbon.

4. Add a calculated field to the grid using the expression OrderYear: Year([Orderdate]), and leave the option Group By on the Total row.

5. Add another calculated field to the grid using the expression OrderMonth: Month([Orderdate]), and leave the option Group By on the Total row.

6. Add a third calculated field to the grid using the expression OrderValue: Sum([UnitPrice]*[Quantity]), and set the Total row to Expression.

7. Save the query with the name **qryDataForCrosstab**.

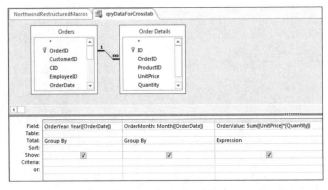

FIGURE 7-65 A query summarizing order data grouped by year and month.

In Figure 7-66, you can see the results displayed by the query by clicking on the View icon on the ribbon and selecting Datasheet View. To cross-tabulate this data, create column headings for the OrderMonth such that for each OrderYear you have a single record.

OrderYear	OrderMonth	OrderValue
1996	7	10441.6
1996	9	3298
1996	10	5749.8
1996	11	17663.2
1996	12	9318
1997	1	13879.6
1997	2	6294

FIGURE 7-66 Summarized data grouped by OrderYear and OrderMonth.

Figure 7-67 shows a new table called OrderSummaryCrosstab that you need to create to hold the cross-tabulated data. The table has a column UserName for recording the name of the user creating the summarized data (which will make the solution usable by several users at the same time) and a column YearOfOrder to record the year of the summarized results. Also, rather than having columns 1,2..12 for the OrderMonth, text (Jan, Feb...) are used for each order month. These are the Number general data types.

Field Name	Data Type
ID	AutoNumber
UserName	Short Text
YearOfOrder	Short Text
Jan	Number
Feb	Number
Mar	Number
Apr	Number
May	Number
Jun	Number
Jul	Number
Aug	Number
Sept	Number
Oct	Number
Nov	Number
Dec	Number

FIGURE 7-67 OrderSummaryCrosstab table for displaying the results of summarizing data.

Next, we need a data macro that can be used to clear any records in the OrderSummaryCrosstab table for a specific user. Start by creating a new data macro called **dmClearOrderSummaryCrosstab**, as shown in Figure 7-68. It has a single, short text parameter called *param_UserName* and uses a For Each loop to select all records in OrderSummaryCrosstab where UserName = param_UserName. Inside the loop, you execute the *DeleteRecord* action to delete each record.

FIGURE 7-68 A data macro to delete existing data from table OrderSummaryCrosstab.

Figure 7-69 displays part of the data macro *dmPopulateOrdersCrosstab*, which will be used when a user selects a year to create a summarized record in the OrderSummaryCrosstab table. This data macro has two parameters: a short text parameter called *param_UserName*, and an integer parameter called *param_OrderYear*.

FIGURE 7-69 A data macro to create the summarized data.

> **Tip** When creating a data macro and entering an action, the availability of the action text is sensitive to the context of where the action is entered. For example, when entering the *SetField* action in the sample code shown in Figure 7-69, the command is available when entering an action within the *EditRecord* loop, but not outside the loop. Care also needs to be taken with the indentation to ensure appropriate actions are positioned within the correct action block. For example, the *EditRecord* action is inside the Lookup A Record In loop, which in turn is nested within the For Each Record In action.

The data macro starts with a Create A Record In macro action, which adds a record to the table OrderSummaryCrosstab based on the two macro parameters for the user and order year.

The data macro then uses a For Each Record In action to filter the query *qryDataForCrosstab* with the *Where* clause qryDataCrosstab.OrderYear = [param_OrderYear]. This outer loop scans through all the matched records for the selected order year. Each record identified will be for a particular month.

Inside the outer loop, you have a Lookup A Record In loop, which filters the data in OrderSummaryCrosstab using the *Where* clause OrderSummaryCrosstab.[YearOfOrder] = param_OrderYear And OrderSummaryCrosstab.[UserName] = param_UserName. This locates the record you created with the first macro action.

Inside the second loop, you execute the *EditRecord* macro action. Then you have a set of tests using IF actions to decide which column needs to be updated. The IF macro action tests to see if `[qryDataForCrosstab].[OrderMonth]` = 1. If this is *true*, it uses the *SetField* action to set the data value in the appropriate column heading—in this case, `OrderSummaryCrosstab.Jan` = `[qryDataForCrosstab].[OrderValue]`. There are 12 IF statements in this section of the code: one for each month in a year. In Figure 7-70, I collapsed the macro actions to show 3 of the 12 comparisons.

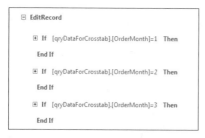

FIGURE 7-70 Collapsed macro actions for three of the tests in the *EditRecord* action.

To execute the macros, you create a blank view on the OrderSummaryCrosstab table caption called **CrossTabData** and add a text box called **txtYear** and a command button called **cmdCrosstab**, as shown in Figure 7-71.

1. Add a blank view called **CrossTabData** to the table caption OrderSummaryCrosstab.

2. Set the data record source to [No data source].

3. Add a label control to the view with a caption of **Year**.

4. Add a text box control to the view, and name it **txtYear**.

5. Add a command button control to the view, set the caption to **Generate Crosstab**, and name it **cmdCrosstab**.

6. Save the new view changes.

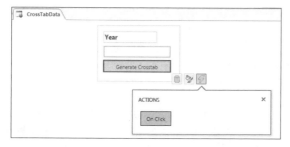

FIGURE 7-71 A blank view with a label, text box, and command button.

On the On Click event for the button cmdCrosstab, add the macro actions as shown in Figure 7-72.

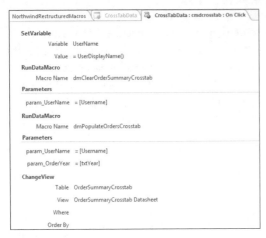

FIGURE 7-72 User-interface macro actions for generating the cross-tabulation of data.

The first macro action is *SetVariable*, which sets the variable *UserName* to the value of the built-in function *UserDisplayName()*.

The second macro action is *RunDataMacro*, which executes the data macro *dmClearOrderSummaryCrosstab*, passing the *UserName* as a parameter. This data macro deletes any records for the user.

The third macro action is *RunDataMacro*, which executes the data macro *dmPopulateOrdersCrosstab*, passing the *UserName* and *txtYear* as parameters.

A final macro action, *ChangeView*, takes the user to a view that displays the resulting data in a cross-tabulation layout.

After saving the changes to this macro and view and refreshing the web app in the browser, enter the year **1997** in the CrossTabData view and click the Generate crosstab button. This will then display the resulting cross-tabulation of data as shown in Figure 7-73.

Datasheet   CrossTabData

UserName	YearOfOrder	Jan	Feb	Mar	Apr	May	June	Jul	Aug	Sep	Oct	Nov	Dec
Andrew Couch	1997	13879.6	6294	1560	12990	4098.05	10060.25	13518	14639.8	12892.98	11649.78	7484.05	23374.86
		0	0	0	0	0	0	0	0	0	0	0	0

FIGURE 7-73 A view displaying the cross tabulation of data.

This is a good example of where you need to use data macros to work around features you might be accustomed to having on the desktop. Another example of where this technique could be applied is in generating a union of data—that is, bringing together two lists of data in a single view.

Side-loading a web app

In Chapter 2, I talked about how to upgrade and deploy a web app and briefly mentioned side-loading. In this section, we look at an example of side-loading in more detail. *Side-loading* is a technique for applying version upgrades to web apps. The advantage of using this technique over the technique that employs the App Catalog (described in Chapter 2 and another example of which is described in the next section) is that it is simpler; fewer steps are required to apply an upgrade.

The disadvantage of side-loading is that you need to lock the web app, a process that means that you cannot work with external data. This technique is better suited to upgrading a single web app, whereas the technique described in the next section is better suited to performing upgrades when you have a number of copies of the web app with different customers.

> **Tip** Side-loading can be used if you want to protect your design because you have a ommercial product. This is because side-loading requires the use of a locked web app. A customer cannot open the design in Access. However, this also means that the customer cannot perform a backup from the desktop or make use of external data connections, because the web app will be locked.

In this section, you will work with two sites. The first site could be your team site, and I will refer to this as the *Production site*. The second site could be a subsite on your team site, and I will call this the *Development site*.

Start by creating a new web app called **SideLoading** on your Production site. After creating the web app, open the web app to customize the design in Access. Add the table shown in Figure 7-74.

Field Name	Data Type
ID	AutoNumber
CustomerName	Short Text

FIGURE 7-74 Creating a table to test the side-loading upgrade feature.

This point is where you would start if you already had an existing web app containing data and wanted to lock the web app and start applying upgrades. From the file menu shown in Figure 7-75, save a snapshot of the web app. This will contain all your data if any data is present in the web app.

FIGURE 7-75 Saving the web app using Save As Snapshot.

When prompted, save this snapshot with the name **SideLoadingVersion1Snapshot**, as shown in Figure 7-76. (This snapshot can contain any existing data.)

FIGURE 7-76 Providing a package title for a snapshot.

From the file menu, save the web app a second time, but this time as a deployment using the option shown in Figure 7-77.

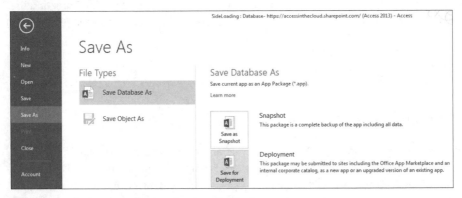

FIGURE 7-77 Saving the web app using Save For Deployment.

Name this file **SideLoadingVersion2Deployment**, as shown in Figure 7-78. (Ensure that the Locked check box is selected. Also, it is very important that you change the version from 1.0.0.0 to 2.0.0.0.)

Caution Side-loading requires the web app that is being upgraded to be locked. It is essential when creating the following deployment package that you select the locked option and ensure that the version number is greater than the version number of the web app you intend to upgrade.

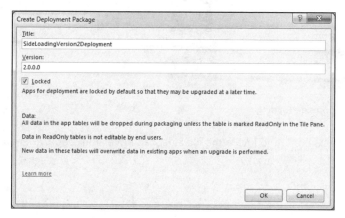

FIGURE 7-78 Configuring a title and options when saving a deployment.

Close access, return to your Production site, and delete the web app SideLoading.

Tip In addition to deleting the web app from the site contents, delete the entry in Apps For Testing if you are using an enterprise subscription. (Or you can delete the entry from the Apps In Testing, which will also delete the web app from the site contents.)

If you do not have an enterprise subscription, you will need to crack open the file SideLoadingVersion1Snapshot.app and edit the version number in the appmanifest.xml file from 1.0.0.0 to 1.0.0.1 before you will be able to upload the snapshot to your site. (The steps to do this are shown in Figures 7-95 and 7-96 later in this chapter.) This is also a procedure you should consider using if you find that you cannot upload a snapshot to a site after deleting the existing web app.

From your Production site, upload the web app SideLoadingVersion1Snapshot. You can then display the web app in the browser and enter some data as shown in Figure 7-79.

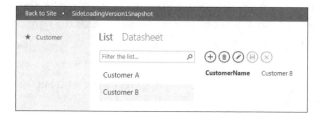

FIGURE 7-79 Entering test data after uploading the snapshot.

Click Back To Site. Upgrade the app from the Site Contents as shown in Figure 7-80.

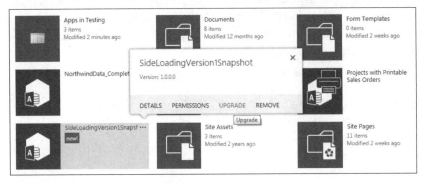

FIGURE 7-80 Upgrading a web app using side-loading.

After clicking on the Upgrade link, browse to locate the file SideLoadingVersion2Deployment.app as shown in Figure 7-81.

FIGURE 7-81 Selecting the upgrade app package.

You might have to wait 5 to 10 minutes or longer for the upgrade to be completed.

During the upgrade, the web app will be read-only to all users and the name of the web app will be shown as SideLoadingVersion2Deployment as shown in Figure 7-82.

FIGURE 7-82 Displaying the web app while updating.

After the upgrade is completed, open the web app in your browser. The data will still be present, but the web app will be locked. The Customize In Access option is not shown. (This is the right side cogs/actions icon that you normally see in the runtime.)

Tip At this point, you have prepared your web app for being upgraded. The web app will contain any data you had in the original snapshot and will now be locked.

You then need to go to a SubSite, which we will refer to as the *Development site*. (Refer back to Chapter 1, "Finding your way around Office 365," in the section "Creating sites and subsites," for details on creating a subsite.) Upload file SideLoadingVersion1Snapshot.app to the Development site. You can't load this onto your Production site because the product unique GUID would conflict. (Remember the rule is that on any TeamSite/SubSite, the GUID must be unique, and across different sites on the same subscription the combination of GUID and Version Number needs to be unique.) Because your Team Site Application is version upgraded to 2.0.0.0 and the snapshot is version 1.0.0.0, this will not cause a conflict.

> **Tip** At this point, you have created your development system, where you can prepare and test upgrades.

After you install this in your Development site, open the web app in Access and add a new field as shown in Figure 7-83.

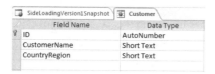

FIGURE 7-83 Adding an additional column in a development/test web app.

After saving the design changes, from the file menu create a new deployment package called **SideLoadingVersion3Deployment**, change the Version setting to 3.0.0.0, and select the Locked check box as shown in Figure 7-84.

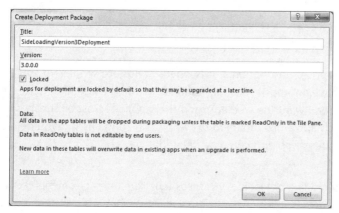

FIGURE 7-84 Configuring a title and options when saving a deployment for upgrading the web app.

Tip By default, when you see this screen the Locked check box is not selected. If you select the check box, after applying an upgrade to the web app, your upgrade will remain locked. If you do not select the box, after the upgrade, the web app will no longer be locked, but you will not be able to continue side-loading other changes.

At any future time for a locked web app, you can create a new deployment with the Locked check box not selected. After the upgrade, the web app will be unlocked. This means that applying locked deployments will keep the web app locked and allow you to continue making upgrades. If you create and apply an unlocked deployment and then want to make further upgrades, you need to go back to the beginning of this section and repeat all the steps to first lock the web app and then create a new development copy of the web app.

Now you can return to the Production site where you have the live system SideLoadingversion2Deployment and apply the upgrade SideLoadingVersion3Deployment by following the steps described in Figures 7-80 and 7-81.

If you have an enterprise subscription and look in the Apps In Testing area, which is shown in Figure 7-85, you will see the latest version of the web app in your team site and subsite.

	App Title		Version	Created	Modified
	NorthwindData_Completed	···	1.0.0.0	Monday at 11:10 AM	Monday at 11:10 AM
	NorthwindData	···	1.0.0.0	Tuesday at 10:34 AM	Tuesday at 10:34 AM
	SideLoadingVersion3Deployment	···	3.0.0.0	Yesterday at 12:44 PM	Yesterday at 1:08 PM
	SideLoadingVersion1Snapshot	···	1.0.0.0	Yesterday at 12:57 PM	Yesterday at 12:57 PM

Apps in Testing
⊕ new app to deploy

FIGURE 7-85 Displaying the Apps In Testing area after upgrading a web app.

Tip If you don't have an Enterprise subscription, this is where things are simpler. In an enterprise solution, you will have an Apps In Testing folder. Don't delete anything here without being sure that you don't want the web app, and that applies across all subsites. Although you can delete a web app while retaining the Apps In Testing entry, if you delete the apps in testing any dependent web app could be deleted.

If you receive an error when upgrading or loading an application, from the site contents click on the web app and then click on the details link shown previously in Figure 7-80. This will then display the screen shown in Figure 7-86. Clicking on the link (if displayed) next to Upgrade Errors or Install Errors will display further details about any recorded errors.

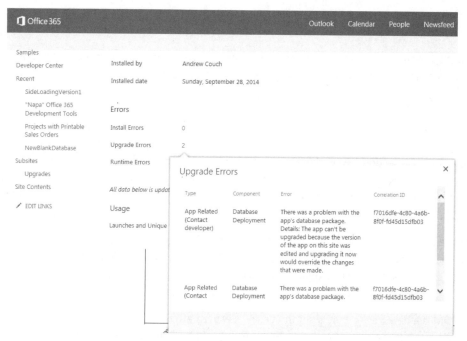

FIGURE 7-86 Displaying information on upgrade errors.

In this example, I used version numbers 1.0.0.0, 2.0.0.0, and 3.0.0.0, but I could have used version numbers such as 1.0.0.0, 1.0.0.1, and 1.0.0.2. As long as the sequence of version numbers is increasing, the numbering is OK. In our example, I also changed the name of the title of the web app as I created the snapshot and deployment files. This means that when you upload or upgrade the web app, the title changes. I could have kept the same title at each stage and given the files different names. That would have meant that the title for the web app in Office 365 would have remained unchanged.

> **Tip** If you want to change the title of a package, you can change the package file extension from *.app* to *.zip* and then edit the appmanifest.xml file and change the title tag in that file. Once you have made changes, the .zip file should be renamed back to the .app file extension. Look back to Chapter 1 in the section "Editing a web app package" to see the steps for doing this.

A second issue you might have observed is that when we performed our upgrade, the name of the web app changed. Again, this is controlled by the name you provide for the app package. In our example, I wanted to make sure you could see every step in the upgrade process, but in a real application you could keep the same name when creating the package but retitle the physical file or folder in which it was held to make sure you do not get confused.

In summary, side-loading is a simple approach to supporting the software design life cycle, where you need to test your design changes before deploying a change to a live system. But side-loading is better suited to a one-off client site, where you could suspend external data for the duration of developing and making a change.

In the next section, we will look at a more advanced approach to upgrading a web app that will allow you to maintain external data connections while still upgrading the web app.

On Deploy Macro

In Chapter 2, in the section "Upgrading and deploying a web app," I introduced the new features for applying upgrades to an existing web app from a development copy of the web app. In this section, I explain the role of the On Deploy Macro (ODM). This is also sometimes called the *On Deploy Data Macro (ODDM)*.

In this section, you will see both how to use the ODM to apply upgrade steps to your data and use the App Catalog to upgrade the web app. I will provide a set of steps similar to those in the last section on side-loading, but one significant difference is that you do not need to have the web app locked. This means you can continue to use links to external data.

The ODM is a data macro that is automatically executed after any schema and other changes have been applied in the upgrade process. If a field is renamed or deleted during the upgrade process, all the data in the field will be lost before the ODM macro is executed.

The ODM can be used to migrate data between tables if you change the database schema, but you need to leave the removal of any old fields or tables until a subsequent version because you cannot use the ODM to restructure tables.

Another use for the ODM is to create test or reference data. In a Deployment package, data in a table is replaced only if a table is locked. If a table is locked, the data cannot be edited through a view (although it can be edited using a data macro).

Caution When you are upgrading a web app using the deployment package, Access prevents upgrading of the app to an earlier version number. You cannot apply a V2 upgrade to a V3 web app. But Access does not prevent you from skipping a version number and upgrading a V2 web app to V4. There is no provision for preventing this kind of upgrade.

The main area to be careful with is if you plan to remove old structures. When attempting to run V3 upgrade steps, you might find that V4 already tidied up and removed the old tables. You could also consider adding your own locked table to hold a version number to better allow for processing logic during an upgrade.

The process of upgrading described in this section is quite complicated, so I will break the steps down into several sequences. The first sequence of operations places your web app under SharePoint version control:

1. Create a web app called **ODM_ExampleV1** (version 1.0.0.0).

2. In the web app, create a table called **tblVersion** for holding details of the software version. Then, after entering a single record, lock the tblVersion table. (This means data can no longer be changed in that table.)

3. Next create a Customer data table into which users can enter data.

4. Next create a snapshot backup of the web app (version 1.0.0.1), and then delete the web app. You do this to prepare to put the web app under SharePoint version control.

5. To activate version control, upload your snapshot to the App Catalog (version 1.0.0.1).

6. Then create a web app in your site based upon the master copy of the web app that was loaded into the App Catalog.

7. Enter data in the Customer data table. (Once the app is under SharePoint version control, I will explain the subsequent steps required to upgrade the application.)

This process is similar to the initial steps for preparing for side-loading, except you do not need to lock the web app and you use the App Catalog to put the web app under version control.

In the following example, you start by creating a new empty web app on your team site called **ODM_ExampleV1**. Then you add a table called tblVersion for holding version information, as shown in Figure 7-87. When adding the VersionNumber field of data type Numeric, change the default subtype to be a whole number.

Field Name	Data Type
ID	AutoNumber
VersionNumber	Number
VersionDate	Date/Time

FIGURE 7-87 Creating a table for holding the software version number.

Next open the table (or switch to Datasheet preview) and add a record for the initial software version, as shown in Figure 7-88.

FIGURE 7-88 Entering an initial version number for the web app.

Close the datasheet. Then use the table selector to lock the table. This prevents data from being directly edited in the table. The Lock setting is shown in Figure 7-89.

FIGURE 7-89 Setting the table Lock property.

Now create a second table called Customers, which will be used later to show how data in a table is preserved and can be updated using the ODM. In Figure 7-90 you can see a sample table. At this point, you don't need to add any sample data to the table.

FIGURE 7-90 Sample table for holding customer data.

From the file menu, save a snapshot of the web app as shown in Figure 7-91.

FIGURE 7-91 Creating a snapshot of the web app containing data.

You will then be prompted to save the snapshot. I entered the title **ODM_ExampleV1** in Figure 7-92.

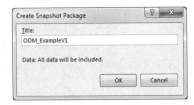

FIGURE 7-92 Adding a title for the snapshot.

Following this, select a suitable file location where the package will be saved.

Close Access and, from the site menu, remove the web app you just created, as shown in Figure 7-93.

FIGURE 7-93 Removing the web app from the Site Contents.

If you are using an enterprise subscription, make sure you also remove the web app from the Apps In Testing area as shown in Figure 7-94. If you remove the entry in Apps In Testing, this will automatically remove the web app.

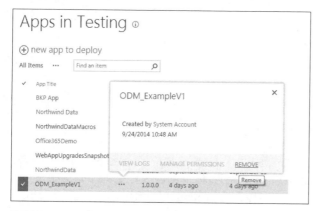

FIGURE 7-94 Removing the web app from Apps In Testing.

Before you upload the snapshot, you need to edit the version number. This is required. If you don't edit the version number, the snapshot will fail at a later step because the default version 1.0.0.0 is already in use. Even when you delete the old version, the following steps are required. Start by renaming the file ODM_ExampleV1.app to **ODM_ExampleV1.zip**, and then open the .zip file to display the contents, as shown in Figure 7-95. Copy the file appmanifest.xml to your desktop or another suitable location.

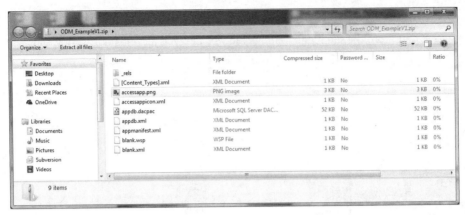

FIGURE 7-95 Renaming the app file to have a .zip file extension, and then opening the .zip file.

Open the appmanifest.xml file with Notepad, and change the Version setting to 1.0.0.1, as shown in Figure 7-96. Then copy this file into the ODM_ExampleV1.zip file, replacing the existing file, and rename the file back to **ODM_ExampleV1.app**.

FIGURE 7-96 Editing the appmanifest.xml file, and changing the version number.

You then follow the steps described in Chapter 2, in the "Upgrading and deploying a web app" section, to upload the snapshot to the App Catalog. Refer to Figures 2-41, 2-42, and 2-43 in Chapter 2 for the set of steps to be followed to do this. After completing these steps, your App Catalog should look like Figure 7-97.

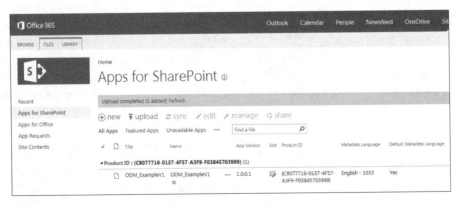

FIGURE 7-97 The snapshot uploaded into the App Catalog.

From your site, you can now add a new app based on the snapshot that was uploaded from the App Catalog. When choosing to add the app, select the From Your Organization item on the left side menu shown in Figure 7-98. This displays the web app that was uploaded into the App Catalog. Click on the app to select this, and choose to trust the application if prompted.

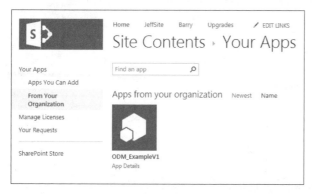

FIGURE 7-98 Loading the web app from your organization apps.

Once this is completed, you can enter some sample data in the web app that has been created in your site, as shown in Figure 7-99. I have entered two records in the Customer table. I will refer to this web app as our *live application*, because in our example users are using it to enter data.

FIGURE 7-99 Entering sample data in the Customer table.

In the next sequence of steps, you will make a copy of the web app and continue your development work in the copy. Then you will use the development copy to upgrade the web app. Here are the steps you need to perform:

1. Create a new snapshot of the live web app.

2. Edit the appmanifest in the snapshot you created to change the version number to **2.0.0.0**.

3. Upload the snapshot to a different subsite, and make new design changes in the development copy of the web app.

4. Alter the design of the development web app. Then create a deployment copy of the new development work version 2.0.0.1.

5. Upload the deployment copy to the App Catalog.

6. Upgrade the live application from version 1.0.0.1 to **2.0.0.1**.

Start by customizing the web app from the previous section in Access and creating a snapshot. You will then be prompted to save the snapshot. Save the snapshot as a file called **ODM_ExampleV1_Deployment.app**, as shown in Figure 7-100.

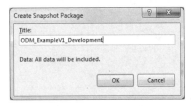

FIGURE 7-100 Creating a new snapshot of the live web app.

Next proceed as described earlier to again edit the appmanifest.xml file. Change the file extension of to a .zip file, open the file, and extract the appmanifest.xml file. Then change the version number to **2.0.0.0** as shown in Figure 7-101.

```
appmanifest.xml - Notepad
File  Edit  Format  View  Help
<?xml version="1.0" encoding="utf-8"?>
<App
    ProductID="c8077716-0137-4f57-a3f9-f03845703999"
    Type="Access"
    Version="2.0.0.0"
    SharePointMinVersion="16.0.0.0"
    Name="ODM_ExampleV1_Development" xmlns="http://schemas.microsoft.com/sharepoint/2012/app/manifest">
  <Properties>
    <StartPage>~appWebUrl/default.aspx</StartPage>
    <Title>ODM_ExampleV1_Development</Title>
    <WebTemplate
```

FIGURE 7-101 Changing the version number in the appmanifest.xml file.

Replace the appmanifest.xml file in the zip file with the new appmanifest.xml file, and change the package extension from .zip to **.app**.

Now that you have your edited app package, install this app into a different subsite than the one you have been using as shown in Figure 7-102.

FIGURE 7-102 Installing the web app to your development subsite.

Next, open the copy of ODM_ExampleV1_Development within Access and customize the design. Create a new table for recording a list of countries/regions called CountryRegion, as shown in Figure 7-103.

Field Name	Data Type
ID	AutoNumber
CountryRegion	Short Text

FIGURE 7-103 Creating a table holding a list of CountryRegions.

Now alter the design of the existing Customer table to look up a CountryRegion from the CountryRegion table, as shown in Figure 7-104.

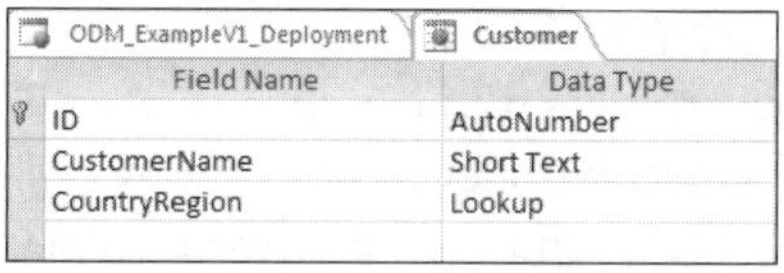

Field Name	Data Type
ID	AutoNumber
CustomerName	Short Text
CountryRegion	Lookup

FIGURE 7-104 The customer table with a new CountryRegion lookup.

Then unlock the tblVersion table, edit the row by changing the VersionNumber and versionDate for the new software version as shown in Figure 7-105, and then lock the table again.

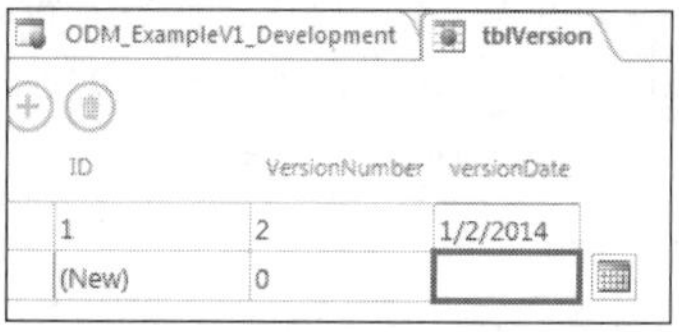

ID	VersionNumber	versionDate
1	2	1/2/2014
(New)	0	

FIGURE 7-105 Editing a new version number to tblVersion.

After you upgrade the version number, you need to again lock tblVersion; otherwise, after the upgrade, tblVersion data will not be updated and the ODM you are about to develop will not work.

You will now create an ODM that will create a new entry, USA, in the CountryRegion table, and then set that as a default value against any existing customer records. This will be executed only as part of upgrading the software to version 2.

From the advanced menu shown in Figure 7-106, select On Deploy Macro.

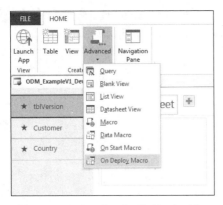

FIGURE 7-106 Creating the On Deploy Macro option.

Figure 7-107 shows the start of the data macro code. You look up a record in tblVersion with a *Where* clause to filter for VersionNumber = 2. When this is *true*, the inner sections of code will be executed. Because the table is locked, during the upgrade the table and all its data will be replaced, which means it will contain the value of 2 for the VersionNumber when the ODM executes.

> **Tip** If you need to know the existing value for the VersionNumber in the web app you are upgrading, you can find out by reading and writing to the table. However, you do not want to have the table locked, because that means the table will be replaced by the time the ODM macro executes. Remember the ODM executes after the data tables have been upgraded. For a locked table, both the table and data are replaced before the ODM is executed.

After the upgrade, CountryRegion will be empty. Using the ODM you create a record in CountryRegion, setting the field CountryRegion.CountryRegion = 'USA'.

Because during development you have been adding and removing records from CountryRegion, you cannot guarantee that the ID will be 1. The next step is to look up the newly entered record in CountryRegion where CountryRegion = 'USA' and set a local variable called *IngCountryID* to the associated primary key ID value.

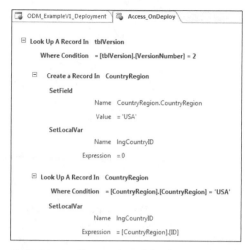

FIGURE 7-107 First section of the data macro code.

The second part of the data macro is shown in Figure 7-108. This consists of a For Each Record action that loops through any records in Customer, setting the CountryRegion field of the Customer table to the *local* variable *IngCountryID*, which was set in the previous macro steps.

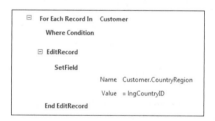

FIGURE 7-108 Looping through the customer records and assigning the CountryRegion foreign key.

In Figure 7-109, I show the macro code blocks collapsed, to make clear the required indentation levels for the macro commands. This shows that inside the Lookup A Record In tblVersion, there is a block to create a CountryRegion record, a block to look up the CountryRegion record, and a For Each loop for processing the Customer records.

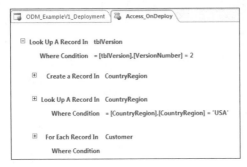

FIGURE 7-109 The indentation levels for the macro actions in the On Deploy data macro.

Save your changes to the ODM macro. You also need to test the ODM. In Figure 7-110, you add a button to the tblVersion view that will be used to execute the *RunDataMacro* action for the macro called *Access_OnDeploy*.

FIGURE 7-110 Adding a button to a view to test the data macro.

In Figure 7-111, you can see after running the data macro that the customer records have been correctly assigned and the new CountryRegion record has been created.

FIGURE 7-111 After running the ODM, data has been correctly assigned new values.

Next you create a deployment package called ODM_ExampleV2_Deployment with version 2.0.0.1, as shown in Figure 7-112. Then you upload this to the App Catalog (following the same steps as performed earlier when you uploaded your initial snapshot of the web app). Then, from the site containing the live system, you apply the upgrade.

Start by creating the new deployment package.

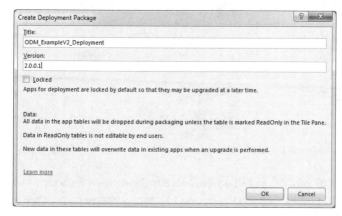

Figure 7-112 Creating a deployment package.

Next upload the deployment to the App Catalog. In Figure 7-113, I show the App Catalog, which contains the original app version 1.0.0.1 and the new deployment upgrade version 2.0.0.1.

FIGURE 7-113 The App Catalog with both versions of the web app.

From the site contents page of the first app you started with shown in Figure 7-114, click on the ellipses button on the web app. This will display a popup window. Clicking on the About link in the popup will allow the web app to be upgraded.

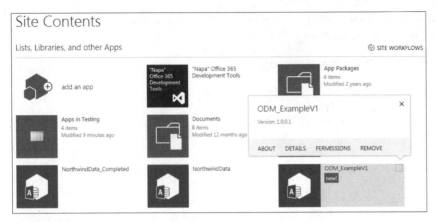

FIGURE 7-114 Upgrading the web app from the site contents page.

In Figure 7-115, you can see the details for upgrading the web app. The screen shows the title for the upgrade. On the right is a Get It button. Click on the button to upgrade the web app. (You might also be prompted to confirm that you trust the application.)

FIGURE 7-115 The App Catalog with both versions of the web app.

The app has been automatically updated. When you open the app, you can see (as shown in Figure 7-116) how the existing records have been assigned the correct value for CountryRegion by the ODM.

FIGURE 7-116 The CountryRegion List view displayed in the web browser.

Using an alias with a macro action

As you worked through more complex examples in this chapter, you might have seen that two commonly used data macro actions, For Each Record In and Lookup A Record In, have options to add an alias to the command. In Figure 7-117, you can see an example of this optional setting for the macro action in the bottom right corner.

FIGURE 7-117 A Lookup A Record In macro command with the Add Alias option.

An *alias* is simply a shortened name, abbreviation, or synonym for referring to the object in the action. In our example, if you create an alias for the name OrderSummaryCrosstab, you can use the alias in the Where Condition and all other nested operations rather than restating the full name.

In Figure 7-118, I added the alias *os* for OrderSummaryCrosstab. Notice that the Where Condition has now been amended to refer to the table by the alias and not the full object name. This is not optional; it is mandatory if you use an alias.

FIGURE 7-118 Adding an alias to a macro action.

One key advantage of using an alias is that for any nested macro actions, you can save on typing by referring to the outer object using the alias rather than the fully qualified object name. However, the restriction is that when you write any nested macro code, you can only refer to the outer object using the alias. Once you start to use an alias, you will be compelled to continue using the alias.

> **Tip** The Where Condition in a macro action is limited to 255 characters. If you are using queries that have a long name, you can easily run out of available spaces in the Where Condition to add your criteria. So when working with nested and more complex data macros, using an alias when you start writing code will save you a lot of pain later if you need several items in the *Where* clause. It is tempting to believe when you are editing a macro and using an alias, that Access is wrong if it displays an error message indicating the macro cannot be saved. However, in every situation where I have seen this, it is because I made a mistake and did not use the alias. Once you start using an alias, you must continue to do so.

If you look under the hood in Azure SQL Database at the resulting stored procedure that is generated, you will notice that using an alias does not alter the resulting TSQL that is generated, with the exception of trace commands, which can be used to debug a data macro (stored procedures) execution. This feature is an aspect of the graphical interface, which is provided to simplify your experience of writing the data macro code.

Summary

In this chapter, you saw the macro programming capabilities in a web app. You also saw that macro programming involves creating two distinct kinds of macros: user-interface macros, which have one set of actions, and data macros, which have a different set of actions.

Macros can be written inside an object—for example, behind a control on a view—or in an event on a table. As an alternative to embedding the macro code, a macro can be created as a standalone object.

Data macros execute as code in the Microsoft Azure SQL Database as either triggers (when written as an event on a table) or as stored procedures (when written as a standalone data macro). Of particular note are the standalone data macros, which are called *named data macros* and can accept input parameters and provide return values to other macros that execute the named data macro. Data macros also have features for tracing their execution. You also saw an example of the On Deploy macro, which has a special role in supporting more demanding upgrade scenarios.

By contrast, the execution of user-interface macros takes place in the browser. These macros can also call the standalone data macros, but they cause the embedded data macros to execute when an action updates, inserts, or deletes data. Data macros cannot execute user-interface macros.

In Chapter 9, we will look in more detail at the Microsoft Azure SQL Database platform, which contains the data macros.

CHAPTER 8

Managing security and a public-facing web app

In this chapter:

In this chapter, we will look at how to make a web app on a public-facing website available in Office 365. This leads on to a more detailed discussion of how to manage security, which should give you some useful ideas for your own applications. The example shown in this chapter is for a site created for the UK Access User Group; the completed web app is also available with the companion content for this book.

Creating a public website

In Chapter 1, "Finding your way around Office 365," I described the different areas in Office 365 where you can place a web app. One topic I did not discuss in that chapter was a public site.

On your sites menu, next to the Team Site icon, is an icon for creating your public-facing website in Office 365, as shown in Figure 8-1.

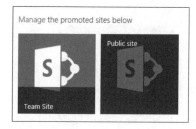

FIGURE 8-1 Site menu icon for developing a public site.

Once you create a site, you can make it available for others to see, and also map a domain name for use with Office 365 and the public site.

When displaying the site, you will need to sign in to display the standard menus for managing Office 365. (Click the Sign In link on the top right of your site to display the site menus.) You can then click the drop-down settings icon (at the top right on the menus), as shown in Figure 8-2, to manage the detailed contents and settings for your site.

FIGURE 8-2 Settings menu for managing the public website.

After choosing Site Settings, you can then choose Site Permissions. The resulting screen is shown in Figure 8-3. In this screen, you can see a new group, Anonymous Users, which has been automatically provided on the public site.

FIGURE 8-3 Site permissions for the public website.

Tip Anonymous users will not need to sign in to Office 365 and will have read-only permissions on a web app. For read/write permissions, a user needs to sign in to the Office 365 site.

Creating a public-facing web app in Office 365

When you go back to the Site Contents page, the settings menu will change to show the options in Figure 8-4. The Add An App option can be used to upload your web app package into the public site. (Alternatively, you can create a blank Access web app.)

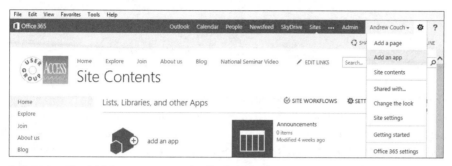

FIGURE 8-4 The Add An App menu option from the Site Contents page.

After you add your web app, you need to hover the mouse over the web app icon, right-click, and select Copy Shortcut, as shown in Figure 8-5.

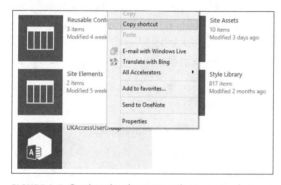

FIGURE 8-5 Getting the shortcut path to your web app.

Your shortcut should look similar to the following:

```
https://ukaccessusergroup-public.sharepoint.com/_layouts
/15/appredirect.aspx?instance_id={7B06C82E-9CF6-4916-99AA-31FE49F60C5F}
```

> **Tip** Your shortcut must look like our example and contain *instance_id*; otherwise, the link will not provide you with read/write permissions when logging in as an Office 365 user. The exact form of the URL is very important.

The final step is to customize one of the pages on your public website by adding a hyperlink to the web app URL, as shown in Figure 8-6.

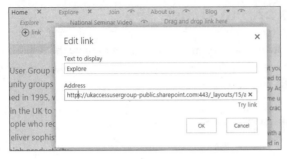

FIGURE 8-6 Adding a hyperlink to the web app.

By following this process of uploading the web app and creating a link, you can have a link on the public website that will launch your web app. If you need to provide documents and files that can be downloaded by anonymous users and other users, these files can be uploaded into folders in the public website Site Contents area. You can then provide links either on site pages or from inside the web app using hyperlinks directed to the Site Contents folders.

Managing security in a public web app

In Chapter 1, in the section "Sharing a web app with external users," I discussed configuring security in a web app. In this section, I will discuss topics specific to managing the security in a public-facing web app. I also will provide you with ideas for adding your own additional layer of table-driven security, which can be used with a public-facing web app and a web app placed on any other kind of site.

In this section, I provide a short case study of creating a security model for a web app that is being placed on a public-facing website. I start by identifying three types of users:

- **Public** Anonymous, read-only access is required for the general public.

- **Administrator** Full permissions are provided for administrators.

- **Members** Members have limited read-write permissions on the data.

By placing the web app in the Public Site area in Office 365, you allow anonymous users to have read-only access to the web app without needing a login.

As long as the URL has been correctly constructed as described in the previous section, administrators (such as the site-owner account) and a limited number of external users have read/write or design permissions according to how you set up the individual account permissions.

In our example, I chose not to use external users for the user group members, because it would have increased the amount of work required to administer security. For the members, I set up a single Windows Live account (and circulated the details to the members). This account has contribute permissions on the website. You could then further limit permissions inside the web app to specific areas of data. With these basics in place, you can then refine the security using a table-driven method for identifying users based on their own email addresses. This provides further control over editing data, because the email address must be validated against a known list of members' email addresses.

This approach would not prevent a user from pretending to be someone else in the group, but because you have a closed community of friendly members, this is sufficient security for your application. You also want to avoid managing individual passwords. This method can easily be generalized so that each member has an individual password if you later decide that is necessary.

The first management table required is a system table, which will hold any external or internal Office 365 email accounts and flag appropriate accounts as having administrator privileges, as shown in Figure 8-7.

ID	WindowsLiveAccount	Administrator
1	user@site.net	☐
2	admin@site.onmicrosoft.com	☑
(New)		☐

FIGURE 8-7 Creating a table to identify Office 365 logins and control permissions.

Next you construct a table containing all the membership email addresses, as shown in Figure 8-8. This table is used to validate a member, and it also acts as a lookup mechanism for tagging records in specific tables as being available to edit by a particular member.

UserID	UserEmailAddress
2	user1@histsite.com

FIGURE 8-8 A table for validating members' email addresses.

Next, add macro code in the On Start macro, which will identify the current user's Windows Live login and match it against the values in tblSystem, setting the following global variables:

- **gAdministrator** A flag indicating whether the account has administrator rights

- **gAnonymous** A flag indicating whether the account is anonymous, read only

- **gUserID** The member's *UserID* if a member validated her identity with an email address

Before turning your attention to the On Start macro, create a standalone data macro to look up the Windows Live login in tblSystem (shown previously in Figure 8-7). This is shown in Figure 8-9.

> **Tip** There are two useful functions for getting information on users: *UserDisplayName()*, which returns a user's logon name, and *UserEmailAddress()*, which returns the user's email address. For anonymous users, the email address will be blank and the user name is "Anonymous User."

The data macro takes a single text parameter called *WindowsLiveEmail* and looks up the record in tblSystem. You declare a local variable named *IsAdministrator* and read the appropriate flag in tblSystem for the matched record. Then the data macro returns this value to the calling macro code (which will be in the On Start macro).

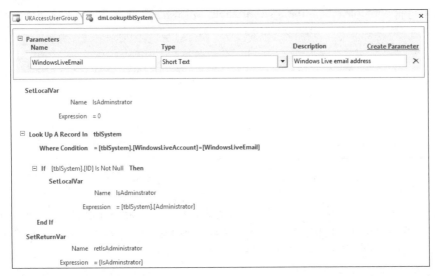

FIGURE 8-9 The data macro *dmLookuptblSystem*, which is used for identifying user permissions.

The first part of the On Start macro is shown in Figure 8-10. This macro sets the three global variables to indicate a user's unique identifier, to flag whether the account is anonymous, and to flag whether a user is an administrator. For anonymous users, the *UserDisplayName()* function returns the text "Anonymous User" and sets the *gAnonymous* variable to *1* (true) and the *gAdministrator* variable to *0* (false). Setting the last variable is not essential, but it helps when reading through the code. The last step is to use the *StopMacro* command. (This is important. You will see that the next code section uses a data macro, and anonymous users cannot execute data macros.)

Tip Take great care that you correctly spell global variable names. There is no spelling checker in the environment, and an incorrectly spelled name will result in an error indicating that a screen control cannot be identified with the name. Global variables cannot be referenced without having first set the variable to a value.

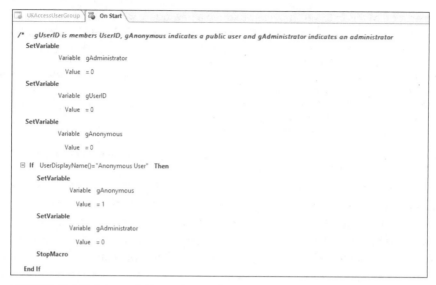

FIGURE 8-10 Initializing variables and managing anonymous users.

The second part of On Start macro is shown in Figure 8-11. This code uses the *RunDataMacro* command to execute the data macro *dmLookuptblSystem*, passing in the parameter *WindowsLiveEmail* set to get the user's logon email address using the system function *UserEmailAddress()*.

FIGURE 8-11 Using a data macro to determine whether a user is an administrator.

I highly recommended that you get used to using Microsoft SQL Server Management Studio (SSMS) to help debug and test the resulting data macro code. SSMS makes the whole business of debugging data macros an easily undertaken task. The trace table features in the product are good, but in most cases you can spot errors by directly inspecting the code (TSQL) generated from the data macro code in Azure SQL.

In the following short extract from the definition of the data macro, you can see that the stored procedure is defined as expecting to return a single OUTPUT parameter and being able to accept a single input parameter:

```
CREATE PROCEDURE [Access].[dmLookuptblSystem]
    @retIsAdministrator Decimal(28,6) OUTPUT,
    @WindowsLiveEmail NVarChar(4000)
WITH EXECUTE AS 'AccessWriter'
AS
BEGIN
```

To test the execution of this in SSMS, you need to open a new query window and declare variables to return values from the stored procedure. Use the following code to test the new stored procedure:

```
declare @retIsAdministrator Decimal(28,6)
declare @WindowsLiveEmail NVarChar(4000)
set @WindowsLiveEmail = 'user@testsite.com'
exec [Access].dmLookuptblSystem @retIsAdministrator
    OUTPUT,@retIsAnonymous OUTPUT,@WindowsLiveEmail
select @retIsAdministrator, @retIsAnonymous
go
```

> **Tip** Debugging data macro code is quite easy, because you have both tracing features and SSMS. Debugging UI macro code, on the other hand, is very challenging; the only way to debug the code is by using message boxes. Thankfully, most UI macro code is quite simple, and your biggest problem is likely to be incorrectly spelling variable names and forgetting to set them to a value before using them in another part of the application.

One of the simplest operations you will want to perform is ensuring that only administrators can view certain parts of the application. To do this, name the table caption for tblSystem "Admin Only," and then create the following standalone UI macro. The result is that if a user selects the table selector and is not an administrator, he will be redirected back to another view called Introduction on the table calendar. In Figure 8-12, the macro code tests the global variable *gAdministrator* and redirects any nonadministrator using the *ChangeView* macro to a safe point on the table selector and displays a different view. To use this macro, you execute the *RunMacro* command in the embedded macro code behind the On Load event. This displays the first view defined on the tblSystem table selector.

FIGURE 8-12 Using a standalone UI macro to redirect nonadministrators.

> **Tip** The *ChangeView* macro command can be a challenging macro to work with because it does not provide IntelliSense for either the Table or View arguments. Also, because the macro designer is modal, you have to close the macro designer before checking on the name of the table and view. When a name is incorrect, the macro command does not generate an error; instead, it fails to work correctly.

Another useful standalone UI macro to create is one that hides all the action bar commands. This means that on lists and blank views you can easily hide all the buttons for changing the data. This macro can be executed from the On Load event on a view. I show an example of this macro in Figure 8-13. Note in the figure I collapsed the *SetProperty* macro commands for clarity. The reason I did not directly use the *gAdministrator* variable in the *SetProperty* commands but instead used the *glState* variable is to make it easier to reuse the code. It is easier to copy and paste this code to create other standalone macro actions that use different logic other than the value held in *gAdministrator* to decide whether to hide or show the buttons.

FIGURE 8-13 Using a standalone UI macro to hide the built-in action bar buttons.

> **Tip** Although you can use a similar technique with a datasheet view to hide buttons, you need to take further actions to prevent a user from saving changes, deleting records, or adding records. (Because a user does not use a button to allow editing of data in the datasheet, there is no button to hide). To prevent a user editing the data, you could create a table After Update trigger to execute a *RaiseError* macro command, but this would be complicated. In this situation, it is easier to create a separate datasheet view for administrators and users, and make the user's datasheet read/only.

Figure 8-14 shows a UI macro that is similar to the last example, with the exception that users can edit a record as long as the record is marked as belonging to the user. Each record has a [UserID] field that can be set when the record is created. Earlier in this section, I defined a global variable to identify the user *gUserID*. The macro then compares the current user ID *gUserID* against the field value [UserID] to decide whether buttons to change the record are available to the user. This macro, unlike the last example, is executed from the On Current event in a view.

```
UKAccessUserGroup    ui_ActionButtons_MemberEmail

  SetVariable  (glState, 0)

  ⊟ If  [gAdministrator]=1   Then
         SetVariable  (glState, 1)

  ⊟ Else

      ⊟ If  [gUserID]=[UserID]   Then
             SetVariable  (glState, 1)

         End If

     End If
  SetProperty  (addActionBarButton, Visible, =[glState])
  SetProperty  (editActionBarButton, Visible, =[glState])
  SetProperty  (deleteActionBarButton, Visible, =[glState])
  SetProperty  (saveActionBarButton, Visible, =[glState])
  SetProperty  (cancelActionBarButton, Visible, =[glState])
```

FIGURE 8-14 Restricting users to editing records that belong to them.

You also need to provide a view where users can enter their email address in an unbound text box before using the application. After checking the email address the user entered against a table of known email addresses, you can then set a value in the global variable *gUserID*.

Figure 8-15 shows the Members Login page, which displays a text box for users to enter an email address and a command button. When the user clicks the command button, the address is validated and the *userID* is saved in *gUserID*.

FIGURE 8-15 Identifying a user using an email address.

In Figure 8-16, I show the code behind the command button, which calls a data macro to validate the user's email address.

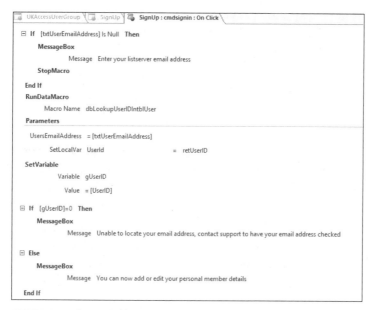

FIGURE 8-16 Command button macro code calling a data macro for validation.

In Figure 8-17, I show the data macro *dbLookupUserIDintblUser*, which checks the email address against values in the table tblUser.

FIGURE 8-17 Using the Lookup A Record In macro command to validate data.

The work in this section allows you to avoid the read-only restriction for public anonymous users by using one or more external user accounts with read/write permission. You then use a table-driven list of email addresses (for which passwords also can be added) that users can use to edit only their own data.

Caution You should take care that the level of permissions you provide to users does not enable them to make other undesired changes on the public-facing website.

Summary

In this chapter, you saw how a web app can be deployed to a public-facing website. Users can interact with the public interface either by using the built-in anonymous account to have read-only use of the application or by logging in to external user accounts the developer creates that grant them wider permissions.

In Chapter 1 and in subsequent chapters, we focused on the team site, but you saw that those sites were available only when you either created a personal invitation to an external user or added permissions for a licensed user. However, in this chapter, you saw how you can increase the number of users who can interact with an application through the anonymous security feature of the public-facing website.

In Chapter 9, "Looking under the hood at Microsoft Azure SQL Database," we will delve deeper into the underlying structure of the back-end database in Azure SQL.

Looking under the hood at Microsoft Azure SQL Database

I mentioned in earlier chapters that behind the Office 365 interface your data is held in an Azure SQL Database. Microsoft Azure SQL Database is Microsoft's cloud platform for the SQL Server database engine. In this chapter, we will look in more detail at what can be learned about the Azure SQL Database back end and get a better understanding of how the design in the web app translates to objects in the Azure SQL Database. Then, in Chapter 10, "Other techniques for reporting," we make use of this information to explore how you can use other technologies to extend your web applications. If you have not already read through Chapter 3, "Converting a desktop database to a web app," you should do so now. You might find that reading through that chapter helps with understanding this chapter, which builds upon topics covered there.

With Microsoft Access, you can create two users: ExternalReader, with read-only use of data, and ExternalWriter, with read/write use of the data. But you cannot use either of these users to make changes to the Azure SQL Database—the design is read-only.

> **Tip** If you are already familiar with either SQL Server or Azure SQL, you will know that SQL Server has a database called the *master*, and in that database within Azure SQL, the firewall rules are maintained. (These rules control the IP addresses that can be used for connecting to the database.) In a web app, you do not have the ability to display or manipulate the master database or directly change the firewall rules. However, you can use the Access interface to either maintain a firewall rule exclusively limiting connections to your current location or open the firewall for connections from any location.

The Access team faces a dilemma in terms of security—they would like to give developers as much freedom as possible, but they need to make sure that a developer does not change the parts of the design that are automatically maintained. The current restrictions mean that you cannot script out a database, use the query plan features to analyze query performance, or add and change objects in the database. This is because these features need db_owners, dbcreator, or sysadmin permissions (which are not available unless you have an on-premise installation). If you had these permissions, you could adversely impact the database. On the other hand, these are features that will engage serious developers.

In my own scalability tests, I uploaded a table with one million rows. This took around one hour to upload. After uploading with the default UI, it was taking 5 to 9 seconds to refresh data, but after adding appropriate indexing the response times became instantaneous. With large tables, you should consider using indexing and filters and, if searching for examples on a List view using the list control, specifying the fields to search. (In other words, to search for *France*, you enter **countryregion:france**.)

SQL Server Management Studio

If you love Microsoft Access, you will also come to admire and love SQL Server Management Studio (SSMS). Although the tool is different from Access (in that it does not aim to provide a user interface), it is an advanced design tool. SSMS is an intuitive and easy-to-use tool, but it is also very sophisticated. So you can get started easily, and as your expertise grows you can explore more advanced features.

Before undertaking the exercises and examples in this chapter, you need to download the appropriate development tools. Unless you have SSMS or full SQL Server on your desktop, I recommend that you download and install SQL Server 2012 Express (which is free). SSMS provides you with the management tools for connecting directly to the Azure SQL Database, and you will have options for creating your own desktop SQL Server databases, which is a technique you will use in this chapter.

Microsoft SQL Server 2012 Express can be downloaded from *http://www.microsoft.com/en-us/download/details.aspx?id=29062*. Among the download options, look for X86 if you have a 32-bit version of Windows or X64 for a 64-bit version. You can also choose between SQLEXPR or SQLEXPRADV for the advanced edition, which includes Report Server. If you want only the management tools, look for a download including *SQL Management Studio* in the name. For the work in this chapter, the minimum requirement is the ManagementTools download. A typical example is to download *ENU\x86\SQLEXPR32_x86_ENU.exe*.

ODBC drivers

If you want to use an Access desktop database you created on your development machine on a different machine to connect to the Azure SQL Database used by Office 365, on the selected machine you need to have installed the latest ODBC drivers. You will need either the SQL Server Native Client 11.0 drivers or ODBC Driver 11 for SQL Server. The SQL Native Client 11.0 driver is an essential requirement when using a Reporting Database or any of the other databases I describe in this chapter that are connected to Azure SQL.

When Microsoft releases a new version of SQL Server, it also releases a feature pack, and the feature pack contains a download for the appropriate ODBC drivers.

If you visit *http://www.microsoft.com/en-us/download/details.aspx?id=29065* and search on the page for *Microsoft SQL Server 2012 Native Client*, you will find links to download either the 32-bit or 64-bit versions of the latest drivers. (When viewing the site page, click the Install instructions to display a list of package features that can be downloaded.)

There is also a newer driver called *Microsoft ODBC Driver 11 for SQL Server - Windows*, which can be downloaded from *http://www.microsoft.com/en-gb/download/details.aspx?id=36434*. This driver incorporates newer features, but it does not have support for OLEDB, which means it does not support the techniques using ADO described in Chapter 3 for uploading attachment data. You might find it useful to download both the older and newer ODBC drivers.

Connecting to Microsoft Azure SQL Database

If you look at backstage for a web app, you will see details of the Azure SQL Database, as shown in Figure 9-1 in the Data Connectivity section.

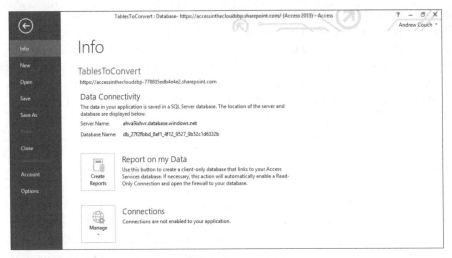

FIGURE 9-1 Displaying data connectivity in backstage.

Near the top of Figure 9-1, you will see the name of your server (*database.windows.net* is the generic part of the name when using Office 365), and below this you will see the database name. Notice that below the Connections title, the text "Connections are not enabled to your application" is shown.

> **Tip** Azure SQL has a firewall that, by default, prevents direct access to the database from any computer. Indirect use from the Office 365 environment is obviously allowed. You can also use the Connections area to manage direct access to Azure SQL.

If you click the Manage button, the options shown in Figure 9-2 will be displayed. Notice that not all the options are available until other options are selected.

The first two options, From My Location and From Any Location, determine from where a connection can be made to the database. These options allow connections from your current IP address or from any location (any IP address).

In the options, there are two types of connections you can make to the database: Read-Only and Read/Write. There are two options for enabling each of these connections, two options for resetting the passwords for each of these connections, and two options for viewing the connection details for each of these connections.

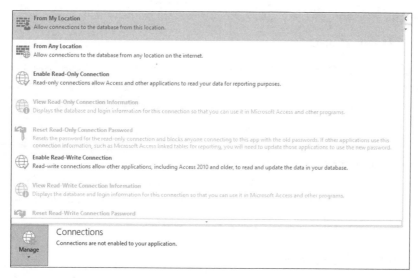

FIGURE 9-2 The database connection options.

To get started, you need to enable a connection from either your location or any location. To do this, click either the From My Location or From Any Location button. After you make this selection, Access closes the connection options and applies those changes to the database. You'll need to click the Manage button again to reopen the database connection options. Next, click the Enable Read-Write Connection button and Access closes the connection options once again. Finally, click the Manage button one last time and then click the View Read-Write Connection Information button. Access displays the SQL Server Connection Information dialog box, as shown in Figure 9-3.

FIGURE 9-3 SQL Server Connection Information dialog box.

 Tip After you make changes to the firewall using the Manage Connection options From My Location or From Any Location shown previously in Figure 9-2, you might need to wait a few minutes for the changes to become available through the cloud.

At this point, it is a good idea to copy and paste the following information into a text file:

- **Server** ahva9ixhvr.database.windows.net

- **Database** db_27f2fbbd_8af1_4f12_9527_9b52c1d6332b

- **UserName**   db_27f2fbbd_8af1_4f12_9527_9b52c1d6332b_ExternalWriter

- **Password**   ^/UeYHfx-t4<PRO

To make a connection using SQL Server 2012, start SQL Server Management Studio (SSMS) and enter the information into the appropriate text boxes as shown in Figure 9-4. You need to ensure that Authentication is set to SQL Server Authentication and then click the Options button at the bottom right of the screen.

Caution When you enter the login information, you must combine the user name and the server name and separate them with an @ symbol. In our example, we entered the following (all on one line): db_27f2fbbd_8af1_4f12_9527_9b52c1d6332b_ExternalWriter@ ahva9ixhvr.database.windows.net

FIGURE 9-4 SSMS Connect To Server dialog box.

Before proceeding, you must click the Options button on the bottom right of the Connect To Server dialog box and select the Connection Properties tab. On this tab, as shown in Figure 9-5, enter the database name and then click Connect to make the connection.

Caution If you don't perform the last step of clicking on the Options button, your connection will fail. The failure occurs because when the database is not specified, the default database used is a special database called *master*, and you do not have any permissions to the master database.

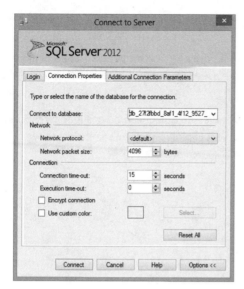

FIGURE 9-5 SSMS Connection Properties tab.

After making the connection, you can then expand and explore the database design in Azure SQL, as shown in Figure 9-6, using the Object Explorer (which you use to explore information on the objects held the Azure SQL Database).

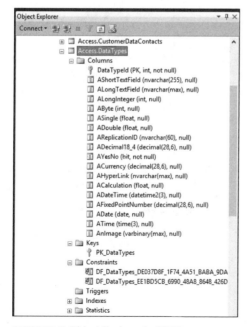

FIGURE 9-6 Object Explorer in SSMS.

Schemas

If you look back at Figure 9-6, you will see that the tables are prefixed with either *Access* or, if you scrolled further down the list, *AccessSystem*. If you have used SQL Server, you probably noticed that tables by default are normally prefixed with *dbo*.

These prefixes are all examples of *schemas*. In SQL Server, an object can be grouped by placing it on a schema. If you look in the Schemas folder in Object Explorer, you will see the list shown in Figure 9-7.

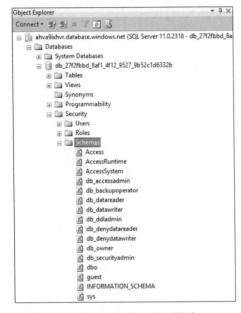

FIGURE 9-7 Schemas displayed in SSMS.

You need to be concerned only with the following three schemas:

- **Access** This schema contains all your tables and other tables, such as the Trace table that is available in the Access UI.

- **AccessRuntime** This schema contains runtime system objects.

- **AccessSystem** This schema contains the system objects.

Security in SSMS

Depending on whether, in the Manage Connections area in your web app, you chose to enable a Read Only or Read Write level of connectivity, if you use Object Explorer to expand the Users tab as shown in Figure 9-8, you will see a user with the name ExternalReader or ExternalWriter.

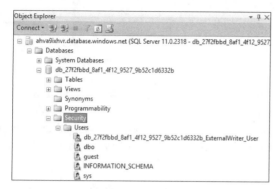

FIGURE 9-8 User security displayed in SSMS.

Tip The two possible users, ExternalReader and ExternalWriter, both have only read-only permissions on the design; this means you cannot directly make any modifications to Azure SQL Database. You might also find that if you try to perform certain standard SQL Server operations, such as scripting out the design of the database, these operations will fail because your account does not have sufficient permissions to undertake the operation.

Linked Microsoft SharePoint lists

In Chapter 1, "Finding your way around Office 365," when we looked at document storage and libraries, you saw how from a web app you could link to a SharePoint list. Now you can look under the hood to see some of what is actually happening.

If you link a web app to the SharePoint Documents list, when you look inside Azure SQL, you will not see a table called Documents. Instead, you will find a view called Access.Documents. The structure for this view is shown in Figure 9-9.

FIGURE 9-9 Access.Documents view displayed in SSMS.

Although the SQL for creating this view creates the columns Name, Modified, Modified By, ID, Created, and Created By, these are not real columns selected from a real table. This is a pseudo-table that can never return any real data. It is created to provide consistency in the web-app design tool. When you display this table in a web-app browser, Access Services will switch to using the real SharePoint list.

This means you cannot make any external use of a linked SharePoint list via the Azure SQL interface.

Manually creating an ODBC DSN connection

Now that you have the credentials to link to the Azure SQL back-end database, you might find that you want to create direct links to the tables from a traditional desktop database. You might want to do this so that you can integrate other existing desktop databases or because you are migrating data.

Before I show the detailed steps for creating an ODBC connection, I need to discuss the different types of connections that can be created. In this discussion, I will avoid explaining User Data Source Names (DSNs), because those are specific to a user and you are unlikely to want to use this option. There are three main types of DSNs: System DSNs, File DSNs, and Machine DSNs. However, there is also another term you will come across: *DSN-less connection*.

A DSN-less connection is a connection that can be made in program code without the need to construct a DSN. The result of using a DSN-less connection is that all the connection details are embedded in a *tabledef* connection string. This means that a DSN-less connection is portable between machines; you don't need to create a DSN on another machine to make the link to the database.

File DSNs produce DSN-less connections. That is, the File DSN is a local set of stored instructions, but when you generate the linked tables all the required details are embedded in a *tabledef* connection string, which makes them effectively DSN-less connections.

System and Machine DSNs are similar, in that the connection string contains a reference to the named DSN. So the resulting linked tables are not portable between machines without the DSN being made available on the target machine.

The advantage of using a DSN-less connection is that you can place a database using the connection on any machine, and as long as you have installed the SQL Server drivers, you do not need to make any other changes. With a System or Machine DSN, you need to also create the DSN on the target machine.

The advantage of using a System or Machine DSN is that if you want to change the target database or the driver, you don't need to relink your tables. You just need to edit the definition of the DSN. So, if you want to switch between test and production environments, these DSNs offer support without the tables needing to be relinked.

> **Tip** The way a Machine DSN (which is created from inside Access) behaves depends on whether you installed Office Pro Plus from your Office 365 Subscription and have a Subscription Version, or whether you downloaded Office Professional 2013 from some other source, such as an MSDN subscription. If you are using a Subscription Version, when you create Machine DSNs (User or System DSNs), these are now held in a special new area of the Windows registry: HKEY_LOCAL_MACHINE\SOFTWARE\Microsoft\Office\15.0\ClickToRun\REGISTRY\MACHINE\Software\Wow6432Node\ODBC\ODBC.INI\ODBC Data Sources. (They are not visible in the external Windows ODBC Administration Tool.)
>
> If you have a retail subscription, creating a Machine (System) DSN creates a System DSN that is visible in the Windows ODBC Administration Tool. In this case, a Machine (System) DSN is the same as a System DSN.

There are two different places where you can create a DSN. You can either use the built-in Windows Data Source Administration Tool or create a DSN connection from within the External Data ribbon tab inside Access.

Here is an overview of the key differences in DSNs:

- **System DSNs**   These are created using the Windows ODBC Administration Tool, and they should be listed in your Machine Data Sources in Access.

- **Machine DSNs**   These can be created only from within Access. The details are stored in registry keys, which means that the DSN can be easily repointed. However, the Machine DSN will need to exist on a target machine for the linked tables to work. Also, see my previous tip for more details on how this can vary depending on your Office subscription.

- **File DSNs**   These are used to produce DSN-less connections, embedding the connection information in the linked table. Normally, you can create these with either the Windows ODBC Administration Tool or from within Access, but for Office 365 you need to create them by first creating a .dsn file. This is because the Windows ODBC Administration Tool interface will not complete the authentication process.

- **In-code DSN-less connections**   This is the most flexible type of connection to create, but it requires Visual Basic for Applications (VBA) programming code.

Tip To create a File DSN, open notepad and enter the following information (using your own credentials):

```
[ODBC]
DRIVER=SQL Server Native Client 11.0 UID=db_0eba538b_ee03_4eb3_bbea_11b492a1090a_
ExternalWriter
Pwd=dM:DqJoSO5anJ#k
Encrypt=yes
DATABASE=db_0eba538b_ee03_4eb3_bbea_11b492a1090a
SERVER=jwsw08hfi8.database.windows.net
```

Save this file with a .dsn extension in the location where your file DSNs are stored (normally, your documents folder). This will then be available in Access as a File DSN.

Before leaving this overview of DSN connections, consider the differences between using the 32-bit and 64-bit drivers. On a 64-bit machine, you can create a DSN using either the 32-bit or 64-bit drivers. If you are using 32-bit Office, you want to use DSNs created with the 32-bit drivers. If you have 64-bit Office, you need to use DSNs created with the 64-bit drivers.

If you have a 64-bit machine, you go through the control panel and select Data Sources (ODBC) in the administrative tools. This will launch the administrative tool located in *%windir%\system32\ odbcad32.exe*. This is the 64-bit driver administration tool. The 32-bit administrative tool is located in *%windir%\ SysWoW64 \odbcad32.exe*. This means that if you are using the recommended 32-bit Office on a 64-bit machine, you will need to use the 32-bit administration tool to create a DSN. (In Windows 7, you need to locate the programs with File Manager, but in Windows 8 you should have links to both administration tools in the Control Panel.) If you use a Machine DSN in Access, this 32/64 ambiguity will not be a problem, because Access will make the correct 32/64 DSN bit selection.

To create an ODBC Data Source, you need to use the ODBC Data Sources program. In Windows 7, you access this from your Start menu by selecting Control Panel and then Administrative Tools. In Windows 8, you can search for the Control Panel application as shown in Figure 9-10.

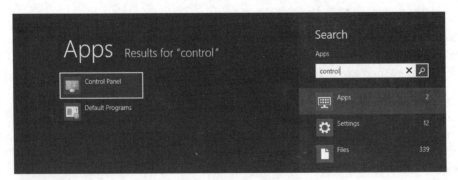

FIGURE 9-10 Search to locate the Control Panel application.

This application will then open on your desktop. Select Administrative Tools as shown in Figure 9-11.

FIGURE 9-11 Selecting Administrative Tools.

You will then see the ODBC Data Sources program as shown in Figure 9-12.

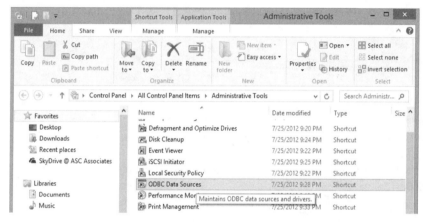

FIGURE 9-12 The ODBC Data Sources program.

In the ODBC Data Source Administrator, click the Drivers tab and scroll down the page. You will see the SQL Server Native Client 11.0 drivers, as shown in Figure 9-13.

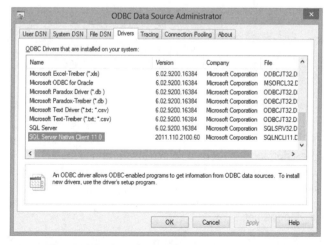

FIGURE 9-13 ODBC Drivers for SQL Server 2012.

Next we look at how to create a new ODBC Connection, which you can then use from a Desktop Access database.

Click the System DSN tab (which was shown in Figure 9-13). This displays the ODBC Data Source Administrator screen shown in Figure 9-14. On the System DSN tab, click the Add button on the right.

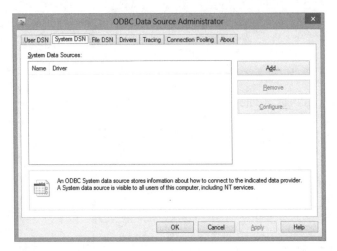

FIGURE 9-14 System DSN tab in the ODBC Data Source Administrator.

Scroll down the list of available drivers (shown in Figure 9-15), select the SQL Server Native Client 11.0 driver, and click Finish.

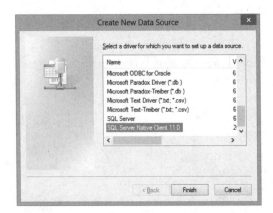

FIGURE 9-15 Selecting an ODBC driver.

Next, enter a name and optional description for your data source (as shown in Figure 9-16), enter the server name, and click Next. Refer back to Figure 9-3 for an example of how to locate and display the values you need to enter here. For your convenience, I show the details again here:

- **Server** ahva9ixhvr.database.windows.net

- **Database** db_27f2fbbd_8af1_4f12_9527_9b52c1d6332b

- **UserName** db_27f2fbbd_8af1_4f12_9527_9b52c1d6332b_ExternalWriter

- **Password** ^/UeYHfx-t4<PRO

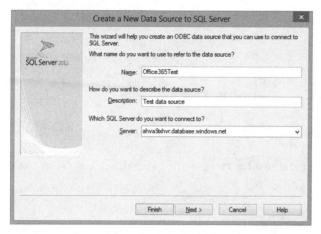

FIGURE 9-16 Create A New Data Source To SQL Server dialog box.

After you enter a name and description for your data source, Access displays the next page of the Create A New Data Source To SQL Server wizard, as shown in Figure 9-17. Select SQL Server authentication, and enter the login ID and password. Notice that as described earlier in this chapter, you need to enter the user name, the @ symbol, and then the server name. Then click Next.

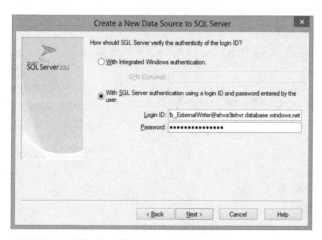

FIGURE 9-17 Selecting SQL Server Authentication.

In the next screen, select the Change The Default Database To check box to change the default database. Then enter the database name in the text box, and click Next, as shown in Figure 9-18.

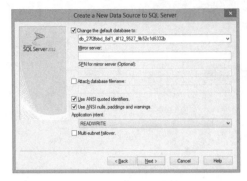

FIGURE 9-18 Using the Create A New Data Source To SQL Server dialog box to change the default database.

The next screen contains a number of more advanced options. Leave the default settings as shown in Figure 9-19. Click Finish.

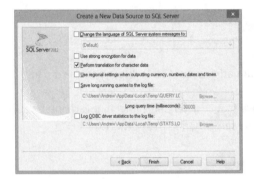

FIGURE 9-19 The optional settings for the Create A New Data Source To SQL Server dialog box.

On the last screen, shown in Figure 9-20, you can test the data source. After testing the data source, click OK. Then click OK to close the ODBC Data Source Administrator window.

FIGURE 9-20 Testing the database connection.

In the next section, you will see how to display a Machine DSN from within Access. The process of creating a Machine DSN is similar to the choices and settings described in this section.

Linking from the desktop to use an ODBC connection

Having created a suitable System DSN in the last section, you can then use this in a desktop database to connect to the Azure SQL Database. Create a new blank desktop database, and then from the External Data tab, click the ODBC Database button, as shown in Figure 9-21.

FIGURE 9-21 Linking to an external ODBC database.

On the next screen, select Link To The Data Source By Creating A Linked Table and click OK, as shown in Figure 9-22.

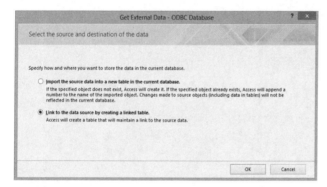

FIGURE 9-22 Selecting to link to the data source.

Use the next screen to select from the Machine Data Source tab the System DSN that you created in the last section, as shown in Figure 9-23, then click OK.

FIGURE 9-23 Selecting the data source.

You will be prompted to enter your password, as shown in Figure 9-24. Enter it and click OK.

FIGURE 9-24 SQL Server Login dialog box.

Select all the tables on the Access schema (as shown in Figure 9-25), select the Save Password check box, and then click OK.

FIGURE 9-25 Link Tables dialog box.

You will be prompted to confirm that you want the password to be saved, as shown in Figure 9-26.

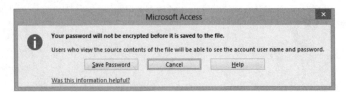

FIGURE 9-26 The Microsoft Access confirmation message box for saving your password for the linked table.

Tip Unfortunately, you will find that you are prompted to make the selection shown in Figure 9-26 for each selected table. You will also find that if you selected to link to the query (or as it is saved in Azure SQL, a view), you will be prompted to select one or more fields to act as a unique identifier. This is because Access has a great feature when it can update data through views: if you make no selection for the unique ID, the link to the view will be read-only.

After completing this, you will have a set of linked tables to the data in Azure SQL, as shown in Figure 9-27.

FIGURE 9-27 Desktop database and linked tables.

Notice that the table connections are all prefixed by the *Access_* schema name. You can remove this prefix either manually or with program code.

Creating DSN-less connections with program code

Although you can use the interactive graphical tools to create connections, it is not difficult to construct your own interface for managing DSN-less connections.

A DSN-less connection gives you detailed control over how the connections are constructed. Two great features you can exploit are as follows:-

- You can easily rename the connections to remove the schema prefix. So, rather than having a linked table called Access_Customers, you have a link called Customers.

- The second advantage is that when you are linking a large number of tables and want to save the password and user name in the connection, you can automate the process.

In the sample database DSNManagement.accdb, I include all the code described in this section and show highlights of the code in the main body of text.

To create a connection string in program code, build up the connection string as shown:

```
' DSN-Less connection
If strConnectionType = "DSN-Less Connection (FileDSN)" Then
    strCon = "ODBC;Driver=" & strDriverName & ";"
    strCon = strCon & "Server=" & strServerName & ";"
    strCon = strCon & "UID=" & strUserName & ";"
    strCon = strCon & "PWD=" & strPassword & ";"
    strCon = strCon & "DATABASE=" & strDatabaseName & ";"
End If
```

The resulting connection string will look similar to the following example:

```
ODBC;Driver=ODBC Driver 11 for SQL Server;
Server=jwsw08hfi8.database.windows.net;
UID=db_0eba538b_ee03_4eb3_bbea_11b492a1090a_ExternalWriter;
PWD=dM:DqJoSO5anJ#k;
DATABASE=db_0eba538b_ee03_4eb3_bbea_11b492a1090a;
```

Here is a useful code fragment for getting a list of available table names from the Azure SQL back end:

```
Set db = CurrentDb
Set qdef = db.CreateQueryDef("")
qdef.ReturnsRecords = True
qdef.Connect = strCon
qdef.SQL = "SELECT * FROM INFORMATION_SCHEMA.TABLES WHERE TABLE_SCHEMA= 'Access'"
On Error Resume Next
Set rst = qdef.OpenRecordset()
```

The code fragment for creating a linked table (tabledef) is shown next:

```
Set tdef = New TableDef
tdef.Name = rst!ObjectName
tdef.SourceTableName = rst!Schema & "." & rst!ObjectName
If blSavePassword Then
    ' force authentication to be saved in the linked table
    tdef.Attributes = DB_ATTACHSAVEPWD
End If
tdef.Connect = rst!ConnectionString

db.TableDefs.Append tdef
Set tdef = Nothing
```

When you make an external database connection to the back-end data source, you have the option to save the password in the connection string. The UI is constructed so that if you decide to save the password you need to confirm this on every table selected. For a larger application, that will become tedious. By making a connection in code, you can avoid this problem by simply setting a *tabledef* property to save the password and user name in the connection string (tdef.Attributes = DB_ATTACHSAVEPWD). The password will be hidden, but the user name is visible in the connection string.

Tip If you do not want to save the password and user name in a connection string, you can make the initial connection to the back end in code. Then, when the user performs an operation attempting to connect to the back end, the user will already be authenticated. Access caches the authentication and uses the information for all subsequent communications with the server.

Extracting information on relationships

To extract information on relationships and other structures in Microsoft Azure SQL Database, you can look at the capabilities of SSMS and see how structural information can be displayed or extracted.

Azure SQL does not have database-diagramming capability, and you will also find that you are unable to script out your design using the built-in Azure SQL tools. However, the following script, *ListRelationships.sql*, uses the *information_schema* views to display a tabular list of relationships in your web app:

```
SELECT
        FK_Table  = FK.TABLE_NAME,
        FK_Column = CU.COLUMN_NAME,
        PK_Table  = PK.TABLE_NAME,
        PK_Column = PT.COLUMN_NAME
   FROM
        INFORMATION_SCHEMA.REFERENTIAL_CONSTRAINTS C
        INNER JOIN
        INFORMATION_SCHEMA.TABLE_CONSTRAINTS FK
            ON C.CONSTRAINT_NAME = FK.CONSTRAINT_NAME
        INNER JOIN
        INFORMATION_SCHEMA.TABLE_CONSTRAINTS PK
            ON C.UNIQUE_CONSTRAINT_NAME = PK.CONSTRAINT_NAME
        INNER JOIN
        INFORMATION_SCHEMA.KEY_COLUMN_USAGE CU
            ON C.CONSTRAINT_NAME = CU.CONSTRAINT_NAME
        INNER JOIN
        (
            SELECT
                i1.TABLE_NAME, i2.COLUMN_NAME
            FROM
                INFORMATION_SCHEMA.TABLE_CONSTRAINTS i1
                INNER JOIN
                INFORMATION_SCHEMA.KEY_COLUMN_USAGE i2
                ON i1.CONSTRAINT_NAME = i2.CONSTRAINT_NAME
                WHERE i1.CONSTRAINT_TYPE = 'PRIMARY KEY'
        ) PT
        ON PT.TABLE_NAME = PK.TABLE_NAME
        WHERE C.CONSTRAINT_SCHEMA = 'Access'
```

The result of running this script on a sample database is shown in Figure 9-28.

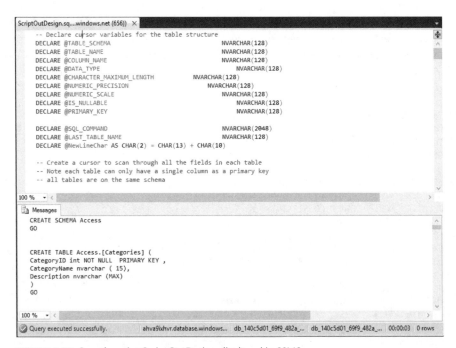

	FK_Table	FK_Column	PK_Table	PK_Column
1	CustomersProductCategories	CategoryID	Categories	CategoryID
2	Products	CategoryID	Categories	CategoryID
3	CustomersContacts	CustomerID	Customers	CustomerID
4	CustomersProductCategories	CompanyID	Customers	CustomerID
5	Orders	CustomerID	Customers	CustomerID
6	Orders	EmployeeID	Employees	EmployeeID
7	Order Details	OrderID	Orders	OrderID
8	Order Details	ProductID	Products	ProductID

FIGURE 9-28 List of tables and relationships in a web app.

In the samples, you will also find a more sophisticated script incorporating the preceding code called *ScriptOutDesign.sql*. (The script is too long to include here.) If you run that script, it will output in the messages window a script of commands that can be used to re-create your tables and relationships, as shown in Figure 9-29.

FIGURE 9-29 Sample script ScriptOutDesign displayed in SSMS.

Copy the message output to the clipboard, create a local SQL Server database in SQL Express, and execute the code in a query window for the new database. You can then create a database diagram, part of which is shown in Figure 9-30.

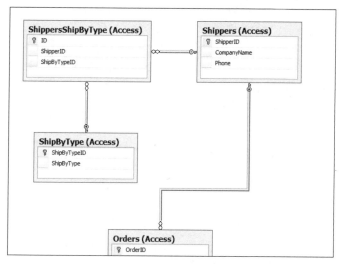

FIGURE 9-30 Part of the database diagram in a local SQL Server database.

Displaying structural information using data access objects

In the sample database NorthwindDAO.accdb, I provided you with sample code that can read the design on Azure SQL and then re-create a local desktop database containing the tables and relationships. The relationship diagram can then be viewed in that database.

To use this sample database, delete the linked table called Info_Customers, shown in Figure 9-31, and import any linked table from a reporting database, such as those created in Chapter 3, in the "Reporting" section, or using any of the techniques described earlier in this chapter for creating a link to Azure SQL.

After importing a link, right-click and rename the linked table Info_Customers, or edit the module code in the subroutine *modDAO_GetConnectionString* to use the name of your linked table. You only need this linked table to provide an ODBC connection string that will then be used to extract the structural information from the database in Azure SQL.

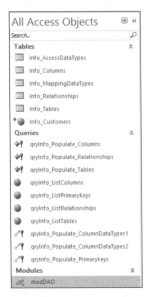

FIGURE 9-31 Contents of the NorthwindDAO.accdb sample database.

The Info_AccessDataTypes table lists constants for the Access column data types, and the Info_MappingDataTypes table provides a list for converting the SQL Server data types to Access data types.

The main processing routine *modDAO_BuildTableSchema* uses a subroutine called *modDAO_GetConnectionString* to read the connection string from your linked table. It then empties three local tables: Info_Relationships, Info_Columns, and InfoTables.

The tables are repopulated by running four append queries; these queries use pass-through to queries to extract the data from Azure SQL. Before the appended queries can be executed, the connection strings need to be set in the pass-through queries *qryInfo_ListTables*, *qryInfo_ListRelationships*, *qryInfo_ListColumns*, and *qryInfo_ListPrimaryKeys*.

As an example, the SQL contained in *qryInfo_ListColumns* is as follows :

```
SELECT TABLE_NAME, COLUMN_NAME, ORDINAL_POSITION,
IS_NULLABLE, DATA_TYPE, CHARACTER_MAXIMUM_LENGTH,
NUMERIC_PRECISION, NUMERIC_SCALE
FROM INFORMATION_SCHEMA.COLUMNS
WHERE TABLE_sCHEMA = 'Access'
and TABLE_NAME <> 'Trace'
ORDER BY TABLE_NAME, ORDINAL_POSITION
```

The subroutine *modDAO_PopulateInformationTables* executes a sequence of queries, which append data into the information tables, map primary keys, and map the data types from Access to SQL Server.

The main routine in the module *modDAO* is shown here:

```
Sub modDAO_BuildTableSchema()
    Dim qdef As QueryDef
    modDAO_GetConnectionString
    ' Empty information tables
    db.Execute "DELETE * FROM Info_Relationships"
    db.Execute "DELETE * FROM Info_Columns"
    db.Execute "DELETE * FROM Info_Tables"
    ' set the connection strings
    Set qdef = db.QueryDefs("qryInfo_ListTables")
    qdef.Connect = strConnection
    Set qdef = Nothing
    Set qdef = db.QueryDefs("qryInfo_ListColumns")
    qdef.Connect = strConnection
    Set qdef = Nothing
    Set qdef = db.QueryDefs("qryInfo_ListPrimarykeys")
    qdef.Connect = strConnection
    Set qdef = Nothing
    Set qdef = db.QueryDefs("qryInfo_ListRelationships")
    qdef.Connect = strConnection
    Set qdef = Nothing
    ' Populate our list of tables, columns and relationships
    modDAO_PopulateInformationTables
    ' Create a target database
    modDAO_CreateTargetDatabase
    ' Create tables
    modDAO_CreateTables
    ' Create relationships
    modDAO_CreateRelationships

    MsgBox "Completed"
End Sub
```

The subroutine *modDAO_CreateTargetDatabase* creates a blank database in your current project folder and sets the variable *tdb* to allow the manipulation of the contents in the new empty database. The code is shown here:

```
Sub modDAO_CreateTargetDatabase()
    Dim strPath As String
    strPath = CurrentProject.Path & "\" & TargetDatabaseName
    ' Creates a target database
    ' Replaces the target if it exists
    If Dir(strPath) <> "" Then
        Kill strPath
    End If
    DBEngine(0).CreateDatabase strPath, dbLangGeneral
    ' Set a reference to the new database
    Set tdb = DBEngine(0).OpenDatabase(strPath)
End Sub
```

The subroutine *modDAO_CreateTables* scans through a list of the tables using data access object (DAO) code to create a new table definition, and then it saves the table definition in the new empty database. For each table, it creates a *TableDef*, and for each column it creates a field that is added to the *TableDef.Fields* collection. Then it creates a primary key index, and it adds the primary-key field into the *Index.Fields* collection. After that, the *Index* is appended to the *TableDef.Index* collection. Finally, the completed table definition is appended in the target database *TableDefs* collection. The full code for this is present in the sample database.

In the final routine, *modDAO_CreateRelationships*, you could have used DAO code to create the relationships, but it is simple to use Data Definition Language (DDL) SQL. The routine is shown here:

```
Sub modDAO_CreateRelationships()
    ' rather than use the DAO it is easier to use DDL
    ' to create relationships
    Dim strSQL As String
    Dim strConstraint As String
    Dim rstRels As Recordset
    Set rstRels = db.OpenRecordset("info_Relationships", dbOpenDynaset)
    Do While Not rstRels.EOF
        strConstraint = "rel" & rstRels!FK_Table & rstRels!PK_Table
        strConstraint = Replace(strConstraint, " ", "")
        strSQL = "ALTER TABLE [" & rstRels!FK_Table & "] ADD CONSTRAINT " & _
                strConstraint & _
                " FOREIGN KEY([" & rstRels!FK_Column & "]) REFERENCES [" & _
                rstRels!PK_Table & _
                "] ([" & rstRels!PK_Column & "])"
        tdb.Execute strSQL
        rstRels.MoveNext
    Loop
    rstRels.Close
    Set rstRels = Nothing
End Sub
```

When you are creating relationships, the SQL will look similar to the following example:

```
ALTER TABLE [Products] ADD
CONSTRAINT relProductsCategories
FOREIGN KEY([CategoryID])
REFERENCES [Categories] ([CategoryID]).
```

Once the code has completed execution, the results can be viewed in the sample database TestRels.accdb (which will be located in the same folder as your current database). Figure 9-32 shows the resulting database window.

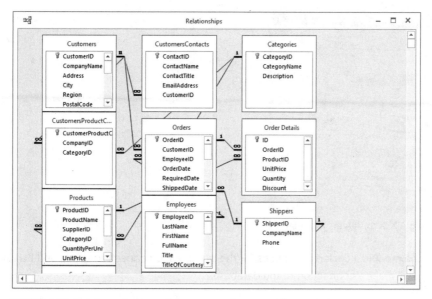

FIGURE 9-32 Database diagram of the extracted structure from a web app.

Caution In the subroutine *modDAO_CreateTables*, you will notice that the code creates a numeric data type *double* for the SQL Server data type *decimal*. This works around a limitation in the DAO code for creating decimal data types in code. It is possible to use either ADO or DDL to improve on that, but this is not necessary for the purpose of extracting a picture of the web-app relationships.

Displaying structural information using ADOX

A further technique for displaying information on the design structure in Azure SQL is to use the Active Data Objects Extension Library. In the sample database NorthwindADOX.accdb, I included a module called *modADOX* that demonstrates how to obtain a list of tables using ADOX.

In Figure 9-33, I added the ADOX library to the references.

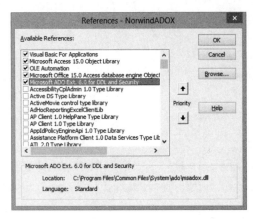

FIGURE 9-33 Adding ADOX to VBA project references.

At the top of the module, I declared variables for the catalog and connection string, and I created a subroutine that will make a connection to the database:

```
Option Compare Database
Option Explicit

Dim cat As ADOX.Catalog
Dim strConnection As String

Sub modADOX_DatabaseInfo()
    modADOX_ConnectToCatalog
    modADOX_GetTableNames
End Sub
```

To make a connection using either Active Data Objects (ADO) or ADOX, you need to construct a connection string like the following:

```
PROVIDER=SQLNCLI11;
SERVER=ahva9ixhvr.database.windows.net;
Initial Catalog=db_27f2fbbd_8af1_4f12_9527_9b52c1d6332b;
Uid=db_27f2fbbd_8af1_4f12_9527_9b52c1d6332b_
ExternalWriter@ahva9ixhvr.database.windows.net;
PWD=^/UeYHfx-t4<PRO;
```

The routine *modADOX_ConnectToCatalog* provides an example of constructing the connection string:

```
Sub modADOX_ConnectToCatalog()
    ' Create the connection string and connect to the catalog
    Dim strServer As String
    Dim strDatabasename As String
    Dim strUser As String
    Dim strPassword As String
    strServer = "ahva9ixhvr.database.windows.net"
    strDatabasename = "db_27f2fbbd_8af1_4f12_9527_9b52c1d6332b"
    strUser = "db_27f2fbbd_8af1_4f12_9527_9b52c1d6332b_ExternalWriter"
    strPassword = "^/UeYHfx-t4<PRO"
```

```
            strConnection = "PROVIDER=SQLNCLI11;" & _
                            "SERVER=" & strServer & ";" & _
                            "Initial Catalog=" & strDatabasename & ";" & _
                            "Uid=" & strUser & "@" & strServer & ";" & _
                            "PWD=" & strPassword & ";"
        Set cat = New ADOX.Catalog
        cat.ActiveConnection = strConnection
End Sub
```

The routine *modADOX_GetTablenames* enumerates the table names, but because we cannot identify the schema for the table names, we added a function to eliminate reporting on Access system tables:

```
Sub modADOX_GetTablenames()
    Dim tbl As ADOX.Table
    Dim col As ADOX.Column
    Dim idx As ADOX.Index
    For Each tbl In cat.Tables
        If tbl.Type = "Table" And modADOX_UserTable(tbl.Name) Then
            Debug.Print tbl.Name
        End If
    Next
End Sub


Function modADOX_UserTable(strTablename As String) As Boolean
' As we cannot get the schema to use for filtering tables
' we need to exclude known system table names
Select Case strTablename
    Case "Trace": modADOX_UserTable = False
    Case "ApplicationProperties": modADOX_UserTable = False
    Case "ColumnProperties": modADOX_UserTable = False
    Case "FieldSchemaCache": modADOX_UserTable = False
    Case "HostProperties": modADOX_UserTable = False
    Case "ObjectDependencies": modADOX_UserTable = False
    Case "Objects": modADOX_UserTable = False
    Case "ObjectStorage": modADOX_UserTable = False
    Case "QueryColumns": modADOX_UserTable = False
    Case "RemotingSchemaCache": modADOX_UserTable = False
    Case "TimeZoneDefinitionBase": modADOX_UserTable = False
    Case "TimeZoneRuleBase": modADOX_UserTable = False
    Case Else: modADOX_UserTable = True
End Select
End Function
```

> **Tip** Because you cannot list information on the keys collection in ADOX, which you would need to list relationships, there are limitations on the information that can be extracted using this technique. However, you could find that using ADO and ADOX are useful in other parts of any application that needs to connect to the back end. One example is in quickly checking that a connection is valid.

Displaying structural information with a query

Of all the methods for getting a picture of your relationships, this has to be the easiest. However, it is also the most primitive, and the results of your layout work cannot be saved. I describe it here because it is so easy.

Because queries understand relationships, you can create a query in a web app to include your tables, and then shrink down the criteria area on the screen and reposition the tables. Then take a screen print and add this to your documentation of the design. I show an example of this in Figure 9-34. If you select a single field, you will be able to save the query. The only problem is that the actual layout position of the tables does not get saved. However, as a quick technique for getting prints of your design, this is a great technique.

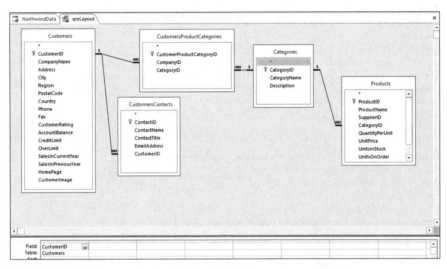

FIGURE 9-34 Using a query to document relationships.

Validation rules

In Chapter 4, "Creating a blank web app and using templates," we looked at adding validation rules to tables. These rules are saved as check constraints in Azure SQL. If you locate your table in Object Explorer and then expand the constraints for a table, you will see the constraints prefixed with *DF*, indicating a default, and *CK*, indicating a check. You script out a constraint by right-clicking the constraint, selecting Script Constraint As, selecting Create To, and then choosing New Query Editor Window. (See Figure 9-35.)

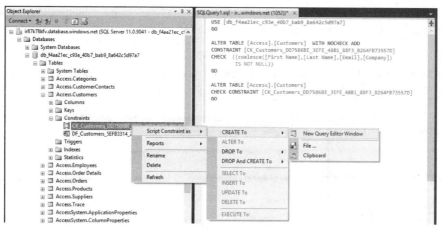

FIGURE 9-35 Displaying a constraint in a new query window.

Data macros under the hood

In the previous section, we looked at how a table validation rule is translated into a check rule in Azure SQL. In this section, we will construct the same rule, but using a data macro to implement the rule. We will also look under the hood to see what is happening.

This is an example that I do not expect you to reproduce, but you should read through the text because it serves as a guide to how you could start to look behind the scenes at what a web app generates in the SQL Azure Database when you write a data macro code. Take one of your own data macros, and apply the principle demonstrated here to investigate what is happening.

Start by writing the data macro shown in Figure 9-36. This data macro will check that after editing a record a value has been provided in at least one of the four specified fields: [First Name], [Last Name], [Email], or [Company].

FIGURE 9-36 An After Update data macro.

You might wonder how the macro knows which customer record should be checked. To answer this question, you need to look at the resulting code in Azure SQL. In that code, you will find that, because the trigger works with virtual tables called INSERTED and DELETED (as will be described later in this section) and these tables hold (in this case) only the single row that has changed, the trigger is very efficient at identifying and processing the single modified record.

This simple macro will generate around 180 lines of TSQL Trigger code, so we will not list the entire code. Instead, we will focus on some of the features you will find in equivalent macro code. Figure 9-37 shows how to script out the macro trigger code so that it can be examined.

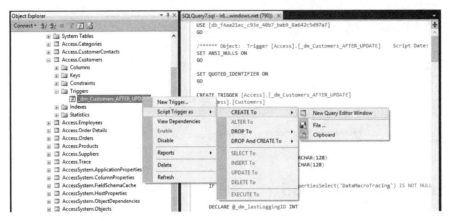

FIGURE 9-37 Example of scripting out the trigger code for a data macro.

In the following explanation, we will outline some of the general programming structures that are used inside the trigger code. The trigger code starts with the following declaration:

```
CREATE TRIGGER [Access].[_dm_Customers_AFTER_UPDATE]
ON [Access].[Customers]
AFTER UPDATE
AS
BEGIN
```

The *Create* syntax names the trigger and specifies that it will handle the After Update event.

> **Tip** The three types of triggers (FOR INSERT, FOR UPDATE, and FOR DELETE) are also known as AFTER INSERT, AFTER DELETE, and AFTER UPDATE because they occur *after* the referential-integrity check and other check constraints have been processed. If the referential-integrity check fails, these triggers do not execute. The reason for this terminology is that SQL Server also supports another set of types of triggers called *INSTEAD OF triggers*, which are not relevant to the explanations in this section and primarily are used to improve view updateability.

The trigger checks to see if macro tracing is enabled and sets an appropriate flag, which is then used at various points to write to the trace table as the trigger executes:

```
DECLARE @_dm_traceOn BIT = 0
IF AccessSystem.ApplicationPropertiesSelect('DataMacroTracing') IS NOT NULL
    SET @_dm_traceOn = 1
```

Following this code, you will observe code that initiates a transaction, or if a transaction is already in progress, it generates a transaction save point:

```
DECLARE @_dm_savePoint as VARCHAR(36)
SET @_dm_savePoint = CONVERT(VARCHAR(36), NEWID())


DECLARE @_dm_initialTranCount INT
SET @_dm_initialTranCount = @@TRANCOUNT
IF @_dm_initialTranCount > 0
    SAVE TRAN @_dm_savePoint
ELSE
    BEGIN TRAN
```

The system variable @@TRANCOUNT counts the number of active transactions.

The main code block is then encapsulated within an error-handling block that has a structure. The BEGIN TRY to END TRY section contains the execution steps, and the BEGIN CATCH to END CATCH section is the exception handler:

```
BEGIN TRY
...
END TRY
BEGIN CATCH
...
END CATCH
```

Inside the programming blocks just shown, you will see the detailed trigger code for implementing the data macro. The trigger code makes use of cursors. The cursors are similar to a VBA recordset in that you define and open the object and then write a programming loop to iterate through the records for processing. Shown next is the sample code for defining a cursor in the trigger:

```
DECLARE _dm_cur1 CURSOR LOCAL STATIC FOR
    SELECT
        *
    FROM
        [DELETED]
OPEN _dm_cur1
```

Typically, below the cursor definition you will find a *while* loop, in which records are fetched from the cursor and processed while *fetch_status* is zero. Once all records have been processed, the cursor is closed and de-allocated from memory:

```
FETCH NEXT FROM

    _dm_cur1
WHILE @@FETCH_STATUS = 0
BEGIN
...
FETCH NEXT FROM
        _dm_cur2
END
CLOSE _dm_cur1
DEALLOCATE _dm_cur1
```

> **Tip** In the code shown here, you will see the use of a table called [DELETED], and you might also see another table called [INSERTED] used in trigger code. These are not real tables; they are virtual tables that contain a before image [DELETED] and after image [INSERTED] view of the data. DELETED shows old values, and INSERTED shows new values.
>
> On an AFTER INSERT trigger (On Insert data macro), you have values only in [INSERTED]. In an AFTER DELETE trigger (On Delete data macro), you have values only in [DELETED], and in an AFTER UPDATE trigger (On Update data macro), values are present in both virtual tables. In the Access UI, because you edited a single record, the INSERTED and DELTETED virtual tables will include only one record. This is how the data macro knows which records to process. It is a built-in feature of Azure SQL. If you wrote your own single block of SQL in SSMS and it updated 20 records, when the trigger was executing, the virtual tables would each contain 20 records showing the before and after images of the data.

The section of code that implements the IF macro statement and generates an error if the validation fails is shown here:

```
IF COALESCE(@_dm_temp2, @_dm_temp3, @_dm_temp4, @_dm_temp5) IS NULL
BEGIN
    IF @_dm_traceOn > 0
        EXEC [AccessSystem].[LogActionTrace] @_dm_macroRunning,
        N'If', N'Coalesce([First Name],[Last Name],
        [Email],[Company]) Is Null', N'', N'', N''
    IF @_dm_traceOn > 0
        EXEC [AccessSystem].[LogActionTrace] @_dm_macroRunning,
        N'RaiseError', N'', N'', N'', N'Last Name, First Name,
        Email and Company are null';
    THROW 50000, N'Last Name, First Name, Email and Company are null', 1;
    SET @_dm_actionRunning = N'Else If'
END
```

If the required condition is not met, the code throws an error. This passes processing to the BEGIN CATCH...END CATCH processing block.

Inside the error-handling block, you will see code like the following:

```
IF @_dm_initialTranCount > 0
BEGIN
    IF XACT_STATE() <> -1
        ROLLBACK TRAN @_dm_savepoint
END
ELSE
    ROLLBACK TRAN
```

The AFTER triggers are executed after all referential integrity and other checking of data is completed, but before the actual physical changes are applied to the data. The code in the AFTER trigger executes in a transaction (although you don't need to begin the transaction with an explicit

BEGIN TRANSACTION statement because that is managed by the system as part of how triggers work in SQL Server).

When the trigger starts, the @@TRANCOUNT will be 1 (unless this trigger has been fired by another trigger in the system—in which case, it will be greater than 1). Near the start of the trigger code, you saw that a saved transaction point is created. If the trigger does not throw any errors, after it completes the @@TRANCOUNT will be decreased by 1 because the transaction commits the changes. (Again, you don't need the COMMIT command because that is part of the system managing the triggers in SQL Server.)

If an exception is thrown, the error-handling code will roll back any changes to the save transaction point. (It also uses the function XACT_STATE to check that it is allowed to perform a rollback.) Rolling back to a save point means that any outer transaction will still remain open.

There is also an alternative action for the error handler. If the variable @_dm_initialTranCount is zero, the trigger error-handling code executes a ROLLBACK, and this causes any open outer transactions to also roll back. (This is different than rolling back to a saved transaction point, which does not affect any outer open transactions.)

Early in the trigger code execution, a flag is checked in a temporary table called *'tempdb..#Context'* (if it exists). If it is a top-level trigger (the outermost trigger), the variable @_dm_initialTranCount is set to zero (and the flag is cleared). This means that if the trigger throws an error, the error handler will execute a ROLLBACK and all pending transactions will be canceled, including any inner transactions that are nested and completed. The temporary table indicates that other triggers can determine whether they are nested transactions or the top outer transaction.

The last command in the error handling is THROW. This command will raise the error handling in the outer code that caused the inner trigger to be executed. The result when you have nested transactions is to cause the execution in the outer transaction to enter an error handler.

This strategy means that, if a top-level data macro raises or encounters an error, all changes are rolled back. Also, if a data macro on a related table encounters an error when caused to fire by a top-level data macro, it will perform a localized rollback to a save transaction point, and then the outer top-level data macro will roll back all changes. This amounts to stating that if any of the data macros encounter an error, all changes are rolled back.

> **Tip** Some of the logic and apparent complexity in the trigger code is the result of actions that must be taken to ensure that all errors are handled elegantly and processing is carefully terminated. When looking at the trigger code, you can focus on a small portion of the code inside the BEGIN TRY..END TRY area to check the logic. Looking at the trigger code can be useful if you are in doubt regarding the detailed operation of a data macro.

If you create standalone named data macros, these are created as stored procedures.

Views and table-valued functions

In some respects, because a web app stores components in Azure SQL, it is a bit unfortunate that a web app makes so much use of the term *view* for a component that is displayed in a web browser and is part of the UI. This is not what is traditionally regarded as a view within the context of a database.

In this section, I will use the term *view* to mean a Azure SQL view. When you create a query in a web app in Office 365, it gets saved in Azure SQL. It will either be saved as a view or as a table-valued function. The choice depends on whether the SQL needs to accept parameters, because these are not supported in views. If the SQL needs parameters, the query will be saved as a table-valued function.

In our first example, we have a simple query, shown in Figure 9-38.

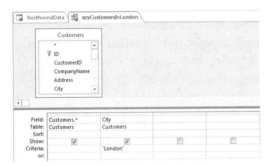

FIGURE 9-38 Example of simple select query.

In Figure 9-39, you can see how this query gets saved as a view in Azure SQL.

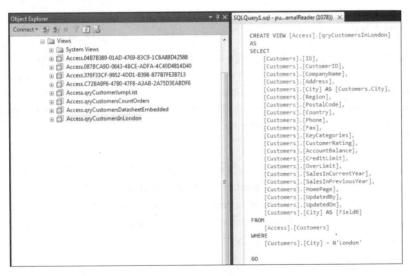

FIGURE 9-39 A simple query translated into a view in SQL Server.

Next we look at creating a simple parameterized query, as shown in Figure 9-40.

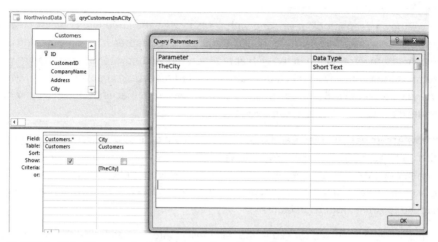

FIGURE 9-40 In this example, the query has been parameterized.

If you look in Azure SQL in the table-valued functions, you will now see how a parameterized query is saved, as shown in Figure 9-41.

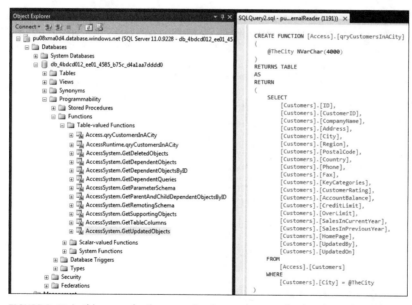

FIGURE 9-41 In this example, the query has been parameterized and saved in Azure SQL.

Summary

In this chapter, we took a deeper look at working with SSMS to view the underlying objects created from the web app design in the Microsoft Azure SQL Database. The chapter started by looking at how you locate the connection information in the web app design tool and how to manage the firewall and security settings used with any connections. I also indicated that you can download the Microsoft SQL Server 2012 Native Client ODBC drivers to allow connections from machines on which you have not already installed the Office 2013 desktop design tools.

I discussed how Access design objects and other Access system objects are arranged in different schemas in Microsoft Azure SQL Database. You also saw how queries in the web app are held as either SQL views or, when using parameters, they are saved as table-valued functions. Further examples demonstrated how standalone data macros become stored procedures and how embedded data macros are mapped to After Triggers on tables.

Several techniques were discussed for extracting relationship information from Microsoft Azure SQL Database, including the construction of TSQL scripts, extracting information using DAO, and working with ADO/ADOX. Remember that a web app does not have any feature you can use to display all your relationships, other than by creating a large query linking all your tables, as described in the chapter.

In Chapter 10, "Other techniques for reporting," we will look at further technologies to extend the capabilities of your web app, which involve similar methods for connecting to the data in Azure SQL.

Other techniques for reporting

The Access web app Runtime Experience lacks one specific feature, which is reporting. In this chapter, we take a look at how you can push the boundaries of what is available to deliver reports in a browser environment, and also fill in some gaps with complementary technologies.

You need to be very careful with your choice of technologies when connecting to the Microsoft Azure SQL Database. For example, if you use older versions of products, such as Microsoft Visio 2010 to report structure or Microsoft Visual Studio 2012, you will fail to make a connection to the data. (Note that Visual Studio 2013 will work as described in this chapter.) This can be because older products expect to extract information by first connecting to the Master database in Azure SQL and, with our web app, we do not have permission to access the Master database.

If you want to follow along with the design steps in this chapter, continue to use the NorthwindData web app used in Chapter 6, "Creating data sources by using queries." You will also find the sample reports in the database NorthwindReportsForSSRS.accdb.

In this chapter, we will look at how to overcome limitations in the standard web-app design environment and extend your applications to include a number of novel features.

Excel and data connections

Microsoft Excel has data-connection capabilities you can use to connect the product to data held in Azure SQL. But these data connections work only from the desktop version of Excel. As you will see in the next section, PowerPivot goes one step further and supports the display of data in a browser window, which is a more appealing feature when you want a browser-based solution.

In this chapter, I will show you how to connect from a desktop Excel 2013 spreadsheet to the data held in Microsoft Azure SQL Database. I assume you have enabled either read-only or read/write connections to your web app, as previously described in several earlier chapters.

Using a desktop Excel workbook, click the Get External Data icon on the ribbon and select the From Data Connection Wizard, as shown in Figure 10-1.

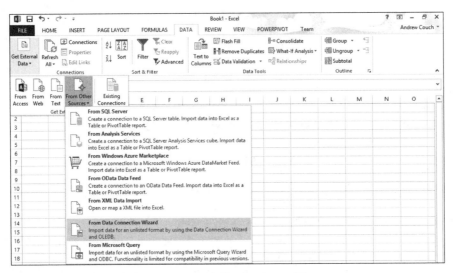

FIGURE 10-1 Making a desktop connection in Excel to Azure SQL.

From the Data Connection Wizard, shown in Figure 10-2, choose the Other/Advanced option and then click Next.

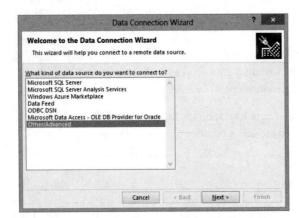

FIGURE 10-2 Choosing the correct option to make a connection.

Caution You might be tempted to choose the From Microsoft Query option or the From SQL Server option shown in Figure 10-1. However, neither of these will work, because they are designed for situations where you have permissions on the Master database when connecting to SQL Server.

In the Data Link Properties dialog box, on the Provider tab, select the SQL Server Native Client 11.0 driver as shown in Figure 10-3. Then click the Next button.

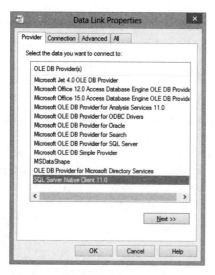

FIGURE 10-3 Selecting the connection provider for connecting to Azure SQL.

In the dialog box shown in Figure 10-4, enter the server name, user name (enter *username@servername*), password, and database name as displayed in the connection properties in Access. Make sure to unselect the Blank Password check box, and select the Allow Saving Password check box.

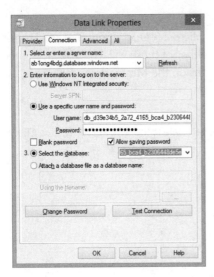

FIGURE 10-4 Entering the connection details on the Connection tab in the Data Link Properties dialog box.

After you click the Test Connection button shown in Figure 10-4, click OK. This continues the Data Connection Wizard, which guides you through the process of choosing your source of data. Accept the default choices. Then select the Customers table as shown in Figure 10-5, and click the Next button.

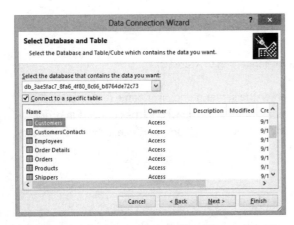

FIGURE 10-5 Selecting a table in the Data Connection Wizard.

You can use the Save Data Connection File And Finish screen, shown in Figure 10-6, to specify a location for saving your connection. You can leave the default selections on this screen or add descriptive text and provide a friendly name for the connection.

FIGURE 10-6 Saving the data-connection information.

Caution There is an option to save your password as text in a file, but this is not a secure solution. Even after you choose to save your password, you might still encounter prompting to re-enter your password.

After you click Finish, the Import Data window, shown in Figure 10-7, will be displayed. Here you can choose from the following options to display your data: Table, PivotTable Report, PivotChart, or Only Create Connection. After making the appropriate changes to your selections (in our example, we selected to view the data as a table then chose an existing worksheet), click OK.

FIGURE 10-7 Choosing how to display your data, and where to display the data.

After you work through any prompting to provide a password, you will see the data displayed in your spreadsheet, as shown in Figure 10-8.

D	E	F	G	H
	ID	**CustomerID**	**CompanyName**	**Address**
	1	ALPHO	Alpine Ski House	Obere Str. 57
	2	BLYON	Blue Yonder Airlines	Avda. de la Constitución 2222
	3	COMES	Consolidated Messenger	Cerrito 333
	4	CONSO	Contoso, Ltd	24, place Kléber
	5	CONSP	Contoso Pharmaceuticals	C/ Araquil, 67

FIGURE 10-8 The resulting table of data displayed in the Excel spreadsheet.

Although it might be appropriate to use the preceding technique to link to the Azure SQL data, these data technologies were not designed anticipating our current web-app technology, where we are connecting to a Azure SQL database and have restricted security permissions. One further restriction is that you cannot use Excel in a browser to display and refresh the data in this spreadsheet.

In the next section, you will see how PowerPivot resolves this problem.

Excel PowerPivot

If you have worked with Office desktop products, you might be used to the idea that you can interconnect a product like Access with Excel, Word, and other Office applications using many different techniques to exploit the strengths of each product. Unfortunately, we have not yet reached this stage of integration with the web-app versions of the products.

Caution Although you can construct a PowerPivot using any kind of subscription and make it work on your desktop, if you want to refresh the displayed data in a browser window as I describe in the final steps in this section, this is possible only with an Enterprise subscription.

Microsoft has invested a significant amount of effort in PowerPivot, which does not suffer from the limitations described in the last section for displaying data in a bowser window. In addition, it offers the benefit of delivering up summaries and charts of data in a web browser, which fits perfectly with a web app, which can then link to display the PowerPivot information in a browser window.

Tip Details for downloading and configuring PowerPivot in Excel can be found online, for Excel 2013 the option can be enabled with the following steps:

1. Go to File > Options > Add-Ins.

2. In the Manage box, click COM Add-ins > Go.

3. Select Microsoft Office PowerPivot in Microsoft Excel 2013, and then click OK. If you have other versions of the PowerPivot add-in installed, those versions are also listed in the COM Add-ins list. Be sure to select the PowerPivot add-in for Excel 2013.

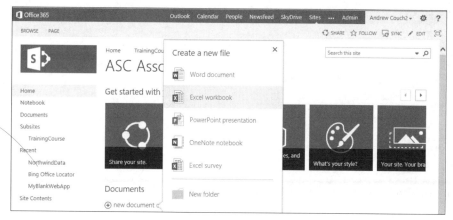

FIGURE 10-9 Creating a new Excel workbook from site contents.

In the popup window shown in Figure 10-10, type a document name and click OK.

FIGURE 10-10 Providing a document name for the new Excel workbook.

The spreadsheet will open in the browser window using the Excel web app. Click the Open In Excel tab on the ribbon, as shown in Figure 10-11.

FIGURE 10-11 Using the Excel web app to open the document in Excel.

If you have installed PowerPivot, click the PowerPivot ribbon, and then click the Manage button shown in Figure 10-12.

FIGURE 10-12 Excel desktop ribbon displaying the PowerPivot tab.

Clicking the Manage button displays the Get External Data drop-down menu, which is shown in Figure 10-13. Click the From Database command in the Get External Data ribbon group, and then select From SQL Server.

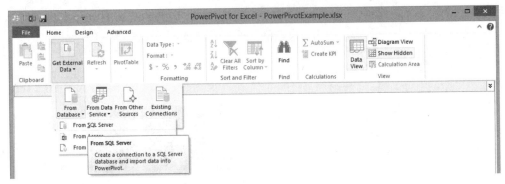

FIGURE 10-13 Selecting From SQL Server as the PowerPivot data source.

Figure 10-14 shows the SQL Server Connection Information dialog box, which can be displayed from the Access desktop backstage menus, as described in earlier chapters.

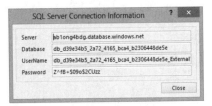

FIGURE 10-14 Access SQL Server Connection Information dialog box.

Figure 10-15 shows the Friendly Connection Name text box filled in with a value of *SQLAzure*. The information shown in Figure 10-14 has been used to fill in the connection information.

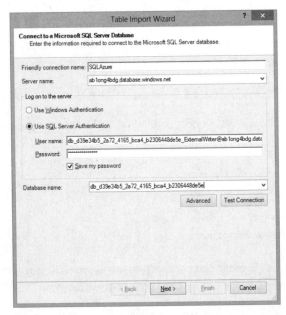

FIGURE 10-15 Completing the connection information in Excel.

Figure 10-16 shows the Choose How To Import The Data page of the Table Import Wizard. It contains two options: Select From A List Of Tables And Views To Choose The Data To Import, which is selected (which is the simpler choice to make), and Write A Query That Will Specify The Data To Import (which allows more flexibility in selecting the data for a report).

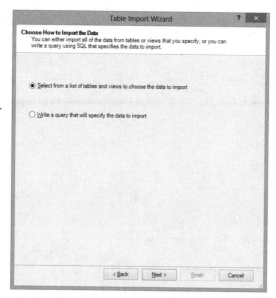

FIGURE 10-16 Deciding whether to import from a table/view or write a query.

The Select Tables And Views page of the Table Import Wizard is shown in Figure 10-17. Here you can select multiple tables. Figure 10-17 shows three example tables selected from the Tables And Views list.

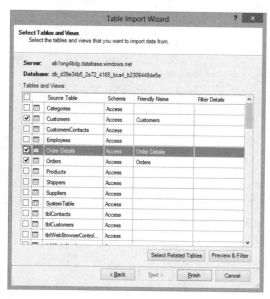

FIGURE 10-17 Selecting tables to import.

After you click Finish, a summary of the import processing is shown on the Importing page. (See Figure 10-18.)

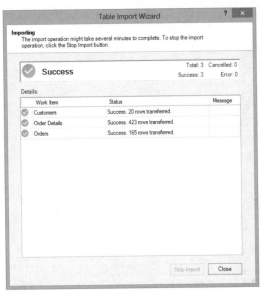

FIGURE 10-18 Reporting back on the success of the import operation.

After you close the Table Import Wizard, your data will be displayed in a table as shown in Figure 10-19.

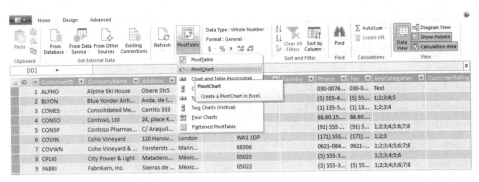

FIGURE 10-19 Creating a PivotChart from a data table.

To prepare a more interesting presentation of your data, select the PivotChart option. You will be prompted with the Create PivotChart window as shown in Figure 10-20. You can choose to create the PivotChart in a new worksheet or at a specific location in an existing worksheet.

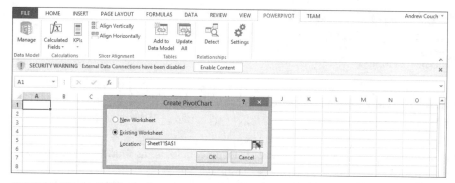

FIGURE 10-20 Specifying the location at which to create a PivotChart.

Figure 10-21 shows an example of selecting from the available PivotChart fields and creating a graphical presentation of the data. You should click the Enable Content button shown next to the Security Warning at the top of the figure to enable the data to be refreshed.

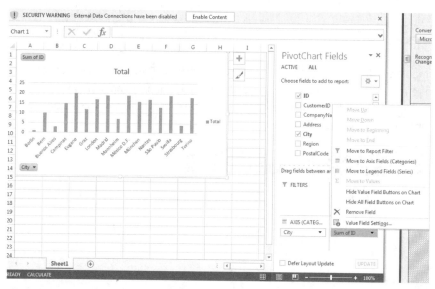

FIGURE 10-21 Creating a graphical presentation using PivotChart fields.

As shown in Figure 10-21, the default operation when selecting a column is SUM(). Clicking the Value Field displays a shortcut menu and selecting the Value Field Settings drop-down option will enable you to change SUM to another more appropriate operation such as COUNT.

Figure 10-22 shows the resulting Security Warning presented after you enable the content. Click Yes to trust your document. You then need to save your work, and you can then close the Excel desktop spreadsheet.

FIGURE 10-22 Trusting a document.

Returning now to your browser window, in your Documents folder as shown in Figure 10-23, click the spreadsheet to display the graph in a browser window.

FIGURE 10-23 Selecting the Excel spreadsheet from the Documents area in Office 365.

With the spreadsheet displayed in the browser window, click the Data tab and select Refresh All Connections to refresh the screen so that it will show any changes in the underlying data in your web app, as shown in Figure 10-24. (Remember, as I mentioned at the beginning of this section, you need an Enterprise subscription to refresh the data.)

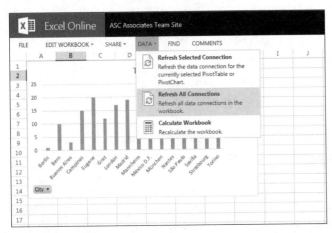

FIGURE 10-24 Displaying and refreshing the data for the PowerPivot results in a browser window.

Tip You could create hyperlink fields from inside your web app to the Excel workbooks saved in your site to display the PowerPivot results in a browser window from within your web app.

Creating a report for SQL Server Reporting Services

SSRS stands for *SQL Server Reporting Services*. There are several methods for making use of the capabilities of SSRS in a web app. If you are using an on-premise solution hosting your own Microsoft SharePoint 2013 environment, you can use your own on-premise SSRS. Another option is to use SSRS within a separate Azure SQL account.

Because the techniques described in this section use the "Remote and non-SQL data source support" feature of SSRS, you cannot make use of these techniques when using either the Web edition or SQL Express Edition with Advanced Services; these features are not supported on those editions. These features are supported on the Standard, Business Intelligence, and Enterprise editions.

> **Tip** If you are deciding on minimum memory requirements for a virtual/dedicated server, note that although SQL Server can exist with 512 MB, you need a minimum of 4 GB of memory to run SSRS.

When you install SSRS, this also installs the SQL Server Business Development Studio (2008R2 and earlier versions) or SQL Server Data Tools (2012). These products can be used to create reports, and the SQL Server Business Development Studio can also import reports from Access databases, converting them to Report Server RDL files. (Note that SQL Server Data Tools [2012] does not support this import feature.) The product associated with 2008R2 and earlier versions is based on Visual Studio 2008, and for 2012 it is now based on Visual Studio 2010.

Working with Visual Studio in a Report Server project involves using new skills and techniques to design reports. In this section, I assume you have installed and configured SSRS, and I want to demonstrate how to link these reports to your web app. It is beyond the scope of this book to delve into the intricacies of designing reports, so I will focus on some tweaking that is required when importing an existing Access report.

There are two methods for displaying a report using SSRS. One of the most popular approaches is to use the Report Viewer control in a Visual Studio project; another approach is to link directly using a URL. (For more information about the latter option, see *http://msdn.microsoft.com/en-us/library/ ms153586.aspx*.)

Managing authentication is an area that requires careful consideration. There are two levels of authentication to consider.

First, when you create a report, the report requires you to use the Azure SQL login user name and password that we used in earlier sections. You can either embed the user name and password in the report or have the report generate a prompt when opened for the user name and password. Because the user name and password form a very long and complicated string and you cannot set up your own user names and passwords, you will either want to embed the credentials or have your own .NET program provide the credentials when displaying the report.

Tip If you embed the credentials and the password then changes, you need to manually adjust the embedded information in each report and republish the reports, which is a time-consuming task.

The second level of authentication is provided by the Report Server used in SSRS; this also requires a login and password.

In this section, you will start by converting an Access report and embedding the credentials to test the report. Then I will demonstrate an alternative solution that uses a .NET Web Forms application to provide the authentication.

Create an Access reporting database linked to the Azure SQL back end. Then import the sample report named Invoice and a query used by the report called Invoices from the sample database NorthwindReportsForSSRS.accdb, which is the original desktop reporting database. The resulting database is shown in Figure 10-25.

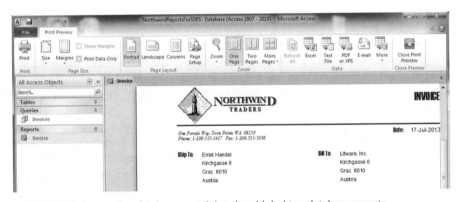

FIGURE 10-25 A reporting database containing the old desktop database reports.

Because the desktop database report you added relies on a desktop query that will not be part of your web app, you need to copy the SQL in the query Invoices into the record source property of the report as shown in Figure 10-26.

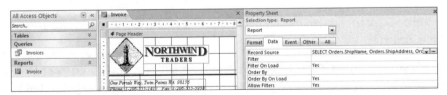

FIGURE 10-26 The report in design view showing the record source property.

> **Tip** You might also need to make changes to the SQL relationship links to allow for any new autonumber foreign keys introduced when the desktop database was converted to a web app. Also, if the report has any module code, set the Has Module property to No, because this will prevent the report from being subsequently imported.

Because you want to use the Access report import feature, use the SQL Server Business Intelligence Development Studio on a machine that has SQL Server 2008 R2 with advanced services. You can do this from the Start menu as shown in Figure 10-27 (or the associated tile in Windows 8).

FIGURE 10-27 Starting the SQL Server Business Intelligence Development Studio.

From the File menu, select New Project as shown in Figure 10-28.

FIGURE 10-28 Creating a new project.

Select the Report Server Project template as shown in Figure 10-29, and provide a name and directory location for the project.

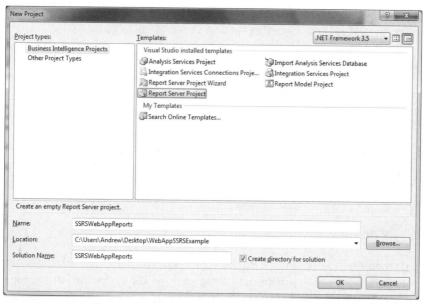

FIGURE 10-29 Selecting the Report Server Project template.

From the Project menu, shown in Figure 10-30, choose the Import Reports option to import an Access report. This will open a window from which you can select the reporting database.

FIGURE 10-30 Importing reports from Microsoft Access.

> **Tip** You should have only the reports you want imported in the target Access database, because the Import Wizard does not allow you to select individual reports.

After you import the reports, you can open a report by double-clicking it in Solution Explorer on the right side of the screen. In Figure 10-31 on the left, you can see the Report Data window. You will be working with this to modify the data source and data set. In the center pane, you will see the detailed report design.

FIGURE 10-31 Imported reports from the desktop Microsoft Access database.

Double-clicking on DataSource1 in the Data Sources folder, which you can see on the left side of Figure 10-31, displays the Data Source Properties window shown in Figure 10-32.

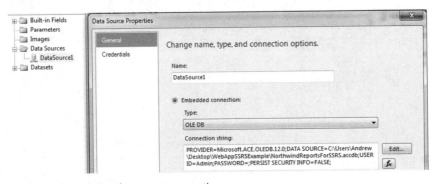

FIGURE 10-32 Existing data source properties.

Change the Type drop-down selection to Microsoft Azure SQL, and then, after acknowledging a warning message regarding the existing connection string, click the Edit button (which you can see at the bottom of the screen in Figure 10-32). This will displays the connection properties shown in Figure 10-33.

Enter the server name, choose the Use SQL Server Authentication option, and then enter the user name with the syntax *username@servername*. Enter the user password, and select the Save My Password check box. Finally, enter the database name and click the Test Connection button to test your settings.

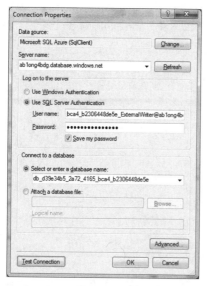

FIGURE 10-33 Completing the connection properties.

Once you are done, click OK on any open popup windows to save your changes and then double-click on DataSet1 in the left panel in the DataSets folder. The result is shown in Figure 10-34.

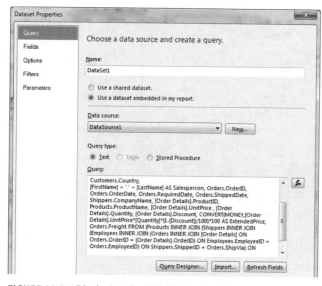

FIGURE 10-34 Displaying the SQL for the DataSet.

At this point, you might want to open the query designer by clicking the Query Designer button shown in Figure 10-34 and then modify the SQL to change it from Access SQL Syntax to SQL Server Syntax. In our example, I replaced a currency conversion, CCUR(Access function with a CONVERT(MONEY SQL Server function and changed the string concatenation symbol from & to + in the expression for SalesPerson.

After saving your changes and saving the report, right-click in Solution Explorer on the top-level item and select Properties, as shown in Figure 10-35.

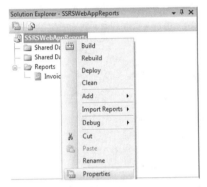

FIGURE 10-35 Displaying the project properties.

The project properties are shown in Figure 10-36. Set the Start Item property to the name of your report, Invoice.rdl, and click OK to close the project properties.

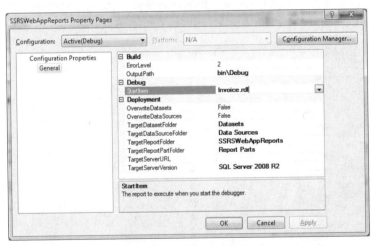

FIGURE 10-36 Setting the Start Item property in the project properties.

You can then click the Start Debugging button, the last button (the right-pointing arrow button) on the right in Figure 10-37, to display your report.

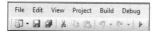

FIGURE 10-37 Displaying the report.

 Tip There is also a preview tab inside the design tool that you can use to preview your report without opening it in a separate window.

The resulting report is shown in Figure 10-38.

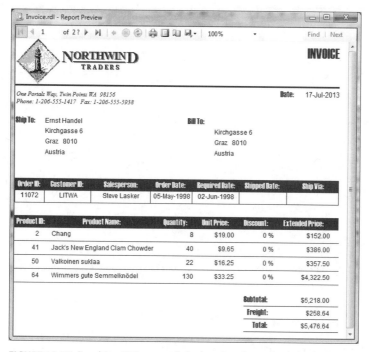

FIGURE 10-38 Resulting RDL report linked to data from the web app in Azure SQL.

To effectively use your invoice report, you need to define a parameter for the invoice number, which can then be used to filter the report to display a single invoice.

 Tip Although a converted report might work, you can have problems with a field that has the same name occurring in more than one place when you try to use more advanced features. For example, in our invoice we have field called CompanyName from the Customers table and the Shippers table also has a field with the same name. Although the report works without a parameter, when you try to add a parameter it will fail. So it is important to rename any potentially duplicated field names.

Next, I show the full SQL for the DataSet1 report, where I renamed `Shippers.CompanyName` as `ShippersCompanyName`. This is very important. I also reformatted the JOIN syntax, but that is a cosmetic feature. After doing this, I also had to alter the control on the report to use the now renamed fields for [Customer_CompanyName] to [CompanyName] and [Shippers_CompanyName] to [ShippersCompanyName].

```
SELECT
Orders.ShipName,
Orders.ShipAddress,
Orders.ShipCity,
Orders.ShipRegion,
Orders.ShipPostalCode,
Orders.ShipCountry,
Orders.CustomerID,
Customers.CompanyName,
Customers.Address ,
Customers.City,
Customers.Region,
Customers.PostalCode,
Customers.Country,
[FirstName] + ' ' + [LastName] AS Salesperson,
Orders.OrderID,
Orders.OrderDate,
Orders.RequiredDate,
Orders.ShippedDate,
Shippers.CompanyName As ShippersCompanyName,
[Order Details].ProductID,
Products.ProductName,
[Order Details].UnitPrice ,
[Order Details].Quantity,
[Order Details].Discount,
CONVERT(MONEY,[Order Details].UnitPrice*[Quantity]*(1-[Discount])/100)*100 AS ExtendedPrice,
Orders.Freight
FROM Orders
INNER JOIN [Order Details]
ON Orders.OrderID = [Order Details].OrderID
INNER JOIN Products
ON Products.ProductID = [Order Details].ProductID
INNER JOIN Shippers
ON Shippers.ShipperID = Orders.ShipVia
INNER JOIN Employees
ON Employees.EmployeeID = Orders.EmployeeID
INNER JOIN Customers
ON Orders.CID = Customers.ID
Adding a parameter to a report
```

Although it is useful to display a report showing all data, you will most likely want to supply a parameter when running a report to filter the available data. In this section, we look at adding a single parameter to our invoice report. This means that from the web app we can display the report and pass in a suitable parameter to filter the information.

Figure 10-39 shows the query designer view, which is selected from the default page of information displayed in the dataset properties. I edited the SQL, typed in the *where* clause `Orders.OrderId = @OrderId`, and then clicked the Run button (the exclamation mark). The query designer recognizes that @OrderID means a parameter value is expected, and a popup window opens for you to enter a value.

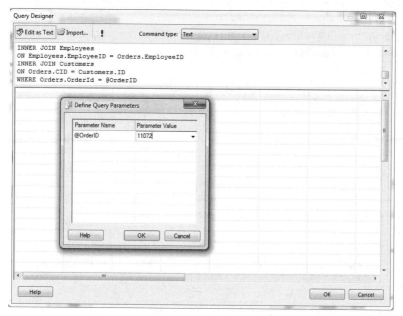

FIGURE 10-39 Creating a parameter in the Query Designer window.

After successfully testing your parameter, click OK to close the query design window and then click OK to close the Dataset Properties window. You will then see, as shown in Figure 10-40, that the parameters folder for the report can be expanded and opened to display a parameter called *@OrderID*. (This has been automatically added for you.) Double-click the parameter, and set an appropriate data type—in our example, it's *Integer*.

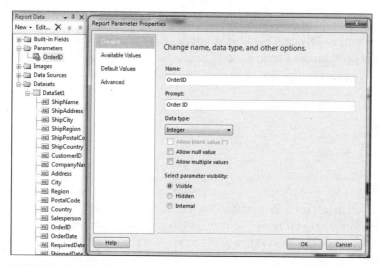

FIGURE 10-40 Defining a parameter data type for the report.

Tip If you re-open and examine the DataSheet properties, you will see that it also has a Parameters section. This links the dataset parameter to the report parameter. In an earlier step when you clicked OK to close your changes to the dataset after adding the parameter, the design tool automatically created a report parameter to match the name of the parameter you created in the dataset and also linked the parameters together.

If you now display your report in the preview window as shown in Figure 10-41, you will see that the parameter prompt is displayed in the top area of the window.

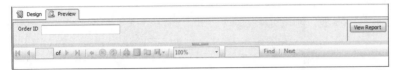

FIGURE 10-41 Prompting for a parameter when displaying a report.

Tip In SQL Server, parameters and variables are defined by prefixing the variable name with the @ symbol.

Publishing a report to SSRS

Before you can make use of your report with a web app, you need to publish the report to SSRS. A detailed description of configuring SSRS and preparing a folder within SSRS to locate your published report is beyond the scope of this book. But I will provide some simple guidance so that if you are not familiar with SSRS, it will help you get started.

On a server that has SSRS installed (for example, where you downloaded and installed SQL Server 2012 Express with Advanced Services), from the Windows start menu select the Reporting Services Configuration Manager from the Configuration Tools folder shown in Figure 10-42. (The Configuration Tools folder is located within the SQL Server 2012 menu.)

FIGURE 10-42 Preparing to configure SSRS.

On the opening screen, you might see a Start button. To start the report server if it is not already started, click this button to start the report server. You need to then work sequentially through the menu items on the left of the screen shown in Figure 10-43 to prepare the report server. When you reach the Web Service URL item, take note of the URLs hyperlink near the bottom of the right side of the screen; this is the URL you can use on the local machine to locate a base path where the reports will be published.

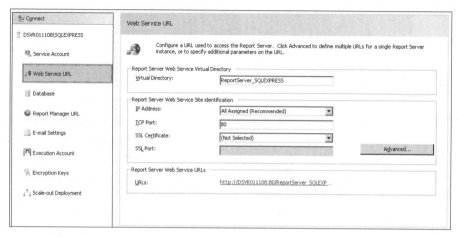

FIGURE 10-43 SSRS configuration steps and Web Service URL screen.

A second important URL to note is shown in Figure 10-44, where the Report Manager URL item is chosen on the left of the screen. Clicking this item opens the Report Manager URL, which you use to create folders for reports, define security, and upload reports.

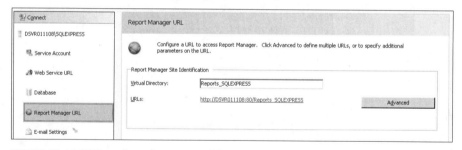

FIGURE 10-44 SSRS configuration steps and Report Manager URL.

Tip There are two methods for getting your reports published into SSRS. The first method is to use the Report Manager to upload a file into a folder on SSRS, and the second method is to publish the report from within the SQL Server Business Intelligence Studio.

Upload your report using the Report Manager into a new folder on SSRS, as shown in Figure 10-45.

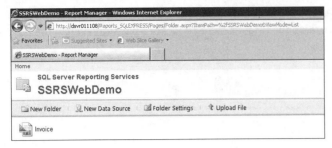

FIGURE 10-45 Working with a Report Manager folder.

Once the report is operating correctly, you will find that it prompts you to log in with the Access ExternalWriter or ExternalReader name and password. (You do not need to add the *@servername* when entering this information.) You can work around this by looking at the report's security properties. (Click the report as shown earlier in Figure 10-45, and select Security from the drop-down list of choices.) Then change the Data Sources credentials as shown in Figure 10-46.

SQL Server Reporting Services
Invoice

Properties
Parameters
Data Sources
Subscriptions
Processing Options
Cache Refresh Options
Report History
Snapshot Options
Security

DataSource1

○ A shared data source

Select a shared data source [Browse]

⦿ A custom data source

Data source type: | Microsoft SQL Azure ∨ |

Connection string: | Data Source=ab1ong4bdg.database.windows.net;init ial |

Connect using:

○ Credentials supplied by the user running the report

Display the following text to prompt user for a user name and password:

[Type or enter a user name and password to access the data source.]

☐ Use as Windows credentials when connecting to the data source

⦿ Credentials stored securely in the report server

User name: | db_d39e34b5_2a72_4165_bca4_b2306 |

Password: | •••••••• |

☐ Use as Windows credentials when connecting to the data source

☐ Impersonate the authenticated user after a connection has been made to the data source

○ Windows integrated security

○ Credentials are not required

[Test Connection]

FIGURE 10-46 Properties for a report.

In Figure 10-47, you can see the report displayed in a browser window presenting data from your web app. In the drop-down list displayed when you click the Export icon on the toolbar, you can see a list of supported formats for exporting your report; it includes XML, CSV, PDF, MHTML, Excel, TIFF File, and Word.

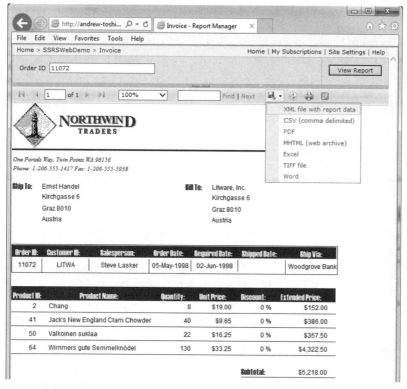

FIGURE 10-47 Final report displayed in a browser showing supported export formats.

Linking a web app to an SSRS report

In our example, you can click the following URL to pass in a parameter value of 11072 to the Invoice report. (For details on case-sensitive settings on parameters, see the Pass A Report Parameter Within A URL link at the bottom of the page found here: *http://msdn.microsoft.com/en-us/library/ms153586.aspx*.)

```
http://andrew-toshiba/ReportServer_SQLSERVER2008R2/Pages/
ReportViewer.aspx?%2fSSRSWebDemo%2fInvoice&rs:Command=Render&OrderID=11072
```

Figure 10-48 shows the result of adding a variable to the On Start macro to define a path for the invoice report (the value for the variable *strInvoiceReportPath* uses the previous URL without the value 11072 at the end of the URL).

FIGURE 10-48 Assigning a global variable to the URL for an SSRS report.

Next add a hyperlink control called *hypInvoiceReport* to your Orders List view, and write an OnCurrent macro in the view to concatenate the report path with the *OrderID*, as shown in Figure 10-49.

FIGURE 10-49 Generating a hyperlink for the report.

 Tip The technique used in this section uses Windows Authentication to grant the user permissions on the Report Server, so this technique is best suited for use in an intranet environment. You can use anonymous authentication to SSRS in a web environment, but the security issues associated with doing that should be fully considered.

Using Visual Studio 2013 with a web app

Visual Studio 2013 offers features that enable Access web-app developers to both build on more traditional technologies to integrate and augment their applications and to embrace completely new technologies by deploying new and exciting features with the Office products and Office 365.

In this section, you will create an ASP.NET application that displays data from your web app. In practice, you also need a website location on the Internet/intranet to publish and host the application. (This is not being held in Office 365.)

Start by selecting the New Web Site option from the File menu in Visual Studio, as shown in Figure 10-50.

FIGURE 10-50 Choosing the New Web Site option.

With Visual Studio, you can create a diverse range of website types using different technologies. For this example, choose ASP.NET Empty Web Site, as shown in Figure 10-51.

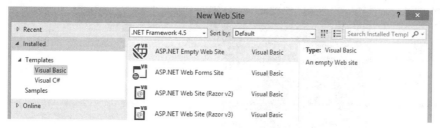

FIGURE 10-51 Choosing the ASP.NET Empty Web Site option.

Before you move on to create content in the website, you'll find it useful to create a link in SQL Server. This link is not stored in your project, but it is a great way to quickly view the tables and SQL views in Microsoft Azure SQL Database.

In Figure 10-52, on the left, you can see SQL Server Object Explorer. If this is not displayed, use the View menu to display this window. Click the Add SQL Server button at the top of the SQL Server Object Explorer. In the Connect To Server dialog box that is displayed, enter your web app database details, as described in earlier chapters.

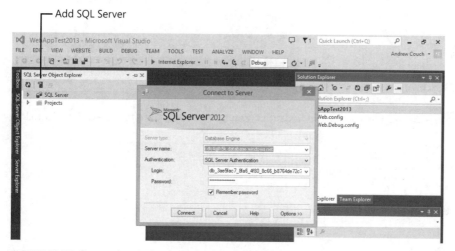

FIGURE 10-52 Connecting to the database using SQL Server Object Explorer.

After connecting to the Azure SQL database, you will be able to browse through the various objects in the database, as shown in Figure 10-53.

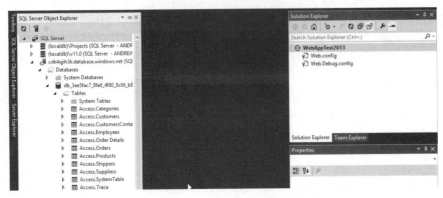

FIGURE 10-53 Viewing the Access tables in SQL Server Object Explorer.

Next, return to adding content to your web site. Click the Website tab to display the drop-down menu, and select Add New Item, as shown in Figure 10-54.

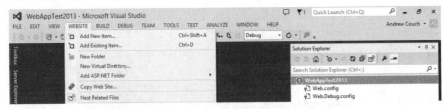

FIGURE 10-54 Adding a new item to the website.

In Figure 10-55, you can see a list of items that can be added to the site. Select Web Form.

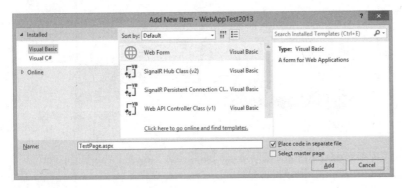

FIGURE 10-55 Selecting to add a Web Form.

Tip A Web Form represents one of the older ASP.NET technologies, but it is a simple technology to work with and has continued to be supported throughout new versions of Visual Studio.

After adding a new blank Web Form to your application, click the Toolbox side menu shown on the top left in Figure 10-56, expand the Data section and scroll down the Toolbox to locate the SQLDataSource icon. Drag and drop this icon onto your new blank Web Form. The Toolbox organizes controls into groups, and you can even add your own groups to the toolbox.

FIGURE 10-56 Adding an SQLDataSource from the Toolbox.

Tip If you intend to invest a lot of time in developing Web Forms, you should look at the free tools available in the ASP.NET Ajax Control Toolkit, which can be downloaded from *http://www.asp.net/ajaxlibrary/ajaxcontroltoolkitsamplesite/*. This is without a doubt one of the most valuable enhancements you can add to your Web Form application.

In Figure 10-57, you can see the new SQLDataSource control added to the Web Form. Click the arrow at the top right corner of the control to display the actions available for the control, and select Configure Data Source.

FIGURE 10-57 Configuring the SQLDataSource.

Tip There are three basic choices you can make for how data is managed in your Web Form. The oldest is SQLDataSource; next in the timeline comes LinqDataSource and then EntityDataSource. These technologies can be mixed in an application, and each has different features. SQLDataSource is the most basic choice, but it is by far the simplest to work with.

Figure 10-58 shows the Configure Data Source window. Because you do not as yet have a connection defined in the application, click the New Connection button.

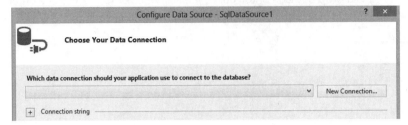

FIGURE 10-58 Creating a new connection.

In the Add Connection dialog shown in Figure 10-59, make the same selections you made in other sections of this book when entering your server name, the details for SQL Server Authentication, and the database name. After that, click the Test Connection button to ensure that these details are correct, and then click OK.

FIGURE 10-59 Adding the connection details and testing the connection.

Your new data connection will be displayed as shown in Figure 10-60. Click Next to proceed.

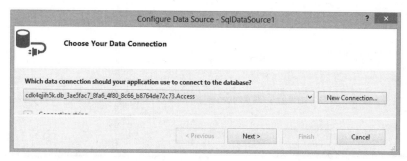

FIGURE 10-60 Specifying the connection to use in the application.

Figure 10-61 shows the prompt you will see to name and save the connection in the website configuration file. Enter a name in the text box, ensure the Yes, Save This Connection As check box is selected, and then click Next.

FIGURE 10-61 Saving the connection string.

In the next window, shown in Figure 10-62, select a table or view from the Name drop-down list and then select the columns to display. This is a sophisticated screen that you use to either write a custom SQL statement or specify (after selecting a table) either a *Where* clause, Order By option, or Advanced option to control how data is updated. After selecting a table and the appropriate columns, click Next.

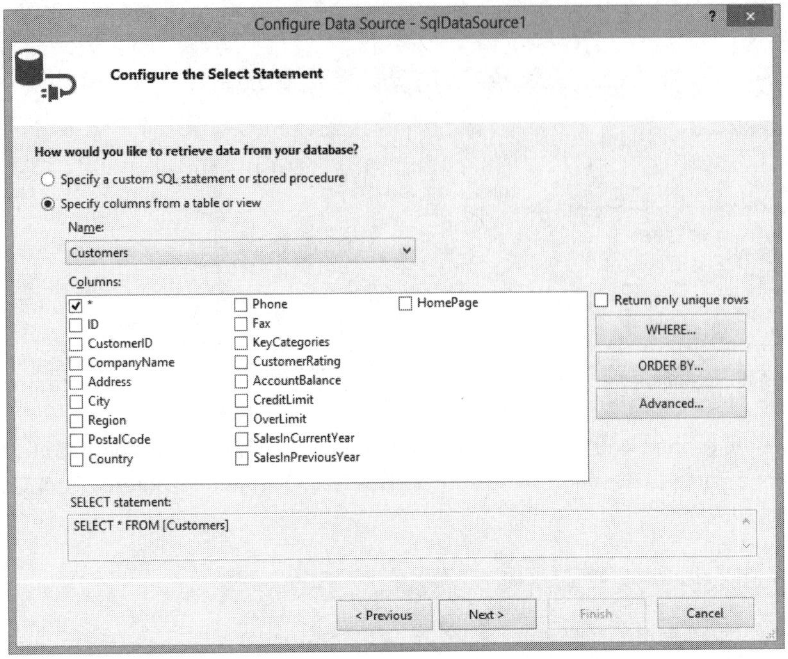

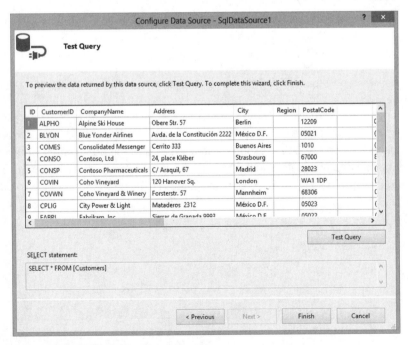

FIGURE 10-62 Configuring a select statement.

Use the screen shown in Figure 10-63 to test and display the results of your SQL Statement. After clicking the Test Query button below the table of data, click Finish.

FIGURE 10-63 Testing the select statement.

Caution You probably already appreciate that the same terminology can have different meanings. In this book, you have seen that a *view* in a web app means a screen in the browser window, while in SQL Server it means the same thing as a *query* in a web app. In Figure 10-63, a SQL statement is referred to as a *query*, although it is not saved as a SQL view.

Return now to the Toolbox as shown in Figure 10-64, and select a ListView control in the Data section. Drag and drop the control onto your Web Form. In a Web Form to display data you need two things: a data source (in our example, an SQLDataSource) and an object for displaying the data (in our example, a ListView).

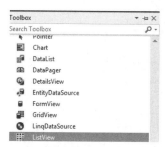

FIGURE 10-64 Adding a ListView control.

Tip The three most popular controls for displaying data are the DetailsView control, which displays a single record-oriented view of the data, a ListView control, which displays a tabulated list of editable records, and an older option called the GridView. A ListView is normally always a better choice of control than the older GridView.

Figure 10-65 shows the screen that results when you click on the top right corner of the ListView control to display the available tasks. Select SQLDataSource1 if it is not already selected in the Choose Data Source drop-down list, and then click Configure ListView.

FIGURE 10-65 Linking the ListView to SQLDataSource1.

In Figure 10-66, you can see that the ListView supports a large number of presentation features. The Professional style is selected in the left pane, but the other settings show the default values.

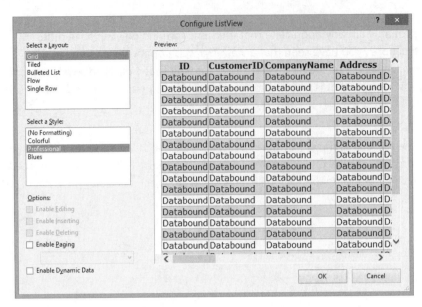

FIGURE 10-66 Configuring the ListView.

Tip Notice on the bottom left of Figure 10-66 that the Enable Editing, Enable Inserting, and Enable Deleting check boxes are not available. You can return to configure your data source by clicking the Choose Data Source option shown in Figure 10-65, proceeding to the screen shown in Figure 10-62 (where you can configure the select statement), and clicking the Advanced button. Then select the Generate Insert, Update And Delete Statements option button. If you then repeat the step shown previously in Figure 10-65 to Configure ListView, the Enable Editing, Enable Inserting, and Enable Deleting check boxes shown in Figure 10-66 will be enabled for selection.

If you need to do this, be sure to do so before you perform subsequent customization on the ListView control, because the control will be regenerated and any custom settings lost.

In Figure 10-67, you can see the fields from the underlying SQL DataSource now displayed in the ListView control. Click the green run button marked Internet Explorer on the ribbon to launch your web page in a browser window.

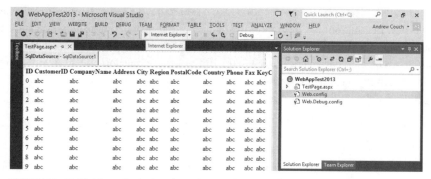

FIGURE 10-67 ListView displaying the column information.

Tip When working in design view, at the bottom left of the Web Form window you will see three tabs: Design, Split, and Source. You use these to view and edit your Web Form either graphically on the Design tab, as markup on the Source tab, or as both a design and source view of the page on the Split tab.

Tip If you look on the right of your Solution Explorer screen shown in Figure 10-67, you will see a Web.Config file. If you double-click to open that file, you will see where the site configuration settings are saved, and you will see where your connection string is saved.

In Figure 10-68, you can see your Web Form displayed in a browser window.

ID	CustomerID	CompanyName	Address	City	Region	PostalCode	Phone	Fax
1	ALPHO	Alpine Ski House	Obere Str. 57	Berlin		12209	030-0074321	030-0076545
2	BLYON	Blue Yonder Airlines	Avda. de la Constitución 2222	México D.F.		05021	(5) 555-4729	(5) 555-3745
3	COMES	Consolidated Messenger	Cerrito 333	Buenos Aires		1010	(1) 135-5555	(1) 135-4892
4	CONSO	Contoso, Ltd	24, place Kléber	Strasbourg		67000	88.60.15.31	88.60.15
5	CONSP	Contoso Pharmaceuticals	C/ Araquil, 67	Madrid		28023	(91) 555 22 82	(91) 555 99
6	COVIN	Coho Vineyard	120 Hanover Sq.	London		WA1 1DP	(171) 555-7788	(171) 55! 6750
7	COVWN	Coho Vineyard & Winery	Forsterstr. 57	Mannheim		68306	0621-08460	0621-089
8	CPLIG	City Power & Light	Mataderos 2312	México D.F.		05023	(5) 555-3932	
9	FABRI	Fabrikam, Inc.	Sierras de Granada 9993	México D.F.		05022	(5) 555-3392	(5) 555-7293
10	GRDES	Graphic Design Institute	Hauptstr. 29	Bern		3012	0452-076545	
11	HUMIN	Humongous Insurance	35 King George	London		WX3 6FW	(171) 555-0297	(171) 55! 3373
12	LITWA	Litware, Inc.	Kirchgasse 6	Graz		8010	7675-3425	7675-342

FIGURE 10-68 Displaying the results in a browser.

Although the processes described in this section require you to have a website outside Office 365, the fact that this is now possible should not be understated. For the very first time, you now have the technology to augment your standard web-app interface with a separate .NET application. When you combine this with the reporting capabilities of SSRS, the options for enhancing and supplementing your web-app design are significantly expanded.

Summary

In this chapter, you saw how to use other products to enhance and extend your web app to provide additional functions and features not available within a web app.

You saw how the flexibility of the Excel PowerPivot can address your needs for graphically presenting data, how SSRS can provide an excellent path toward developing more traditional reporting, and how Visual Studio enables you to extend the experience by building complete solutions integrated with your web app.

This raises some interesting questions: just how much functionality should be present in the web app versus how much should be available through other tools, and to what extent should a web app integrate with those other tools?

In finishing this chapter, I am drawn to consider an analogy with the Access desktop product. In very early versions, there was not the integration that we enjoy today, where the desktop Office products seamlessly integrate through a common programming language (VBA). But that was before cloud technologies were developed. Now we have a new playing field, so it is very difficult to guess how future integration will develop. It looks like Visual Studio 2013 will offer new features for integrating with Office 365.

Using apps for Office with Access

Apps for Office have been available for use for with Microsoft Office products such as Excel and Outlook, but it is only with Office 2013 Service Pack 1 and Office 365 that these features are now available for use with Access web apps.

An app for Office that is tailored to Access can be used only in the web app environment and not in a desktop database. In this chapter, I will continue to refer to the applications discussed in earlier chapters as *web apps*, meaning a web app created with Access, and I will refer to an app for Office, which is suitable for use in Access, as an *app for Access*. I will use the term *app for Office* when discussing these features in the wider context of Office.

I start by explaining the basic ideas behind an app for Access and how to use these components in a web app. Then I will provide an outline of how you can create your own app for Access to extend your web app.

You can use apps for Access to significantly extend the features and functions of your web app and integrate with other systems. In this chapter, you will progress from understanding the basic concepts and capabilities to using these apps, and I will finish the chapter with an outline of how to develop your own apps.

At the time I was writing this chapter, these new features were still at an early stage of evolution in the product. Much of this chapter provides a simple overview of where future developments with this technology are focused.

Apps for Access concepts

The apps for Office experience enables you to use the same component in both the runtime environment of a web app and the traditional desktop environment (although for Access it is not supported in the desktop environment).

In this section, I will introduce a number of new terms and terminology that play a key role in integrating with an app for Access. I start with a brief outline of what I mean by an *app for Access*. In

Figure 11-1, you can see that an app for Access consists of two key elements. The first element is the *app manifest*, which is an XML file that contains settings describing the app and an indicator of where the app will be hosted. The app manifest can be either obtained from the Office Store or uploaded by you into the App Catalog (as I described in Chapter 1, "Finding your way around Office 365," in the "App Catalog" section). The second component resides on a web server and refers to a webpage that contains both the HTML and JavaScript that forms the body of the app.

> **Tip** When using an app for Access, you are not dependent on having a DLL or EXE file installed on your system, and you do not have to rely on using Active-X technologies.

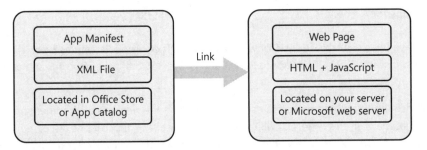

FIGURE 11-1 The components of an app for Access.

If you choose to use an app for Office from the Office Store or contribute an app to the Office Store, there are a number of important questions to ask. For example, what are the licensing implications of bundling the app for Access in your web app, will a contributor to the Office Store continue to support the hosting platform, and how can the app for Access be upgraded?

If you decide to contribute your own app for Access to the Office Store, you will need to continue to meet any associated hosting costs and plan for both licensing and the continued support for the app.

Having now described the basic components of the app for Office, I want to next point out that an app for Office can take one of three forms:

- **Task pane** This is not supported by Access.

- **Mail app** This also is not supported by Access and is specific to mail applications.

- **Content app** This is supported by Access.

> **Tip** A great feature of this technology is cross-browser support, and browsers that support EDCMAScript 5.1, HTML 5, and CSS should support the interface, which includes Internet Explorer 9, Chrome 13, Firefox 5, and Safari 5.06, or later versions.

You can use an app for Access to develop a component that can do the following:

- Read content from your web app

- Write content to your web app

- Handle application and user events in your web app

These features will enable you to create a rich interaction between the app for Access and your web app.

In the next section, I will describe how you can use an existing app for Access from the Office Store.

Consuming apps for Access

You can either use a standard app for Access from the Office Store or, by using the corporate catalog as will be described in the next section, work with your own app for Access or one developed for your company.

Start by creating a List view for the Customers table caption in the NorthwindData web app you created in earlier chapters, and name the view **Bing Map Example**. Remove the relic control, and adjust the layout to look like the example shown in Figure 11-2.

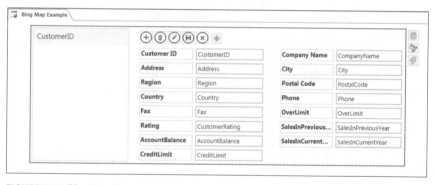

FIGURE 11-2 Bing Map Example list details view.

At the time of this writing, an app for Office can be added only to either a List or Blank view. The controls are not supported on either a Datasheet or Summary view.

With your web app open in the browser window, display the view into which you will be adding the app for Access. Then click on the settings icon to display the drop-down list and select Apps For Office, as shown in Figure 11-3.

FIGURE 11-3 A view open in the browser window and Apps For Office selected from the settings.

A popup window will display a list of apps for Office that are available in your organization. Your list might contain additional options to those shown in Figure 11-4. Click on the Store link if this is not already highlighted, and then scroll down the list to locate the Bing Maps For Access app. Click on the app to select it. A screen will then prompt you to trust the app. Click on the Trust It button to add the app to your view.

FIGURE 11-4 Popup displaying available apps from the Office Store.

The app will then be added to your view as shown in Figure 11-5. In this example, the app displays a Select Data button, which you click to define the data to display on the map. This app was developed by Microsoft to demonstrate what can be achieved using an app for Office. The app can display data points on a Bing map based on geographical locations.

FIGURE 11-5 A Bing Maps For Access app added to a view.

> **Tip** The layout of the app can be altered in the desktop design tool—for example, to enlarge the area displaying the map information.

In this example, clicking the Select Data button will display the Choose The Data For This App dialog box, which is shown in Figure 11-6. On the left is sample data to help guide you through the process of binding the app to your data.

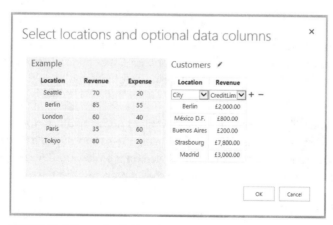

FIGURE 11-6 Popup for linking the app to data in your web app.

In Figure 11-6 on the left is sample data. This should help you understand the type of data that is expected in the app. On the right, I used the drop-down field to choose City as the location, and then in the Revenue column I chose CreditLimit as a numerical field to display the data. You use the +/– buttons to the right of the column-selection drop-down lists to add or remove data columns. Ensure that any unused columns are removed by clicking the minus (–) button. (I removed a single unused column.) Click OK to save your changes.

In Figure 11-6, next to the table name Customers, is a small pencil icon. Click this icon to choose an alternative source of data, binding the app to either a table or query. Every time you display this view, the data displayed in the app for Office will be automatically refreshed from the data in your web app, as shown in Figure 11-7.

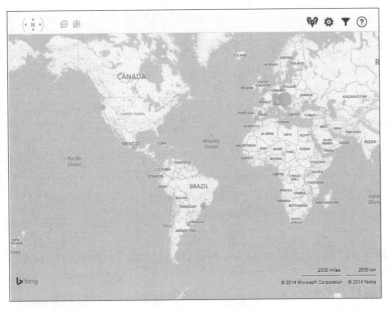

FIGURE 11-7 The app for Office displaying data points.

At the top right corner of the app are several icons you can use to change the presentation features of the map. (These features will be unique to a particular app for Office and are provided by the developers of this particular app for Office.) You can alter the binding of the map to display data from a different source.

If you edit your view in Access, you will see a control on the view titled Apps For Office. You can resize the control to adjust the map area or use the Delete key to delete the control. If you already have the web app open in Access but cannot see the control displayed on the view, close Access and, from the browser, choose to customize in Access using the option shown previously on the top right in Figure 11-3.

Developing apps for Access

An app for Access can be created using either Microsoft Visual Studio 2013, which features more advanced developer features, or "Napa" Office 365 Development Tools.

At the time I was writing this chapter, the URL for downloading Office Developer Tools for Visual Studio 2013 was *http://aka.ms/OfficeDevToolsForVS2013*. The URL for downloading Office Developer Tools for Visual Studio 2012 was *http://aka.ms/OfficeDevToolsForVS2012*. These downloads add templates for creating an app for Access.

When you are developing an app for Access, the coding involves making use of an Office API. Support for the different API calls can vary depending on the product for which the app is targeted. For example, there are differences between the API calls used when working with Microsoft Excel and those used when working with Access.

Figure 11-8 shows the Start Page screen for creating a new project with Visual Studio.

FIGURE 11-8 Creating a new project with Visual Studio.

Figure 11-9 shows the available choices for the type of project to create. From the available templates, open the Office/SharePoint folder in the left pane and select the App For Office 2013 template that shows up in the center pane. (In the right pane, you can see that Visual Basic is the type of project that will be created.)

FIGURE 11-9 Choosing the App For Office 2013 template.

After you select the template, the Choose The App Type page of the Create App For Office wizard is displayed, as shown in Figure 11-10. Use this page to select the type of app for Office to be created. Choose the Content option to create a content app, which is the only type of app supported by Access.

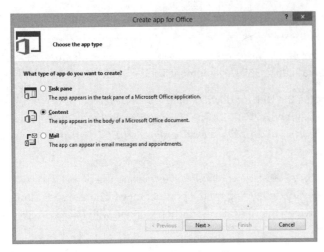

FIGURE 11-10 Selecting the type of app for Office to create.

Click Next to display the Choose The App Template And Host Applications page, as shown in Figure 11-11. Here you select the type of template to use, either Basic App or Document Visualization App. The Basic App provides a minimal amount of startup code. Choosing Document Visualization App will provide you with more template code to help you get started. Under the question, "Based on the template above, in which Office applications do you want the content to appear?" select Access to create the app for Access.

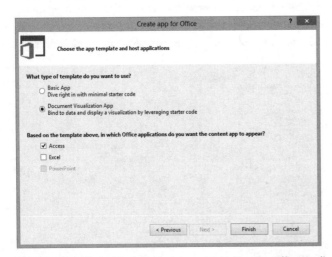

FIGURE 11-11 Choosing the template and selecting the Office application.

Tip If you choose to create an app for multiple Office products, you need to ensure that the API calls used are available in each of the products.

After completing these choices, Visual Studio will create a project that contains a number of files. Figure 11-12 displays the app manifest file for the project.

FIGURE 11-12 Displaying the app manifest for the project.

 Tip In the app manifest, the *Host* tag indicates the app for Office that is being used. A single app can be targeted against more than one type of app for Office, although you need to allow for any differences in supported features in a given product's API. In our example, the *Host name* tag is set to Database. If we needed to add support for Excel, we would provide a second *Host name* tag with the name Workbook.

Figure 11-13 shows the home.html page, where the visualization content of the app will be displayed.

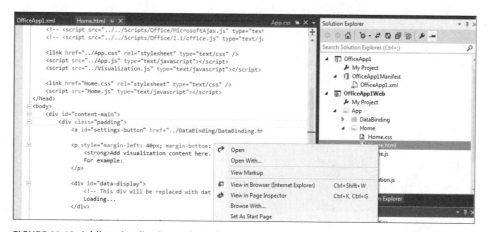

FIGURE 11-13 Adding visualization code to the app.

Right-click on the app shown highlighted in Figure 11-14, select Set As Startup Project from the available choices, and then click on the green arrow on the toolbar or press F5 to run the project.

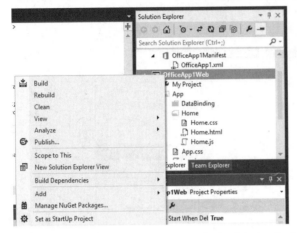

FIGURE 11-14 Setting the startup project in the Solution Explorer.

Visual Studio will then display your app running in a browser window as shown in Figure 11-15. This page is hosted on your local machine and can be used when testing and developing the app.

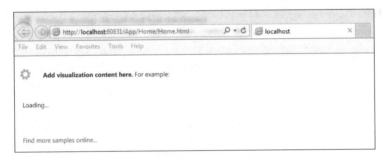

FIGURE 11-15 Displaying the app in a browser window.

 Tip If you refer back to manifest shown in Figure 11-12, you will see attributes for setting the *SourceLocation* where the app is hosted.

At this point, you have used only the default visual studio template, which contains place holders in the Home.html page. Look back to Figure 11-13 to see the comments "Add visualization content here" and "Loading..." for an indication of where to add content.

Before you can use the app for Access in your web app, information needs to be uploaded into the App Catalog in Office 365 or your on-premise installation. It is not the actual webpage that gets uploaded but the app manifest that will direct the app to the *SourceLocation* where the source code resides for the app.

For further examples of creating an app for Office, visit *http://msdn.microsoft.com/en-us/library/office/dn605904(v=office.15).aspx*.

A useful source of information is "JavaScript API for Office" located at *http://msdn.microsoft.com/en-us/library/office/fp142185(v=office.1501401).aspx*. There you will find the object model for the API. Figure 11-16 shows the roadmap of the API that you can find at this site. You can easily zoom in to focus on any area of detail.

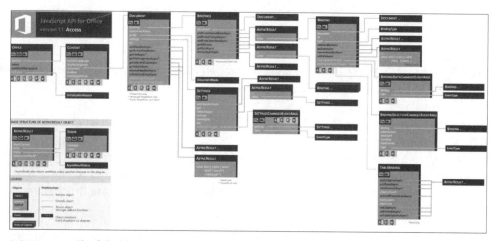

FIGURE 11-16 The full object map for Access apps for Office.

Clicking *http://msdn.microsoft.com/en-US/office/dn449240* takes you to the API Tutorial For Office page. This tutorial provides several examples of the new JavaScript API for Office being used to interact with an Excel spreadsheet. An example is shown in Figure 11-17.

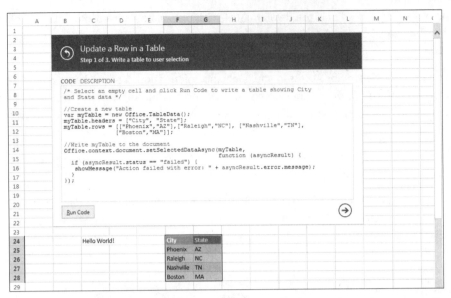

FIGURE 11-17 Working with the API Tutorial For Office in a browser window.

The tutorial shown in Figure 11-17 is a great way to start investigating the capabilities offered by the Java Script API when developing an app for Access.

Summary

The new app for Access features look like they will offer developers who need to add more functionality to an Access web app a set of great new tools once they are available in the Office Store.

These features are also aimed at developers who want to develop their own app for Access. At present, there is limited public information on how to use the API when building an app, and the best sources of information are to be found in the on-line Excel tutorial described earlier in this chapter.

Index

Symbols

W

Y

About the author

Andrew Couch has been working with Microsoft Access since 1992 as a developer, trainer and consultant. He is a joint founder of the UK Access User Group, which has been running for over 13 years. He has been a Microsoft Access MVP for the past 7 years.

Andrew has been involved with Access web apps from early on and has been working with members of the Microsoft team to communicate information on exploiting the power of this new technology.

Other publications with Microsoft Press include *Microsoft Access 2013 Plain & Simple* and *Microsoft Access 2010 VBA Programming Inside Out* and he is a co-author of *Microsoft Office Professional 2013 Step by Step*.

In addition to consulting and regularly speaking at community events, Andrew has developed the Migration Upsizing SQL Tool (MUST), which allows users to easily convert Access databases to SQL Server by using an Access-based application. Due to the success of MUST, which is used by over 200 companies, SQL Translation capabilities and WebForm code generators for .NET were added to the product range. He also provides free technical articles for Access at *www.upsizing.co.uk/TechLibrary.aspx.*

Now that you've read the book...

Tell us what you think!

Was it useful?
Did it teach you what you wanted to learn?
Was there room for improvement?

Let us know at http://aka.ms/tellpress

Your feedback goes directly to the staff at Microsoft Press,
and we read every one of your responses. Thanks in advance!